THE WHOLE WORLD GUIDE TO CULTURE LEARNING

J. Daniel Hess

INTERCULTURAL PRESS, INC.

For information, contact:
Intercultural Press, Inc.
P.O. Box 700
Yarmouth, Maine 04096 USA

Book design and production by Patty J. Topel
Cover design by Lois Leonard Stock

Printed in the United States of America

99 98 97 96 95   2 3 4 5 6

Library of Congress Cataloging-in-Publication Data

Hess, J. Daniel. (John Daniel), 1937-
    The whole world guide to culture learning / J. Daniel Hess.
      p.   cm.
    Includes bibliographical references.
    ISBN 1-877864-19-6
1. Foreign study. 2. American students—Foreign countries. 3. International education. 4. Experiential learning. 5. Returned students—United States. I. Title.

LB2375.H47   1994
370.19'62—dc20
                                  94-28819
                                      CIP

Table of Contents

Preface ix

Introduction xi

Part A Building Perspectives for Culture Learning 1

    Chapter 1 Culture Learning 3

    Chapter 2 Attitudes and Character Traits That
       Promote Culture Learning 11

    Chapter 3 Methods in Culture Learning: The
       Action-Reflection-Response Strategy 21

    Chapter 4 Methods in Culture Learning: Reflection as Cultural Analysis 27

    Chapter 5 Culture Learning, Values, and Ethical Choices 35

Part B The Culture-Learning Process 45

  I. Beginning Well

  Introduction 47

  Guide 1 Getting Ready to Go 49

  Guide 2 Pretesting Your Dispositions 52

  Guide 3 Managing Your Pace 55

  Guide 4 Meeting Your Hosts 58

II. Settling In

    Introduction 63

    Guide 5 Orienting Yourself to the City Center and Getting Around 65

    Guide 6 Finding Help 70

    Guide 7 Asking Questions 73

III. Getting Early Glimpses of the Host Culture

    Introduction 77

    Guide 8 Noting Differences 79

    Guide 9 Reading the Signs 84

    Guide 10 Interpreting Nonverbal Cues 88

    Guide 11 Identifying Agendas 91

IV. Living with a Host Family

    Introduction 97

    Guide 12 The People 99

    Guide 13 The House 101

    Guide 14 Roles 103

    Guide 15 Routines 106

    Guide 16 Expectations 109

    Guide 17 Interactions 112

    Guide 18 Neighborhood 115

    Guide 19 Evaluation 118

V. Moving into the Cultural Milieu

    Introduction 121

    Guide 20 Naming Your *Cucarachas* 123

    Guide 21 Reviewing Critical Events 126

    Guide 22 Learning the isms 130

    Guide 23 Dancing Their Rhythms, Telling Their Time 133

    Guide 24 Dealing with Culture Shock (Part I) 138

    Guide 25 Dealing with Culture Shock (Part II) 141

VI. Exploring Value Systems

    Introduction 145

    Guide 26 Identifying American Value Orientations 147

    Guide 27 Observing Host Values 152

    Guide 28 Studying Influences on Values 155

    Guide 29 Using the Arts in the Study of Values 159

Part C Techniques for Culture Learning 163

  I. Journal Keeping

    Introduction 165

    Guide 30 Enumerations 169

    Guide 31 Vignettes 172

    Guide 32 Critical Reviews 174

    Guide 33 Narratives 177

    Guide 34 Topical Essays 180

    Guide 35 Character Profiles 183

    Guide 36 Personal Essays 187

  II. Explorations

    Introduction 191

    Guide 37 A Plaza Study 193

    Guide 38 Studying Institutions 196

    Guide 39 A Study of Religious Institutions 201

    Guide 40 Field Trips 206

    Guide 41 Shopping 209

    Guide 42 The Uses of Photography 211

    Guide 43 Generating Your Own Explorations 214

  III. Case Studies

    Introduction 217

    Guide 44 Connections 219

    Guide 45 A Rock Concert 221

    Guide 46 Shoes 224

    Guide 47 Eclipse 227

    Guide 48 Money Manipulation 229

    Guide 49 Language Idiot 231

    Guide 50 My Host Father 233

    Guide 51 Dating and Sexual Relationships 235

Part D. Returning Home 241

    Introduction 243

    Guide 52 My Fellow Americans 245

    Guide 53 Reentry Experiences 248

    Guide 54 Culture Learning at Home 251

Bibliography 255

Preface

Three years into my teaching career, we (my family and I) were invited by Goshen College to open a study-service program in Costa Rica. Our innocent acceptance of the assignment fundamentally changed the boundaries of both my career definition and my cultural orientation. In the following twenty-five years, we directed thirteen trimesters of study service in Costa Rica. As we helped our students attain their goals, we, too, became culture learners. Gradually, my orientation became multicultural, and the territory of studies that I called my specialty came to include the large field of intercultural communication.

I don't regret the redirection into cross-cultural studies, nor the movement from ethnocentricity toward multiculturalism. The social, intellectual, emotional, and spiritual rewards have been many—including the privilege of writing this book.

The seeds were sown in Costa Rica in social interactions with friends and neighbors, in our acculturation into "Tico" life, and in the discussions and activities that made up the study-service curriculum. Residencies and visits to other places in Central America, Spain, and Thailand, along with our coming into contact with the vast literature of intercultural communication, nurtured our culture learning.

Throughout the days of writing and revising, I've been grateful for the many witnesses to this work, people who not only surrounded me, but spoke into the text a word or sentence or chapter.

The first and most important ones are those who have shared friendship with us overseas. Mima and Juan Vianey, Doris and Jorge, Zenón and Lilia, Humberto, Ellie, Sonia, Edwin, Rodrigo, Flor, Maylie and Alfonso, Jaime and Lali, Paco and Pilar, Corrine, and many, many others.

And those who, upon introducing and interpreting their culture to us, demonstrated the discipline and compassion of humane world citizens: Henry Paul and Mildred Yoder in Cuba; Vernon and Dottie Jantzi in Nicaragua; in Honduras, Amzie Yoder and, later, Linda Shelly; and Aulden Coble and Dave Kaufman in Costa Rica. Included in this listing are people who worked with refugees, such as Henry Neufeld in Thailand and Mabel Paetkau in Canada.

Goshen College is imprinted deeply into these pages: the international students on campus; the 250 students who learned with us in Costa Rica; the Goshen College faculty who led similar study-service units across the globe; the Goshen College International Education Office, and specifically, Ruth Gunden; the early leaders in Goshen's international program including Henry Weaver, Paul Mininger, Arlin Hunsberger, and J. Lawrence Burkholder; and colleagues in the English and Communication departments.

How can one adequately thank the community of scholars who comprise the bibliography at the end of this book and those others whose ideas were informally handed down from person to person and unknowingly used here? Among the names who have shaped my understanding of intercultural communication are Margaret Mead, Edward T. Hall, Eugene B. Nida, Marshall R. Singer, Larry A. Samovar and Richard E. Porter, John C. Condon, William B. Gudykunst and Young Yun Kim, and Dean C. Barnlund.

My work takes place in community. In Goshen the Becks, Hertzlers, and Yoders are my center of reference. In Chapel Hill and Raleigh, "The Weekenders" include the Boos family, the Bushes, Greg, Jon, Eric, Pam and the North-Martins. The Indiana Consortium for International Programs provided some financial assistance for an earlier version.

Mennonite Central Committee, no matter where it's located on the globe with its program, points true north.

David S. Hoopes and his colleagues at Intercultural Press deserve the highest commendation for knowledge of the subject, editorial coaching, and professional collegiality. And thanks to my family, each of whom models for me how to be a culture learner.

Introduction

Most people who go abroad encounter the things about their host culture which disturb them. Reaction to these aspects of the culture can sometimes color their entire experience in the country and turn it grey. To adapt satisfactorily and to effectively exploit the opportunities for culture learning, it is necessary to face the challenges of overcoming negative responses that are so prevalent among people moving into a new culture. One of the best ways to overcome these negative responses is to name them, look them in the face, and come to terms with that which cannot be changed. That is what this book is about—facing squarely the difficulties inherent in cross-cultural experience so that the sojourner can reap the rewards in culture learning.

Let's start with you. You might be a student enrolled in an American college or university, who wants to spend an academic year abroad. Perhaps you're just taking a short vacation trip to Mexico. Or you've volunteered to work with a nongovernmental organization for three years in East Africa or are going to teach English in Thailand. Maybe you're a missionary nurse headed for Bolivia, or you're a volunteer social worker in India.

Whether you sling on a backpack and go vagabonding, set off with your family on a corporate assignment abroad, or register to study in a national university, you probably aren't the type who'll be content to live in the North American ghetto in the foreign city, sleep every day till noon, drown out the world with your boombox and favorite CDs from back home. Whatever your motivation for going abroad, I suspect that you will want to devote yourself to the serious task of learning another culture, developing relationships with the people you meet, communicating effectively, and adapting to the environment so as to make your time abroad as enjoyable and productive as possible.

Having said all this, it is our expectation that this book will be especially valuable to students who are going on their own or with organized study abroad programs. The methods addressed here rely heavily on experiential learning as practiced and valued at both the college and secondary levels. It calls for the intellectual discipline demanded of students in a more or less structured educational environment. It expects its users to be ready to adopt an inquiring frame of mind which characterizes all good students.

This book is directed toward students—those going on their own or in organized programs—and students come in all ages, shapes and sizes. Thus, if you have an inquiring mind, this book ought to go along with you, even if you travel light. It is a manual on culture learning.

What you will find in these pages is not an academic treatment of cross-cultural communication but a collection of materials drawn from the experience of living abroad. The book is not based so much on theory as on practice. You may best understand it by thinking of it not as original ideas to carry you safely on your travels, but instead as reports of previous trips, supplied by people who have already been there, to enlighten you about the possibilities of culture learning.

The book is divided into four parts. In **Part A** you will find five essays that serve as a foundation for the rest of the book. Chapter 1 gives a definition of culture learning. Because there is a great difference between "just traveling" and culture learning, it's important that we have a common understanding of this core concept. Chapter 2 describes the attitudes and traits displayed by the person worthy of being called a culture learner. Chapter 3, while not presented in argument form, argues nonetheless that the best place to do culture learning is in the living classroom of culture itself, in situ, there with your hosts—morning, afternoon, and evening. Culture learning requires not only action, but also a thoughtful reflection upon what happens. Chapter 4 discusses the topic of cultural analysis, and chapter 5 focuses on cultural relativity and values. Yes, culture learning is holistic in its scope, touching on social behaviors as well as on central meanings. The five chapters frame a perspective for your subsequent "look" at culture.

Part B elaborates the culture-learning process. The materials are presented as practical guides. This section is essentially a workbook designed to help you stop, look, listen, and learn. The guides are grouped in sections such as "Beginning Well," "Settling In," "Getting Early Glimpses of the Host Culture," and "Moving into the Cultural Milieu." One set of guides is written especially for overseas sojourners who reside with host families. Another focuses on the study of cultural value systems.

Highlight the sentences you want to remember, scribble in the margins, respond to the assertions, argue with the opinions, answer the questions, and make up new ones. For education's sake, don't handle this book gently; it is not marked "fragile."

Part C fills your toolbox with additional instruments and supplies for you to craft your culture learning. An important series of guides tells you about, and models, journal keeping. In my opinion, a journal ranks in importance with a passport; if you are going to lose one or the other toward the end of your trip, you'll hurt less if you lose the passport. It can be replaced.

A second series of guides in Part C suggest various projects of cultural exploration. How can you use these guides? Simple—do the explorations. Or design your own alternative activities that get you up in the morning and out onto the street. A third series presents a number of case studies for your careful study.

Part D anticipates your return home. Though that may seem too far in the future for you to think about now, it is included because now is the time to start thinking about your return and because, eventually, you will see reentry as the final phase of your international culture-learning experience.

Keep in mind that the materials are prepared for a novice traveler, a beginner in cultural adjustment. If you've lived overseas before, you'll likely find some sections of the book elementary. But don't discard it. One can always get deeper into cross-cultural learning, and there are ideas and information here that will help you move beyond your current level of understanding. Don't worry about whether this book fits your particular circumstances. Novice or old pro, student or volunteer, traveling in a group or on your own, you will find ways to increase your learning, improve your ability to communicate with strangers, and enhance your intercultural experience.

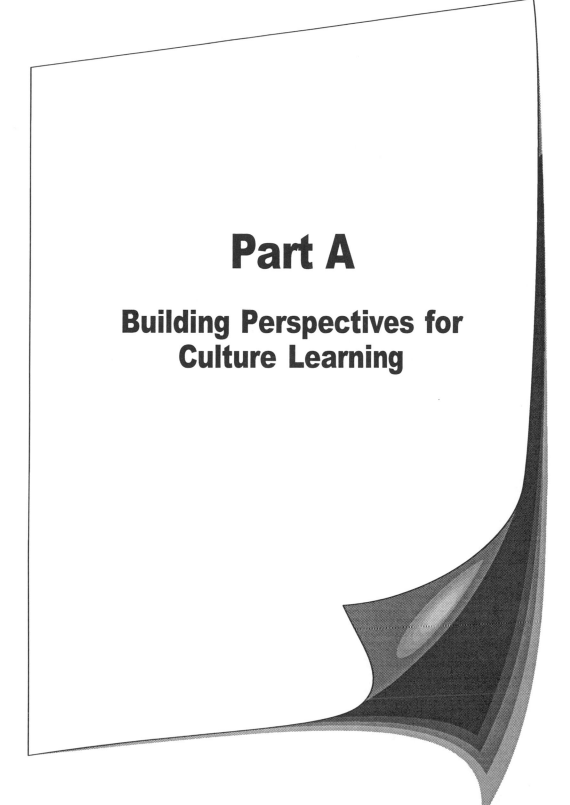

Part A

Building Perspectives for Culture Learning

Chapter 1

Culture Learning

The Whole World Guide to Culture Learning is dedicated to helping sojourners communicate across cultures. Not all travelers come naturally to culture learning. Not all who travel to and reside in foreign countries, even those who remain for five, ten, or more years, take on the task of comprehending the way of life of their hosts. To be sure, most people who leave home for an international trip bring home stories of their adventures and descriptions of the people they saw. Some may talk about the quaint habits, the new foods, and strange costumes encountered along the way. They show their snapshots and purchases. But this booty doesn't confirm that culture learning has taken place. For many, the gap between their native culture and the foreign culture remains unbridged. "East is East and West is West and never the twain shall meet," said Kipling. In the twentieth century, a science-oriented communication specialist has proclaimed: "There is no such thing as cross-cultural communication" (Martin 1976).These words sound scary, as do the attitudes they reflect.

To counter the possibilities of cultural separation, alienation, and even hostility that stem from such attitudes, we want to argue in these pages for the value of culture learning and the significance of intercultural communication and to help each reader become what Eric J. Leed (*The Mind of the Traveler* 1991, 2) calls "the brokers of contacts" among cultures—that is, people who not only know how to study cultures but also how to move comfortably from one culture to another and how to help other sojourners to bridge cultural gaps.

What is culture learning? Who does it? When? How? Why should a person

3

want to engage in culture learning? What is the result of culture learning?

Chapter 1 serves as a general tour of the subject of culture learning. It introduces crucial concepts and prepares you to follow the discussions and to use the guides which follow. Let's get started.

What is culture?

Culture learning has to do with (1) culture, (2) learners, and (3) a learning process. We'll begin with culture. It's a bit difficult to define precisely, but here's a definition you may find useful:

> Culture is the sum total of ways of living, including values, beliefs, esthetic standards, linguistic expression, patterns of thinking, behavioral norms, and styles of communication which a group of people has developed to assure its survival in a particular physical and human environment. Culture and the people who are part of it interact so that culture is not static. Culture is the response of a group of human beings to the valid and particular needs of its members. It, therefore, has an inherent logic and an essential balance between positive and negative dimensions. (Hoopes 1979, 3)

You may think of culture as the subject matter of culture learning in the same way that plant life is the subject matter of botany—or poetry the subject matter of literature. However, culture as "something to be learned" is a little difficult to get your mind around. On a continuum ranging from fluff stuff to the killers (students know how to rank their courses), the content of culture learning places among the more demanding of the disciplines. The reason for the difficulty is not that there's a lot to memorize, but rather that the material is elusive. Not only are people generally unaware of their own culture (they take it for granted), but they are also outsiders to the other's culture, naive and innocent of what the natives take for granted.

Four years after the end of the so-called Cultural Revolution in the People's Republic of China, I tried to teach a group of Chinese professors about culture and its influence on human behavior. The biggest challenge of that course was to come to a common understanding of the concept of culture. Although they spoke of their own cultural revolution (which was hard for me to fathom), the sense of culture as an indigenous and dynamic way of being seemed a strange idea to them. The word culture is frequently used, but its significance often hides itself from people.

Culture learning and cross-cultural adaptation

Culture learning can be seen as part of the process of cross-cultural adaptation that people experience when they go abroad to live. The study of this subject goes back to work done by Sverre Lysgaard (1955) and John Taylor and Jeanne E. Gullahorn (1963) in which the theory of the U curve—and subsequently the W curve—of cross-cultural adjustment was formulated.

The U-curve theory was based on the observation that most people when they live for some time in a foreign country go through a series of transition

4

stages that, when graphed, form the shape of a U. They start out in a state of excitement and interest (often called euphoria), begin to experience difficulties in functioning in the culture, reach a nadir of dissatisfaction and discontent, and then begin to pull out of it, until they finally reestablish a stable emotional state of being. The W curve (literally "double U") was suggested by the fact that when long-term sojourners return home they go through a similar kind of reentry adjustment.

This process is also referred to as culture shock, especially when the bottom of the adjustment cycle (or U curve) is reached. The principal cause of culture shock lies in the encounter with differences—but not just the exotic differences of the immediate senses, the sights, sounds and smells of the new environment. It is the differences in the way the society is organized and in the values, behaviors, styles of communication, and patterns of thinking that cause the problem, since so much of what makes up these basic cultural characteristics is automatic and unconscious and is assumed to be universal. When we encounter differences in these basic ways of being, we are thrown off without knowing why. Things mean something different from what we expect. Our behaviors are misunderstood. Our sense of who we are becomes confused. The cues by which we govern our behavior and identify ourselves at home are gone or mean something different. At the simplest level, a gesture which to you means "OK" may in another culture, Brazil, for instance, be an obscenity. At a deeper level, you may instinctively avoid political arguments with people outside your family and be offended when a Dane challenges you on political issues. Or you may solve problems by using information and instruments you have, where a Frenchperson would think you shallow if you didn't start with a clear theoretical framework.

The reaction to culture shock varies from person to person but may consist of such things as irritability, depression, loss of sleep or appetite (or, conversely, compensations such as overeating), anger, loss of self-esteem, and others. It may result in the person wanting to go (or sometimes actually going) home or developing a very hostile stance toward everything about the host culture. The emergence from this stage of culture shock occurs as you *learn* the host culture. As the values which your hosts live by become more identifiable and appear more reasonable, as the customs and expected behaviors become familiar and you can engage in them comfortably and in a manner which gets the response you want, the emotional problems of culture shock begin to dissipate. The cues become decipherable; you can interpret and predict what is happening or going to happen around you. You feel better about yourself and your hosts. (For more on culture shock, see Guides 24 and 25.)

Culture learning and cross-cultural adjustment are therefore closely linked in the experience of the person living abroad. The pursuit of culture learning speeds you along the road to effective cross-cultural adaptation. The pursuit of effective adaptation provides the context and content for culture learning.

The culture-learning continuum

A number of scholars have suggested that there is a culture-learning continuum along which people can be seen to progress. Most of these continua show a movement from ethnocentrism to some form of multiculturalism. They are useful in

5

enabling you to identify where you and/or others are located in the stages of development and growth described. One of the most interesting and useful models has been proposed by Milton J. Bennett and is called "A Developmental Model of Intercultural Sensitivity" ("Towards Ethnorelativism" 1993).

In Bennett's model, the progress of an individual from ethnocentrism to what he refers to as "ethnorelativism" depends on how she or he deals with cultural differences, which in turn defines the level the person is at in the developmental process. Bennett identifies six stages in that process:

1. Ethnocentrism—a simple denial that the differences exist. The pure ethnocentric believes that the whole world is like him or her, but pure ethnocentrism is a rarely found state of being.

2. Defensiveness—the perception that the differences one encounters are threatening. Barriers are raised and negative judgments made against those who are different.

3. Minimization of the perceived differences—the perception that the differences are not very great or very important. "We're all alike under the skin," is the minimalist's rubric.

4. Acceptance—the recognition that differences exist, that they are substantial and important, and that they can be both positive and negative.

5. Adaptation—the willingness to accommodate and adjust one's behavior to the patterns and styles of another culture.

6. Adoption and integration—the merging of selected aspects of another culture into one's own cultural identity or patterns of thinking and behaving, becoming a bi- or multicultural person.

Successful culture learners inevitably push themselves along this continuum, although their progress is rarely without setbacks and temporary regressions. Identifying where you stand on it can give you an indication of the degree of progress you are making in your culture-learning endeavors.

Peter Adler, in his seminal writings on cultural identity (1974, 1975, 1977), elaborated on the final stage of the culture-learning continuum. The passage through culture shock and cross-cultural adaptation, Adler suggests, is accompanied by a stressful challenge to and change in the identity of the sojourner. But the sense of isolation and questioning of self that results from the experience is not to be seen as a call to despair. It is instead a springboard for the creation or evolution of a new identity which is "inclusive of life patterns different from [one's] own....We can call this new type of person multicultural because he [or she] embodies a core process of self-verification that is grounded in both the universality of the human condition and the diversity of cultural forms" (1977, 157).

But what do these abstractions about cross-cultural learning and identity mean in practical terms for the culture learner? They do not suggest, nor do we recommend, that you engage in morbid introspection throughout the time of your travel or residence in another culture, but rather they indicate the need for a regular and careful processing of the stuff of culture as one undoes and resets the culture boundaries in the mind and heart. You may and should ask, what are the components of this culture that you are using to shape who you are? (See Guides 11, 19, 21, 26, 36, and 54.)

Culture learning and communication

One of the processes to which every learner must give attention is intercultural communication, which involves much more than learning and speaking a foreign language.

Edward T. Hall, in his classic study, *The Silent Language* (1981), to which we will refer again in another context, argued succinctly that "culture is communication," meaning that all the ways of behaving, thinking, valuing, and organizing within the context of a culture are special to that culture and communicate something about it. They constitute a "silent language" or what is sometimes referred to as the cultural code. Here we focus particularly on nonverbal communication, but with a meaning much broader than mere gestures and physical expressions.

When you enter a cultural environment different from your own, you encounter a whole new communication system. Even if you know or understand the language, there are many ways people communicate with each other and give meanings to behavior, which are special to that culture. They may laugh when they are unhappy, for instance; body odors may be valued, touching may be taboo, privacy may not be respected, dependency on others may be a virtue. While not much will be absolutely unique, these cultural characteristics will exist in different combinations and intensities and, at the deepest level, will be anywhere from significantly to radically different from your own.

The basic problem lies in the fact that in your own society when you attempt to communicate with someone, there is a broad base of shared cultural experience—values, customary behaviors, ways of thinking and perceiving—that provides the context for the message. This base enables each of you engaged in the process of sending messages back and forth to interpret what you see and hear in very nearly the same way. At the simplest level, if an American is chatting with a passing acquaintance and one of them ends the conversation by saying, "Let's get together sometime," each one understands there is no obligation to do so—and in most cases not even an expectation that it will occur. The foreign student in the United States frequently expects the getting together to take place, because he or she doesn't understand American communication styles and patterns of personal relations.

At a more complex level, culture defines the obligations people in the society have toward each other. In many there are elaborate rituals of reciprocity in giving gifts or paying the bill on social occasions. Americans tend to be wary of and avoid social obligations of this sort and the personal entanglements they involve. Because of the value placed by American culture on independence and self-sufficiency, they are more likely to want to pay their own way.

While at a distance these kinds of differences may not seem so problematic, when they are multiplied by all the dimensions of culture and when you are in the midst of them and in a state of confusion, they can scuttle your best efforts to communicate effectively.

Even if people speak the same language, as, for instance, the Americans, Australians, and British do, beneath the linguistic surface each finds the other very different in the assumptions they make about life, in the values they hold dear, in their behavior patterns and ways of thinking—so much so that they are often amazed at the conflict and disagreement which occurs in cross-cultural encounters. Australians, for instance, suppress recognition of outstanding individual achievement while Americans glorify it. When Australians start cutting Americans down to size, watch out.

In a country where the language is foreign to you, even if you speak it—unless you learned it as a child growing up in that country—there will be major dimensions of the culture you will not understand. There will be nonverbal cues you will not pick up until you have been there a long time or study systematically as a culture learner.

It is important then for the overseas sojourner to recognize that there is a cultural code as well as a linguistic code to be learned and that the more attention given to learning it and the more rapidly it is learned, the quicker the person will progress along the culture-learning and cross-cultural adaptation paths. (Guides that address communication issues include 7, 9, 10, 17, and 49.)

Culture learning and values

There are two major dimensions to the values question in the culture-learning experience. One relates to the fundamental role of assumptions, values, and worldviews in determining the cultural patterns the stranger encounters. The other involves the question of value relativity: how can you be clear about values and ethics when your basic ideas of right and wrong differ significantly from those of your hosts?

The latter question will be dealt with extensively in chapter 5. Here we will examine how values affect the practical pursuit of knowledge in a foreign culture. Our assumptions about the world and the values by which we decide what is right and wrong, good and bad, are buried deeply within us. They were put there over the long period of time we were children and were acculturated into the society of our family, friends, neighbors, teachers, mentors, and other important people in our lives. They are believed and followed so instinctively that most of the time they are out of awareness. In fact, the nearer one is to the ethnocentric end of the culture-learning spectrum the more one will assume that one's own values are natural and universal.

Even for those who accept the proposition that other cultures have different values, it is still a shock to discover how many the differences are and how significant.

The reason for the inescapability of this cross-cultural surprise is that it is difficult to be aware of the values that govern our lives until they are contrasted with different ones, until we are removed from the environment in which they are "natural." It is like not realizing how necessary oxygen is to our survival until we are deprived of it.

To give a specific example, many Americans have no idea that the kind of individualism valued by Americans is, in many cultures, valued very little, and in some is actually considered a negative trait. Many have no idea that American concepts of personal privacy and private property are not held by people in a number of other countries. Many have no idea that what one personally achieves is in some countries valued much less than one's social status or family connections.

Students of intercultural relations have called these values and beliefs "cultural baggage," which we carry with us everywhere we go but without realizing we

8

have it. We'll come back to cultural baggage later.

The point is that the culture learner must be ready to encounter differences in very important values when she or he goes abroad, and must be willing to suspend judgment and observe the nature and significance of the differences before reacting within a right/wrong, good/bad framework. (See Guides 26-29 for exercises in exploring values, both one's own and those of others.)

The process of culture learning

Culture learning is the effort to gain insight into how cultural strangers live. That means, of course, that one must do more than memorize a few key words of their vocabulary or mimic a few of their interesting behaviors; it involves much more than just hanging around until you catch on. Rather, one must come to know the basics of the culture—the worldviews, values, ways of thinking, styles of communication, and patterns of behavior that are shared. In the Philippines, for example, that may mean learning the complex values embedded in the concept of harmony in human relationships: *Pakikisama*, getting along with others; *Hiya*, maintaining self-respect, having and saving " face," and fearing shame; and *Utang na loob*, the balancing of obligations and debts. Each culture one attempts to learn offers mysteries of this kind that must be understood.

Culture learning, when done properly, calls for cognitive, affective, and behavioral knowing. Cognitive learning is typically associated with traditional classroom mastery of a subject through conventional intellectual discipline. The subject matter might include the theory of culture, a description of people and their customs, and analyses of cultural differences. For example, one may study the Japanese use of the go-between, or mediator, in situations of social negotiations. The concept may be introduced, described, and illustrated by a teacher. Typically this type of instruction and learning takes place in a classroom setting.

Affective learning is of a different kind. Mildred Sikkema and Agnes Niyekawa talk about affective learning in terms of active rather than passive understanding, "the development at gut level of an attitude of acceptance, respect, and tolerance of cultural differences" (1987, 4). In learning affectively about the Japanese tradition of the go-between one not only describes and defines it intellectually, one has an emotional response to the experience and feels the subtlety of the role played by the go-between and its importance in maintaining the social harmony which the Japanese value as much as if not more than the Filipinos.

Behavioral learning presents an equal challenge—to learn so well that one lives differently than one did before as a monocultural or ethnocentric person. Ultimately, the learner begins to behave in ways that save face in the Philippines or, in Japan, he or she calls upon a go-between at just the right moment. All education should have such transforming behavioral effects. We all know, however, that straight A's in exams at school do not necessarily predict how one lives after graduation. So it is that culture learning isn't completed until the learner is transformed.

You should not be surprised, then, that the most effective and efficient culture learning takes place not in the classroom, but on-site—in a store, on the job, at a host family's dinner table, in an intersection where people of differing cultures bump into each other. It takes place in various social situations where you

9

encounter people behaving in the normal context of their culture. Thus, obviously, you can best learn about Brazil in Brazil. The way to learn about kibbutzim is to go live and work in a kibbutz. The term used in this manual to describe this type of on-site learning is the *action-reflection-response strategy.* In brief, this strategy is a tool to help turn ordinary (and sometimes extraordinary) events of life into instructional modules. You teach yourself using your own experiences in the foreign setting.

The dynamics of culture learning

Recently a friend of mine went overseas for a year. As expected, she suffered culture shock. But the letters she wrote to me (and others) while she was there indicate that she will be numbered among culture learners. As you read several excerpts from these letters, notice how she shifts from newcomer to a committed learner. The first excerpt is lifted from a passage about how tough the initial month was.

> I miss desperately the people and activities left behind; I'm moody and cry easily; frustrated with situations (family, neighborhood, university) that don't suit me, I begin to think about and question my aspirations, my goals.

Her candid confession, arising from the painfulness of culture shock, is understandably focused upon herself. And then within two weeks comes another letter that shows a shifting of her focus that surely must have required extraordinary effort.

> In the next six weeks I'm going to be doing intensive language study—writing, reading and I'll be translating either a book or some articles. I see writing in this language as transportation to get to other options—I'm looking forward to ecology studies, for example. (Also nutrition, art and literature.) I need this year—all of it: the immersion into a culture that now intrigues me even more, the introduction to a world of emotions I'd never felt before....

She will become a culture learner through her language and ecology studies and through her interests in the specific subjects she lists, but equally important, she will become a culture learner through gradually coming to terms with and understanding the emotions she is experiencing. This learning will not occur through passive endurance but through an active investment of herself.

Culture learning, then, is not only a prescription for overcoming culture shock, but a process of growth and transformation. Whereas some people go home early and others build a wall to keep out the host culture, and still others make grudging accommodations to the strange customs, the successful culture learner commits to a journey from a monocultural beginning point to a larger world in which he or she develops new perspectives, learns new mental, emotional, and behavioral responses, and builds intercultural bridges—in short, becomes a new cultural person.

All of this is easier said than done. A culture is a powerful force, created over a long period of time for its own members. A culture is contained and coherent, with its own internal logic and unspoken laws. It is dynamic. Its energy is capable of thwarting you or of making your culture learning an exciting passage.

Chapter 2

Attitudes and Character Traits That Promote Culture Learning

Attitudes

Whether you succeed in bridging the chasm that separates cultures and that Kipling found so striking depends largely on the kind of sojourner you choose to be. What is the difference between those who effect a meeting of cultures and those who do not?

J. Lawrence Burkholder, who flew relief supplies into China during its civil war in the late 1940s and later became a professor at Harvard and then president at Goshen College, has characterized the curious traveler as "one of the most delightful persons of Western civilization," but he hastens to distinguish these "Marco Polos" of the Western world from the self-centered modern tourist. The traditional traveler, according to Burkholder, "learned new customs, ate strange foods and met different races, heard legends, observed religious customs and formed deep friendships.... The traveler said, in effect, 'I want to know you and your culture because you have something to offer me and my people'." In contrast the tourist "adopts a quick, packaged schedule, makes a standardized trip, lives out of suitcases, observes historical monuments, and collects souvenirs. The tourist stops, snaps pictures, and defends his or her pocketbook" (Showalter 1989, 27-28).

Similar is the executive who stops to do business in six cities in five days and experiences the world only in the rarefied atmosphere of first-class plane cabins, high-priced hotel rooms, and expensive restaurants. Burkholder calls on us all to be travelers of high quality rather than self-centered tourists on a junket.

As noted in the last chapter, all travelers carry cultural baggage—a set of assumptions, values, attitudes, and behaviors that may slip through customs checks unobserved and accompany them everywhere they go on their journey. These attitudes are their intellectual and emotional apparel. Unlike the contents of their luggage, however, this cultural baggage is rarely taken out and examined, seldom altered to fit the different conditions encountered in their travels, and almost never evaluated to see if it is appropriate or adapted to what they are doing.

You will find described here four attitudes that go a long way toward ensuring success in your cross-cultural travels and interactions. They are (1) a high regard for culture, (2) an eagerness to learn, (3) a desire to make connections, and (4) a readiness to give as well as receive.

A high regard for culture

The first attitude has to do with how you regard culture. Do you have a high regard for culture or a low one? The person with a low regard for culture perceives cultural differences as a social handicap to be gotten rid of. Several years ago in an orientation class for a group going to three countries (coincidentally all beginning with B—Bangladesh, Bolivia, and Burkina Faso), the participants discussed their participation in a weekend of educational service in an inner-city ghetto. They closed the session with prayers, during which one person asked God to "make culture as nothing, so that we can love and serve." The prayer suggested that cultural differences were an impediment to their good intentions.

A person with a high regard for culture, on the other hand, sees the diversity of peoples on the earth as good and the social dynamic that produces that diversity as a valuable and productive force.

Venturing into foreign cultures and among strangers is seen as an opportunity to comprehend the wide diversity in human existence and to find new options for human relationships.

An eagerness to learn

A second attitude pertains to your feelings about change. Do you want, during your travels, to remain stable and fixed, preserving what now is, or do you want to be changed by the experience? A cross-cultural setting can be a violent tidal wave that you brace yourself against or it can be a classroom of first rank. There, in a context that takes away the familiar props that help you preserve your routines, something extraordinary occurs. You are jolted, sometimes shocked, given unfamiliar cues, forced onto unknown paths. The newness, the strangeness, the unpleasantness—it is often unpleasant—arouse unfamiliar feelings. You find that your old ideas don't work. Things are not what they seem to be.

The traveler who welcomes this kind of challenge in hopes of learning new facts, gaining new understandings, changing old opinions, shaping new interpretations, and making new commitments is, in those very acts, positioning himself or herself to learn.

Many illustrations could be given. Sojourners with a mind to learn discover the importance of knowing what Taoism is, which are the South African writers of note, who the Shiites are, where European surveyors drew boundaries for Arab peoples, why the Shining Path is attacking foreigners in Peru, and what "magic realism" is. They may want to learn the crafts of a country, understand better how the legal system works, or explore the subtleties of negotiating or bargaining in a different cultural context. Given a curriculum of this social dimension, the person who embarks on culture learning can never return home the same, for the impact of the "textbook" in this course is to redefine the boundaries of personal commitment forever.

A desire to make connections

A third attitude to be recommended for the effective sojourner is the desire to make connections. Here's an example of two different kinds of traveler: one stays close to the travel group and moves around only in the tourist bus, never venturing out of sight of the tour leader; the other is at the edges of the group, taking early morning walks, trying to talk with the shopkeepers, and using a free afternoon to travel independently to an archeological site in order to find out how the diggers do their work.

Compare two kinds of Americans living abroad: one lives in an American enclave, buys food at an American commissary or where the storekeeper speaks English, attends American social and cultural events, and reads books and magazines from the States; the other moves in with a local family for the first few months in order to learn the language, attends wild Tuesday night soccer matches, sitting in the section of bleachers where the die-hard fans congregate, and drinks coffee regularly in the local cafe.

These descriptions highlight the differences in association patterns. While I don't agree with L. John Martin, who, as noted before, says that "there is no such thing as cross-cultural communication" (1976), it is certainly clear that travelers who remain totally isolated from the people of the host culture, ignorant of their customs, and bent on defending the sanctity of their own cultural norms, will find communication difficult. Intercultural living *is* a risky proposition. Not all the natives are perfect hosts, nor are all travelers friendly guests. Not all merchants are honest, and not all cultural characteristics are benign. When strangers discover that the cultural chasm is deep and wide, not all of them have the will to persevere nor the skills to build bridges and find common cultural ground. Sometimes, even with the best of efforts, communication breaks down, culture shock sets in more or less permanently, and people become enemies. If two people are totally estranged, there can be no communication. If, on the other hand, the partners in communication work hard to establish a common ground of some sort and make the effort to form a connection, they will succeed in creating their own unique common culture. The second person described in each of the examples at the beginning of this section is forming the associations necessary for culture learning.

A readiness to give as well as receive

The fourth attitude for the effective traveler is a meaningful sense of reciprocity and the willingness to engage in mutual or cooperative interchange.

Travel, by its nature, tends to be self-serving. One makes a trip in order to have fun, to see the world, to satisfy curiosity, to make money, to escape responsibility, to earn college credits, to be with one's spouse, or to seek a better life. One returns home with advantages for having traveled.

13

It's a lot to ask such a traveler to try to associate with foreigners, to build a common cultural ground, to make the first attempts at communication. It's asking even more to propose that as a traveler you set up exchanges with strangers and arrangements for sharing that enrich both parties so that other people benefit as much as you do from your travel.

However idealistic this may sound, people who display the imagination to locate opportunities for interacting with strangers, the courage to make the first moves, the graciousness to begin receiving what the strangers have to offer, the resourcefulness to give of themselves to strangers, and the patience to allow such reciprocity to have its own rewards demonstrate attitudes most conducive to culture learning and cross-cultural adaptation.

Reciprocity has its problems, of course. What your host culture would like to give you may not be what you really want. You hope your colleague at the office in Tokyo invites you to go skiing with him during Christmas vacation; instead his Christmas gift to you is a Japanese print. You intend your house call to the Greek acquaintance to be merely a brief inquiry about the youth hostels; he insists on your staying the entire day, a day that you had hoped to spend alone with your American friends. You contract with a guide to take your group to see the waterfalls; he takes you, instead, to a town festival that features a parade because he thinks the festivities to be more important than the waterfalls.

Further, what your host culture would like for you to give them may not be what you are ready to give. The Filipino family that hosted you so generously now seems to expect your continued association with them, even your support (and hosting) of their children. The president of the club who eagerly agreed to talk with your group about the changing role of women in the country has now asked you to make a personal contact with the American consul on her behalf. She wants a two-year visa to the United States.

Effective reciprocity begins in events that may seem trivial, but which represent effective cross-cultural communications. Reciprocity may become institutional or national in scope. A town that hosts American students requests and is reimbursed not with money but with an ambulance that is made in the students' college town. The two cities become sisters. The countries eventually modify their systems of tariffs to effect fairer trading with each other.

In summary, the traveler with a positive attitude toward cross-cultural reciprocity thinks of a trip, from beginning to end, not in terms of personal gain but rather in terms of opportunities for sharing. That kind of attitude helps cultures bridge their differences.

Character traits

What kind of personality does a successful culture learner have? Are there differences in the character traits of the person who is not only willing but eager to become a culture learner and the person who retreats from the challenge?

International program directors wish they had some answers to this question. A widely known and respected international service program was recently asked by its field representative for sixteen volunteers. The home office came up with them, but one dropped out at the airport just before departure from the United States. When the team arrived in the country, two volunteers turned around and went home. A couple of days later during the first orientation sessions, two more left. Two more were asked to leave before they had even settled in to their assignments. Nine of the sixteen remained for the work. "What a waste of time and energy!" the field representative said. "The home office ought to improve its screening."

Indeed, it should. For a number of years I have assisted in the orientation program of another international agency, smaller than the one referred to above. Typically this latter agency has about a thousand people in the field, many of them overseas. To characterize those assignments, I turn to words such as demanding, dangerous, undefined, complex, exhausting, and significant. Yet the rate of early returnees is extremely low.

Why would Agency A lose seven of sixteen volunteers in one assignment and Agency B lose so few?

The answer is not obvious. Administrative competence of the organizations is not the critical factor. Both agencies are run well. Education level is not the answer. Agency A volunteers have a higher average education than Agency B, many with master's degrees. Economic levels, skill levels, language facility, length of orientation—none of these factors satisfactorily explains the adaptability and success of one group of volunteers in contrast to the other. The answer lies instead in the fact that Agency B looked for certain character traits in the people it selected, traits that predisposed them to success in cross-cultural situations. Agency A did not.

Character traits which influence intercultural competence

What are these traits? While researchers have explored the predictability of intercultural success, the data continue to be tentative, somewhat contradictory, and quite general. We, therefore, don't know if there is an ideal intercultural personality, but we have some clues. I also have my own experience of working with overseas educational and service programs for many years. What I've tried to do here is describe the kinds of persons I have found to be most successful in our programs, and have come up with ten preferred traits (expressed as comparatives).

1. A curious rather than a passive person. I'm referring to the group member who, on a trip to the hot and noisy sugar mill, pushes nearer to the guide to shout questions about the factory process, about sugar cultivation, and about the industry, while others follow on behind.

2. A trusting rather than a suspicious person. In a journey to another culture, an individual entrusts himself or herself to others. There's no other way to get through the journey.

3. A brave rather than a fearful person. On occasion I have had difficulty distinguishing bravery from daring and even foolhardiness among the rascals I have worked with, and yet this kind of valiant explorer soon climbs higher than the cautious ones.

4. A secure rather than a guarded person. The individual who has a strong self-concept will likely be confident in new situations. Insecure individuals feel threatened rather easily.

15

5. A laid-back, relaxed person rather than an impatient one. This has to do with time—some people can bend easily to accommodate the pace of the local environment. Others can't.

6. A teachable rather than a finished person. It's easy to detect the difference. One person has already closed the book. The other is ready for new experiences and new understandings, ready to change and grow.

7. A friendly rather than a diligent person. The latter has a list of things to accomplish while the former gives first place to people.

8. A humble rather than a haughty person. Arrogance produces "the ugly American." Humility corresponds with genuineness.

9. A compassionate or empathetic person rather than an insensitive one. I'm not talking here about the do gooder, but rather the person with the capacity and the will to identify with the circumstances of others.

10. A person with a sense of humor rather than a humorless one. Yes, laughter is the best medicine overseas also.

Even while this informal list was being tested over the years by firsthand experience, it grew as I read the work of practitioners and scholars who have tried to define intercultural competence. L. Robert Kohls in his widely used *Survival Kit for Overseas Living* (1984) identifies sixteen traits that contribute to cultural adjustment, most of which overlap with my list. Several deserve special mention here.

11. Low goal/task orientation. Kohls says that a person who is less compelled and preoccupied by a work assignment is likely to be more open to social interactions and consequently quicker to adapt to cultural challenges.

12. Nonjudgmentalness. This has to do with a person's ability to "roll with the punches" without making early and prejudicial evaluations of people and situations. This person has a high tolerance level for differences encountered.

13. Flexibility, adaptability. The ability to make basic changes in thought patterns, experience new ways of feeling, and adopt behavioral changes. The contrasting trait is rigidity.

14. Communicativeness. How could I have failed to put this item on my first list? It has to do, of course, with verbal and nonverbal aptitudes—listening, observing, and responding. One's ability to be perceptive relates to one's capacity to be insightful.

15. Warmth in human relationships. Kohls is referring to something beyond communication skills. By using the term "warmth" he is directing attention to a particular kind of personality affect that encourages comfortable interaction.

16. Motivation. It's rather obvious that a person who truly wants to be a sojourner will be a better culture learner than one who is forced into the situation.

17. Self-reliance. The person of positive self-concept, integrity, and courage will adapt most easily to the challenge of culture learning.

18. Ability to fail. Kohls considers this trait to be one of the most important. The person who is tolerant of his or her own mistakes and tries to learn from them, rather than bemoan imperfections, has more potential for rapid and effective adaptation in new situations.

Finally, I'd like to call particular attention to several character traits that seem to commend themselves powerfully. They are a person's (1) breadth of affiliation, (2) tolerance for ambiguity, (3) general receptivity, and (4) capacity for empathy.

Breadth of affiliation

The kinds of affiliations a person has may be seen as a trait contributing to intercultural competence. It has to do with belonging and pertains to the groups one becomes a part of, the social configuration that gives a person a social identity. One is affiliated with family, school, church, region, and possibly an ethnic community. Occasionally in class I ask students to record all their affiliations. These lists eventually include 50, 75, and even 100 items.

The nature of one's affiliations contributes significantly to one's readiness (or lack thereof) to meet strangers, inasmuch as the group's disposition to outsiders impresses itself upon each individual (Stewart and Bennett 1991). Each cultural group holds a set of attitudes about distant and dissimilar cultures; affiliated group members are likely to hold the same attitudes.

Xenophobic groups—those fearful or contemptuous of strangers or foreigners—provide a scaffolding to support their ethnocentric disposition. They support prejudices, build fences, and discourage their members from venturing into strangers' lands. In contrast, culturally tolerant groups urge their members to meet strangers and provide support when doing so.

The success rate for Agency B described earlier in this chapter (see p. 15) has a great deal to do with affiliation. Its constituency is positively motivated for cross-cultural contacts. It is not unusual for those constituents to travel, live, and work overseas. There is even an expectation in churches, homes, and communities of that constituency—even among its youth—of spending one, two, or three years in an overseas service assignment.

In sharp contrast is the agency that has to deal with a constituency not positively motivated for cross-cultural contacts, where families have rarely ventured out of their own communities, where people are not hospitable to strangers of other ethnic origins or races, and where learning foreign languages and studying other cultures are considered boring subjects in school.

Tolerance for ambiguity

Ambiguity is another element in the intercultural experience to which scholars have given attention (Brislin 1981; Dodd 1987; Grove and Torbiörn 1993; Gudykunst and Kim 1984b; Ruben 1977). It too is presented as a function of multiculturalism and is expressed something like this: one measure of a person's potential for multiculturalism may be indicated in his or her capacity to tolerate or accommodate ambiguity.

Consider its opposite. A person with little tolerance for ambiguity insists upon clear definitions, precision, predictability, satisfied expectations, and, above all, knowing with certainty what is happening or is about to happen. Such a person needs to know prior to the field trip whether there will be warm showers, when breakfast will be served, whether the water will be safe to drink, and when the group will return.

Here's a specific case. Marjorie, a student abroad, happily invited her host family to a roller-skating party sponsored by her college. Because of her limited facility in using the local language and because roller-skating was not yet a well-known recreation (only a couple of rinks in the country), she gave her host parents a printed invitation and explanation. She concluded by their expressions that they accepted the invitation and shared her enthusiasm. Sunday, the day of the skating party, arrived. To Marjorie's surprise, the parents announced in the morning that the family was going to the country for a picnic. But what about the skating party, Marjorie tried to ask. They assured Marjorie that they'd return in the afternoon for roller-skating. Thereupon they—along with Marjorie—left for the outing. In the afternoon, they said they'd soon be returning to the city, but they didn't. An hour later they repeated their intention of packing up, but they didn't. They finally began their return to the city when the roller-skating party was over.

Why did the family say they would go to the party and then pursue other plans? Was it intentional? Was there a religious scruple against the event? Perhaps the father, who was somewhat authoritarian, didn't want to go, and so ruled the family according to his wishes? Maybe the family was socially ill at ease with other host families? Did they think it would cost them money? Were they timid about trying to skate?

The situation—while it was in progress—tested Marjorie to the extreme. Would she, or would she not, accommodate this ambiguity? On the one hand, she could allow herself to be upset by the confusion and express her disappointment and frustration with their inconsistent behavior. On the other, she could acknowledge to herself the continuing presence of mysteries in this foreign land, accommodate the strange and incongruous behavior, and make the most of a family outing, hoping that someday she would better understand.

General receptivity

To illustrate the idea of receptivity, I use the metaphor of gatekeeping. The keeper of the gate has the responsibility of letting something in, or of shutting something out. By nature and training, most of us are expert gatekeepers, and we keep most of what happens around us out. For example, we are exposed to a multitude of advertisements and commercial messages daily. Some studies say the number adds up to more than 1500 for an urban dweller. With so many messages hitting us, we'd go crazy by 10:00 A.M. if we weren't expert at screening the messages out. Our attention is selective in what we consciously hear, see, feel, and taste (indeed, technically it is called "selective perception").

So it is with social and cultural issues. Located inside a cultural group, we keep the gates. As I read the daily paper, for instance, this kind of gatekeeping is going on constantly. I pause to read what has happened in my town, but skim the events of a neighboring village. I am more receptive to news of my country than news of others.

This natural tendency has important consequences. As we screen things out, we circumscribe the kinds of information that will affect us. Those limited pieces of information shape our view of the world. So we exercise our gatekeeping skills, trying to make wise decisions of what to keep out and what to let in.

To become multicultural, there must be a measure of receptivity not only in allowing new information through the gates, but also in revising our view of things once we absorb it. An ethnocentric person lives according to the gag line: "My mind is made up, don't confuse me with the facts." A multicultural person, on the other hand, is always ready to modify a sense of the world and of him- or herself on the basis of new evidence. This readiness is more than a superficial tolerance of things strange. Rather it implies a willingness to change a frame of reference so as to see things from another's point of view.

Capacity for empathy

Another key component of the multicultural personality is the ability to empathize (Bennett 1979; Broome 1991; Casse 1981; Luce and Smith 1987; Stewart and Bennett 1991). Empathy is related to, but distinct from, sympathy. If you have sympathy, you express pity or sorrow for the distress of another person. The sympathy, however, is determined by how you would feel if you were in that person's place. It is oriented to one's self. Since, you might say, I typically feel this way about such things, my friend probably feels this way too.

If you have empathy, on the other hand, you can identify with the feelings of the other person on that person's terms. "Empathy relies on the ability to temporarily set aside one's own perception of the world and assume an alternative perspective," say Stewart and Bennett. "Self-interest and purposes are held in check as one attempts to place oneself in the immediate situation and field (but not in the shoes) of another" (1991, 152).

An empathetic person picks up seemingly disconnected cues and makes coherent sense out of them. Many of these cues arise not so much from the words or explicit gestures of the other person, as from the social and cultural context in which the other person lives. As scholars try to articulate this concept of empathy, I recall the empathetic participants in our programs overseas—those who were less concerned about their own first-day nervousness than about the insecurities of the host family as its members welcomed a stranger into their homes. On field trips they were the ones to empathize with the tour guide whose voice quivered because she had never explained the factory before to a group of visitors. Empathetic volunteers seemed to learn quickly which child at the orphanage needed to be held and hugged.

The multicultural personality

This chapter has emphasized the importance of attitudes and character traits in the culture learner. Even in the absence of a definitive model of the culturally competent person, the attitudes and traits do comprise a tentative picture that at least can be contrasted with the attitudes and traits that discourage culture learning. For example, see chapter 1 on the way a person can be "located" on the culture-learning continuum.

As you will recall from that explanation, the culture-learning continuum is marked at one extreme by ethnocentrism and at the other by multiculturalism (or ethnorelativism). At the ethnocentrism extreme is the person fully immersed in his or her own culture with no sense that there are other valid sets of perceptions, structures of thought, or attitudes and behaviors. To this person the possibility of connections with a world beyond one's own culture is ruled out. An ethnocentric personality is defined and fenced in by the norms of one particular ethnicity.

In contrast, the person at the multiculturalism end of the continuum is culturally mobile. His or her own sense of self is molded continually by new cultural contacts and new relationships. (See Bennett "Towards Ethnorelativism" 1993; Bochner 1981; Gudykunst and Kim 1984a; Kim 1988; Sarbaugh 1988; Triandis 1990.)

Young Yun Kim, who has researched and written extensively on intercultural issues, has explored what she calls the "intercultural person."

> The intercultural person represents a type of person whose cognitive, affective, and behavioral characteristics are not limited but are open to growth beyond the psychological parameters of his or her own culture.... With an openness toward change, a willingness to revise our own cultural premises, and the enthusiasm to work it through, we are on the way to cultivating our fullest human potentialities and to contributing our share in this enormous process of civilizational change. (1991, 401-11)

The notion of a culture-learning continuum can be especially helpful for the person inclined to be categorical. It is not a question of whether one is or is not qualified to be a culture learner. It is more helpful to think of every potential culture learner as located at some point on the continuum, but not forever fixed at that position. Rather, each is capable of growing, of moving on the continuum toward ethnorelativism.

Chapter 3

Methods in Culture Learning: The Action-Reflection-Response Strategy

In the previous chapter, we discussed the *attitudes* and *traits* which contribute to successful culture learning. In this chapter and the following one we turn our attention to the *skills* needed for productive culture learning.

This chapter is devoted to one particular model well suited to culture learning, the action-reflection-response strategy, which is perhaps more commonly known as experiential learning.

Although the language of this chapter comes from the discipline of education, the material applies to all travelers and sojourners, including those who are not formally designated as students.

To define the action-reflection-response strategy, let's contrast it with another one, the theory-application model. This latter model uses a two-part sequence: first, you learn a theory; second, you put that theory into practice. The theory-application model pervades Western colleges and universities, learned societies, science, industry, and theology. While the applications of this model vary widely, students using it are expected to listen, to absorb, and sometimes to memorize, for they later will have occasion to apply what they have learned. The following assumptions support this model: (1) learning is a rational process, dominated by rigorous thought; (2) learning is linear—things happen in sequence; (3) the best learning is efficient, with wasteful and costly trial and error eliminated; (4) learning is hierarchical, in that the specialist with knowledge becomes the teacher of those without knowledge.

In rather sharp contrast, action-reflection-response learning features three elements in a sequence quite different from the previous model:

Action. You may call it praxis, practicum, field experience, learning on the job, doing it, or any other appropriate term.

Reflection. This is the process of attaining greater knowledge of something as a result of thinking through the action, a process made possible through gaining more information about, assimilating, and accepting ownership of the experience.

Response. The new knowing isn't enough; there must be a corresponding attitudinal or behavioral modification.

The process is exemplified by the history of liberation theology. Normally, theological concepts are generated as theories and then translated into lay language and applied—the theory-application model. In contrast, when Latin America gave birth to liberation theology following the Pope's visit to Colombia in 1968, North American seminaries were slow to recognize it as genuine theology, largely because the process was "confused." Liberation theology began in praxis (a code word for the experience of living in oppression and thus identifying with those who are oppressed) and then moved into *conscientización* (code word for the experience of coming into awareness of suffering, into the awakening of conscience over issues of injustice) and later into efforts to redress the grievances. Only then, and not before, did the reading of Scriptures begin to make sense. The message of the Bible took on meanings that would have been impossible to extract without the benefit of the prior experience. In other words, the action-reflection-response model altered the sequence of learning. The theory followed the practice.

Today, liberation theology is very much a part of the seminary scene. European as well as North American theologians join in the dialogue. In the meantime, teachers have found usefulness in both models of learning and, of course, know the limitations of each.

Action-reflection-response learning in intercultural settings

We frequently ask people in highly structured overseas educational programs why they, who have invested so dearly and traveled so far to learn about a foreign culture, now sit in classrooms and read textbooks. Clearly, one can obtain valuable information about one's host country from books and lectures. They are also useful at certain stages of the language-learning process. But for culture learning there is no substitute for direct encounter.

The intercultural setting is both the classroom and the text for culture learning. In every contact a visitor has within a new environment there is potential for learning.

Even fairly routine experiences are material for the action-reflection-response learning process. Some experiences of students in overseas study and service-learning programs suggest where these opportunities lie.

Sojourners who are not students will need to identify other more relevant examples. Guide 21 may give you some ideas to help you get started.

What follows is an illustration of the action-reflection-response strategy involving a kind of instant replay of important and/or memorable experiences. It is called "reviewing critical events."

Reviewing critical events

In televised athletics, the instant replay contributes to more accurate sports analysis. Prior to replays, the fan experienced a play so briefly that the memory of the particulars was sometimes closer to fantasy than fact. Cameras can now show a reenactment from several angles and in slow motion. Thanks to instant replay, a critical event in sports can be made both more understandable and more enjoyable.

In intercultural encounters, too, there are critical events, the understanding and management, if not enjoyment, of which can be improved by a kind of instant replay we call "reviewing critical events." Some of these events are exciting, many are memorable. Occasionally they are baffling, some are hurtful. Almost all have their moments of frustration. Unfortunately (or perhaps fortunately!) there are no cameras involved in these reviews of critical events. But there are ways to give our intercultural encounters a second run-through that allows us to experience them in slow motion, so to speak, and to be able to analyze them in greater detail and understand them better.

Most travelers abroad don't have to be coaxed to tell stories of their encounters with the strange and foreign, ranging from asking incorrectly for food in a restaurant to accidentally insulting an important official. What is less usual, however, is a systematic study of these misadventures. It is here that our instant replay comes in. Reviewing critical events includes the following steps:

1. recognizing what a critical event is,
2. reconstructing the event,
3. getting more information about it, and
4. making new interpretations and shaping new behavior as a result of it.

Let's go through a critical event step-by-step, identifying how each step is crucial to the end result.

Step 1

Recognizing the critical event. It is understandable that a stranger in a foreign land can sometimes be under such stress as to be unable to isolate any one critical event out of the grand confusion. Most can, however, delineate particular moments of frustration which can be called back for replay.

> One morning in downtown San José, I became conscious of how angry I felt. I realized that I was angry because my day had gotten off to a bad start when I was pulled over by a traffic cop, who scolded me for kindly stopping my car to let two old men walk across the street.

The act of being stopped by the officer and my subsequent anger was a critical event.

Step 2

Reconstructing the critical event. In a critical event there is a setting in which people are acting or interacting in a more or less routine way. Something happens which breaks the routine, something unexpected that intensifies or modifies the action and draws out different behaviors. A drama of some sort unfolds. Eventually there is a climax to the action, for good or bad, and then a denouement in which there may be apologies, congratulations, efforts to pick up some of the pieces—or it may be an event in which the denouement occurs entirely within the individual as he or she mulls over what happened.

> You see, I jumped into my Toyota, having fourteen chores neatly listed on an index card in my shirt pocket. I headed for town and as I came past Calderón Guardia Hospital, I noticed two men—certainly older than seventy—with hospital gowns on, standing by the curb, wanting to cross from the hospital to the row of doctors' offices on the other side of the street. But Latin drivers, being the way they are, rudely drove through, prohibiting the two feeble men from crossing. Generously, and might one say gallantly, I stopped the car right in the middle of the two lanes, so that no careless, insistent driver of a delivery truck or bus could get around and hit the men. I motioned them; they hobbled across, to the accompaniment of many horns. Once they were on the other side, I resumed... only to be whistled to the curb by a traffic cop who scolded me for what I did. So there we had a Latin American policeman, probably a corrupt, bribe-taking cop, supporting the chaotic and dangerous habits of Latin American drivers. Naturally, I was furious.

I retell the event as I experienced it, including all of the facts and feelings that I can remember.

Step 3

Getting more information. Once you have reconstructed the event as well as you can, it's time to get more information. This new data can come from a variety of sources. In the first place, your telling the story to another person may elicit comments or possibly some questions whose very interjection forces you to recall additional data. More typically, you involve an informant, someone qualified by experience in or knowledge of the culture, to provide more information about the nature of and background to the event. Invariably this informant helps you see things you had not seen before.

> This is dumb, I said to myself. Here I am in San José, burning up in fury and thus not able to get my fourteen chores done. Why not deal with the critical event of the morning? So I retrieved my car from the parking garage (it had been there a total of five minutes) and drove back to the hospital, parking near the cop. I walked over to him, and introduced myself—"the person you pulled over"—and when he looked stunned I pointed out my car. Oh, yes, he recognized me, but gazed at me without expression. Why, I asked him, did he pull me over? I, a foreigner, was puzzled by his action. I

thought I was doing a kindness. Now I returned, because I wanted to learn, so as not to repeat the offense. His face relaxed, he touched me on the arm. "Mister...you see, this is a hospital... and those are doctors' offices...and this hospital complex is located here in Barrio Aranjuez...its streets, you can notice, are very narrow... we have traffic problems, many impossible traffic jams.... But Mister, there is only one street leading into the Barrio, and on that street come the ambulances from Cartago, from Tres Rios, from Guadalupe, Moravia, and Coronado. If the traffic is stalled, the ambulances can't get through. So I am stationed here to keep traffic moving. As for patients needing to go to the doctors' offices, they are clearly instructed to come to this corner, and I help them across. Mister, can you understand?"

What good luck I had. One of the very persons involved in my critical event was still available to serve as informant. Problem was, I had to show my embarrassment right in front of him.

Step 4

Making new interpretations of the event. When you have accumulated information, preferably from several different points of view (it won't always be as easy as it was for me), the facts illuminate each other and bring to light new aspects of the event. At this point, if you can face the fact that your ability to perceive reality, especially in cross-cultural situations, is limited, you can begin to make new interpretations and possibly some behavioral adjustments.

I was dumbstruck, by both his manner and his facts. He was not the scolding traffic officer, but a personable Costa Rican, filled with goodwill and no small amount of charm. I thanked him, and as I walked away, I began to recall the judgments I had earlier made: Latin drivers, my own superiority, police stupidity and corruption. As I thought of my set of interpretations, I recognized how completely I was absorbed in my own cultural cocoon, my own day's agenda, and my own righteousness. The anger that I had earlier felt now changed into an altogether different feeling—embarrassment and chagrin, although as I drove downtown again, I was rather pleased that I had the courage to go talk with the police officer and further my own culture learning.

Examining critical events, even with reconstruction and additional data and reinterpretation, won't always ease the stress of intercultural misadventures. Nor will critical events always reveal their complexities to you, as did the incident above. Some critical events, no matter how hard one works to understand them, leave you angry, diminished, and even permanently scarred. But they are the exception. The majority of critical events beg to be used for learning about and coming to understand and enjoy the strangers you meet in your intercultural experience.

Action	Reflection	Response
routines surrounding the use of the bathroom in a new family household	reviewing and analyzing by oneself critical events and personal encounters with host nationals and/or the host culture	integrating more effectively into one's host family
planning and departing on field trips		building relationships with local people
undertaking independent study projects on aspects of the local community or the host culture such as how farming is done	gathering additional information about the context in which these events and encounters occurred	changing attitudes, opinions, values, and philosophies
interviewing host nationals about local issues	reading about intercultural and other relevant issues	reshaping one's understanding of U.S. foreign policy
working with a local agency	keeping a regular journal	rewriting personal financial budgets
providing social services to disabled veterans	discussing individual experiences in daily or weekly group meetings or seminars	revising career plans
		modifying choice of college major
	giving follow-up reports to the group on subjects discussed earlier	

Summary

Methods of learning vary widely. What we may suppose is the best or universal way to teach children is likely to be a way shaped largely by a teacher's creativity and the force of the child's culture. In the West, we have relied on versions of a theory-application sequence to learning. We adhere to that sequence in a variety of ways, including the use of lecture followed by discussion.

Intercultural settings provide appropriate occasions to engage in another kind of educational approach—action-reflection-response learning. Anyone in an intercultural setting can use this model for culture learning and personal growth. The critical events which happen universally to travelers and sojourners abroad are the supplied action. All the individual has to do is add the systematic analysis of it.

The approach favored in this book is based on and encourages the use of the action-reflection-response strategy. While here we have focused on the reviewing of critical events, later exercises will introduce yet other approaches to and styles of this strategy.

Chapter 4

Methods in Culture Learning:
Reflection as Cultural Analysis

Learning a second language as an adult is a different process from learning one's first language as a child. The first one comes naturally because, according to Noam Chomsky, at birth one is programmed to learn any language (1972). As a person grows older, the original state of language preparedness is changed and limited. Language learning gradually becomes a more difficult task, shifting from a natural to an artificial process.

So it is with culture learning. A child learns the first culture naturally and unconsciously. An adult learns a second culture only with considerable effort. If the learning is to be truly effective, it must entail, as mentioned earlier, not only cognitive, but also affective and behavioral changes.

Milton J. Bennett reminds us that successful culture learning is more than acquisition of new skills (1986, 179). A mastery of culture demands new awareness and attitudes. The same sentiments are expressed by David Hoopes:

> The critical element in the expansion of intercultural learning is
> not the fullness with which one knows each culture, but the degree
> to which the processes of cross-cultural learning, communication
> and human relations have been mastered. (1979, 20)

Particularly challenging for the culture learner is the mental and emotional processing indicated by the term *reflection* in the action-reflection-response strategy. How does one effectively grasp the meaning of a critical event and the essence of a new culture, understanding it in sufficient depth not only to appreciate its dynamic complexities but also to function comfortably as a participant?

The term reflection labels a collection of activities we commonly refer to as analysis. But the word "analysis" may, because of our preconceptions about what it is, hide as much as it reveals of the full range of activities we are calling reflection: searching, finding, seeing, identifying, naming, categorizing, classifying, interpreting—these are only a small part of reflection.

What, then, is the best way to reflect upon—or analyze—intercultural experience so that it ultimately yields a holistic pattern of culture learning? In this chapter, we examine a few samples of cultural analyses produced by scholars in the field. This brief walk-through is not intended to be a comprehensive review of the literature on the subject, an extensive discussion of methods, but rather a citing of models that a beginning culture learner might try to imitate in a fashion appropriate for making on-site inquiries. Some of the later guides in the manual build upon these examples.

Field observation

Margaret Mead, one of the twentieth century's leading anthropologists, followed in the footsteps of Ruth Benedict to clear a path in the use of field observation in anthropological research. Mead's accomplishments will endure even though later scholars improved on the validity, reliability, and objectivity of her methods.

Mead proposed to learn about the life of adolescent girls in selected so-called primitive sites in the Southwest Pacific by going there, observing, making careful notes, trying to find recurring behaviors, identifying patterns in those behaviors, and finally making some generalizations that fit what she saw (1963).

In another significant study, Mead observed three cultures—the Arapesh of New Guinea, the Manus of the southern coast of the Admiralty Islands, and the people of Bali. Her goal was to investigate the relationship of geography, subsistence, and communication in each setting and subsequently to determine how each respective community organized its social controls (1948).

What can today's culture learner gain from Mead's early work? The value of disciplined observation. The kind of research Mead did—and the kind we are recommending in the action-reflection-response strategy—demands, in the first place, a careful defining of what one is looking at or looking for. To focus on selected aspects of a culture or particular relationships is likely to yield more than a vague, undifferentiated attempt to be aware of culture. Second, it requires apprehending with all of the senses what a culture reveals about itself. Third—and Mead raised this to both a science and an art—it calls for making minute observations on which to build a generalized description of the culture. One must always do this task tentatively, ready to admit new and contradictory information. It can take a long time and a great deal of careful observation to gather the information which makes the data add up to a coherent description. Quite a few of the guides in the latter part of this book are designed collaterally, if not primarily, to help you become a better observer. See especially Guides 12-18 and 37-41.

Factor analysis

Edward T. Hall has produced a series of classic books about the dimensions of culture in which the most important similarities and differences lie. Reference was made earlier to his work on the relationship of cultural context and meaning; here we refer to an earlier product of his fertile mind. Like Mead, Hall was a culture observer. And like Mead, he knew the importance of focusing his attention on particular aspects—let's call them factors—of culture. His work, then, became a form of factor analysis, a term used here in a nonstatistical sense.

For example, Hall identified communication as a cultural activity. He knew, of course, that people of all cultures send messages back and forth, so he set himself the task of finding out what was common across cultures in this message sending. He concluded that all cultures, while their messages might be different, used similar primary message systems. He then developed a kind of factor analysis of primary message systems:

1. Interaction—messages having to do with verbal and nonverbal exchanges between people as they maintain contact with each other, such as greetings or conversations.

2. Association—messages having to do with grouping and affiliations.

3. Subsistence—messages having to do with making a living, the job, chores, eating, etc.

4. Sexuality—messages having to do with dating and mating, procreation, and survival.

5. Territoriality—messages having to do with the structure and use of space.

6. Temporality—messages having to do with the definitions, functions, and use of time.

7. Learning—messages having to do with acculturation, assimilation, and the passing on of a heritage.

8. Play—messages having to do with diversionary activity, laughter, games, etc.

9. Defense—messages having to do with self and communal protection, war, fighting, etc.

10. Exploitation—messages having to do with the handling of tools, the manipulation of material properties (*The Silent Language* 1973, 57-81).

Hall's model has in subsequent years been reformulated by other scholars, but the notion that there can be ways to factor out any one aspect of a culture becomes a valuable tool for the culture learner. Each factor can then become a new field for further inquiry, as Hall himself has demonstrated in his book-length studies of the use of time (*The Dance of Life: The Other Dimension of Time* 1983) and space (*The Hidden Dimension* 1966).

Beginning culture learners might try to make a factor analysis of some kind, perhaps of words and gestures that people use to express "How are you?" and "I'm fine, thank you." Or they might explore the kinds of structures that families live in—single-family houses, row houses, apartments, etc. Or they can examine the major means of conveyances people use to get from home to work each day. As you can see, factor analysis can help you ferret out information that a casual observer would miss. (See Guides 23, 34, and 38 for projects related to an analysis of factors.)

Ethnography

The term ethnography may be broadly defined as the description of cultures, or, in somewhat more restricted terms, as a particular way to go about the task. I am using the term in the latter sense. Ethnography is the study and description of culture from inside it, or from the culture's own point of view. In contrast is the study of culture from the outside, using outside models and methods, perspectives, categories, definitions, and interpretations.

The culture learner can get a good introduction to ethnographic studies from the writings of James P. Spradley and David W. McCurdy (1972). These are the procedures: you define a cultural scene for your study; you go inside it to find cultural informants; you observe what is happening; and you ask questions that will elicit from the informant a response which reflects that particular culture's ways of perceiving, its internal logic, its social system, its value patterns, and so forth. You use what Spradley and McCurdy call *structural* questions to allow the informant to define the culture in its own terms. From the culture itself, then, you elicit the cultural meanings.

Spradley and McCurdy have studied many cultures, subcultures, and cultural scenes in this way, including those of tramps, hitchhikers, and high school girls. Using the information gained from inside the culture group itself, they attempt to build taxonomies that show how the people of the culture define and categorize themselves. Here is a hypothetical case of a taxonomic definition of a kindergarten, as seen and expressed by the kindergarten pupil whom we shall name Tina.

A taxonomy of kindergarten as Tina sees it

people	pulls hair and hits	cries	snacks with me	sits at my table
Randy	yes	no	no	yes
Peter	no	yes	no	no
Anna	no	no	yes	yes
Kimberly	no	yes	yes	no

This taxonomy is used to illustrate that the insider's structures and categories are likely to be different from the outsider's. One might imagine the outsider wanting to impose categories of socioeconomic status, sex, intelligence, verbal skills, age, and family structure. Further, the taxonomy suggests to the ethnographer what kindergarten means to Tina and her classmates. Hitting, pulling hair, and crying might be principal shapers of meaning for the children themselves.

An example of a widely read and appreciated ethnographic study of this kind is Thomas Kochman's *Black and White Styles in Conflict* (1981). Kochman shows the close relationship between language and behavior in the African-American community by entering into the culture and allowing its own meanings to inform his interpretations. An outsider, using outside white definitions of "colored people," would not have been able to grasp what Kochman did.

Guide 6 offers some suggestions on finding cultural informants for this type of study.

Analysis of cues, symbols, and signs

Cultures reveal themselves by way of "words and things." Every culture has its conventions, verbal and nonverbal, for conveying meaning. Let's look at one particular cultural scene from this perspective.

Recently, as I entered the classroom on the first day of the trimester, I became aware—with hardly a visual sweep of the room—that the students were not seated in a random and meaningless disorder. As usual, there was the large clustering in the middle, more or less in front of me. Then there were some others: one lone person in the front row, almost against the instructor's table; three people in the back row behind the others; a student off to the right; and a student off to the left and against the wall, with vacant chairs between him and the others. Of the students on the fringes, I was most aware of the chap on the left. His body was turned a bit toward the wall. His gaze was directed straight ahead or toward the wall. He maintained no contact with classmates. He was an African American.

Only later did I learn that the student off to the right had come back to college after being out for a period of time and had recently been to a rehab center. Of the three in the rear, one dropped out after the first class period, the second was Catholic (the campus was predominantly Protestant) and a commuter who, because of not living in the dorm, had few friends on campus, and the third, I soon found out, wrote essays about depression. The student up front was hard of hearing.

The students in the center of the class were, one might say, in the center of this cultural scene. Those at the edges were in some manner marginal. While the details of my students' integration into and estrangement from the campus scene were not clear to me when I first entered the classroom, I did nonetheless feel that something meaningful was being presented to me, that there was some kind of nonverbal message here.

The first essay from Greg, the African-American student, was filled with pain and violence but did not reveal much of himself. He read it in class. As he became more comfortable, he wrote more candidly. In one composition, he told of walking out of a local grocery store and seeing a van-load of young women quickly roll up the windows and lock the doors in fear as he approached his car which was parked next to theirs. On another occasion he gave a presentation on black hairstyles and talked of their significance. He abandoned the chair by the wall and mixed with the main body of students. The other students who had seated themselves marginally to the rest of the class at first also changed their seating during the course of the semester, moving sometimes closer, sometimes farther away.

At the end of the term, I learned that a student who sat from the beginning in the middle with the in-group was quite disappointed in the class and expressed criticism that bordered on hostility. The root of the problem: none of her essays was ever read publicly or duplicated or shown on the overhead projector for class discussion. It was coincidental; none of her writing had seemed appropriate for discussion by the full class. But she took it as a signal; she felt there was a message in the exclusion of her essays—just as I had felt there was a message in the way the students seated themselves on the first day.

In that classroom, there were many more exchanges of meaning, conveyed verbally and nonverbally. Sometimes I caught the signs, sometimes I didn't. As a teacher I have been trying to pay better attention to all of the signals—the chair that a student selects, where the eyes focus and their intensity, the clothing and how it is worn, the handwriting in their essays, the kind of interaction with class-mates, the form of entering and leaving the room—because the number and kind of elements that make up a communication act are far more diverse than I had ever imagined. And if I understand more of the messages that are being given off in a classroom—and understand them better—I think I can be a more effective teacher.

Cultures are similar to that college classroom. Every culture has its way of signing (commonly referred to as nonverbal communication). To the insiders, the sign system is natural, largely unconscious—almost like breathing. Meanings are given to subtle cues. A word takes on special connotations. A gesture comes into use and gradually changes its meaning and then is discarded. To an outsider, this sign system will likely seem impenetrable because the outsider has had no part in making those meanings in the first place. Several guides address the topic of sign analysis: 5, 9, 10, and 23.

Myth analysis

Joseph Campbell was one of a number of scholars who have used myth analysis in recent years to understand cultures. (An example of his many works is *The Power of Myth* 1988). The list ranges from Edith Hamilton who studied Greek myths (*The Greek Way* 1971) to Leszek Kolakowski, a professor from Poland who has written about modern cultures in *The Presence of Myth* (1989). The list in-cludes widely recognized names such as Roland Barthes, Bruno Bettelheim, Mircea Eliade, Jacques Ellul, Northrup Frye, Carl Jung, and many others.

Myth analysis tries, through the study of a people's myths, to understand their way of life, what they know and believe, how they relate to nature, what they do with inexplicable happenings, how they adjust to change, and how they under-stand basic human phenomena such as birth and death. Myth analysts study the "wisdom" that flows from generation to generation, often couched in story, anec-dote, fairy tale, legend, and sayings.

Campbell, for example, has studied the hero (*The Hero's Journey* 1990) and the goddess (*In All Her Names: Four Explorations of the Feminine Divinity* 1991) as mythic figures. These studies help the scholar to understand what a culture val-ues in its men and women, and how it defines roles, develops its expectations, and articulates its rules and sanctions.

While the culture learner is likely not to be an accomplished myth analyst, this field of activity suggests to even the beginner using current clues (wall hang-ings, superstitions, statues downtown, the TV serial, the explanation for the earth-quake) to discover some of the myths upon which the culture is founded (see Guides 8, 16, 22, 27, 28, and 47).

As a final note, it is helpful to recognize that learning by analysis is the Western way to learn, as Camille Paglia reminds us in *Sexual Personae* (1990).

> Science is a method of logical analysis of nature's [culture's] opera-
> tions.... Western science is a product of the Apollonian mind: its
> hope is that by naming and classification, by the cold light of intel-
> lect, archaic night can be pushed back and defeated.

Name and person are part of the West's quest for form. The West insists on the discrete identity of objects. To name is to know; to know is to control.... Far Eastern culture has never striven against nature in this way. Compliance, not confrontation is its rule. Buddhist meditation seeks the unity and harmony of reality. (5)

One might suggest that the West learns by taking things apart, the East by putting things together. Culture learning, however, takes things apart *and* puts things together. The methods of analysis described here, combined with the action-reflection-response strategy, do not end with things in pieces and with the person paralyzed. Rather, they lead into an attitudinal and behavioral response that we hope may be characterized by the word *growth*.

Chapter 5

Culture Learning, Values, and Ethical Choices

Culture learning at its best is inclusive, not only in the scope of one's involvement (cognitive, affective and behavioral), but also in the range of life that is brought into the curriculum. Culture learning includes everything—a people's history, industry, art, institutions, communication patterns, and values. It is the issue of values that calls for further discussion in this chapter.

A study of cultural values suggests three major questions:

1. Must you forsake the values of your culture and people when you aspire to be a multicultural person?

2. Are you entitled to judge the host culture's value system?

3. Does cultural relativity lead to a deterioration of values or, indeed, to moral chaos?

To begin these explorations, let's do a classroom exercise. Below are eight behaviors; please rank them in the order of their moral rightness.

- a woman slipping $20 to a traffic officer who intends to give her a citation

- a man urinating by the road

- a woman talking to another driver from out of the car window at a traffic light

- a woman throwing a dishpan of water out of the window and onto the street

- a man arguing vehemently on the verge of violence, raising his fists at the driver of another vehicle that had hit him
- a woman kicking a cow off the path so that she can continue on her way
- a man setting up a rock barrier so that people cannot continue using the street
- a woman spreading out a sheet on the sidewalk, on which she intends to show items for sale

If you are an American from Iowa you are likely to have considered most of the items to be a little odd, although you'd see nothing wrong in talking to another driver from out of your own car window, and surely you'd chase off the cow without pangs of conscience. On the other side, you'd say that some of the items are unacceptable, such as setting up a rock barricade or paying off the cop. Urinating in a public place can lead to an arrest. It would be crude to throw kitchen water out the window. And in downtown Keokuk, they don't even allow bicycles on the sidewalk, much less a huckster.

But if you complete this exercise not in an American classroom but in India, you will react much differently to the example concerning the cow. The cultural setting complicates the exercise. Hindus don't kick cows, which hold sacred status in India. In Spain, people would tend to value saving face at the moment of a car accident, even if it means a raised voice or a clenched fist. They also don't think it unseemly to urinate beside the road. There are communities where protests rather frequently take the form of blocking off a street.

Is any one of those items ethically right? It depends. Is any one of those items wrong? It depends. In both cases it depends on culture. Within the boundaries of a cultural scene, morality is more or less understood and agreed upon. But across cultures, one can hardly predict moral preferences because communities differ in what they consider to be taboo in their management of morality. Myron W. Lustig explains the situation:

> As you can see, *value* and *culture* are inextricably linked. Each can be understood only in terms of the other because values form the basis for cultural differences. In a sense, a culture's values provide the basic set of standards and assumptions that guide thought and action. By providing its members with shared beliefs and assumptions about the "right" and "proper" ways of behaving, cultures provide the context within which individual values develop. (1988, 56)

A first-time consideration of morality-across-cultures can be unsettling, even shocking, as though the person has opened a door—and just beyond, found a corpse. Questions arise: "Are you saying that morality is relative?" "Are rightness and wrongness merely situational?" "Does this mean that I must discard my values when reacting to another culture?"

Exposure to a new culture causes many people to explore value systems for the first time; discoveries often lead to reexamining the foundation of their own ethical structures. Such an inquiry is liberating for some and frightening for others, especially those in need of assurance that in a world where so much seems to cave in to relativism, there remain some stable and enduring verities. Is it inevitable that cultural studies lead to the destruction of conscience?

No, culture learning doesn't have to lead to a deterioration in values or to moral chaos. Let's look first at ethics and, specifically, how culture and ethics are related. Then I'll suggest an agenda for the further study of values-across-cultures.

Metaphors and frames of reference for ethical analysis

The metaphors or frames of reference we use in our probing of difficult issues serve to structure our thoughts about those issues. Consequently it is important to select the metaphors and frames of reference very carefully, but also, in the words of Robert Frost, "know when to get off" them (1973).

One frame of reference used in thinking about ethical issues is the etic-emic dichotomy. Lustig elaborates on the distinction. Mental programming that is "shared by all humanity" and "essentially universal," he says, comes under the rubric of etic activity. Mental programming that is formed within a specific culture and unique to it comes under the category of emic activity (1988, 55-56). A dualism of the local and the universal is thus introduced into thinking about ethical behavior. According to this dichotomy, some conduct is guided by particular situations, other conduct is governed by general principles. Such a dualism allows a dialogue between the two ethical sets, though it leads at times to contradiction, tension, and warfare between them. For example, within the same community there may be two ethical standards concerning the killing of a human being. One opposes killing human beings, including capital punishment for crimes committed, as immoral based on what is believed to be a universal principle. The other standard, local in origin, might support capital punishment for certain kinds of crimes even while accepting as a general proposition that killing people is immoral. Some within the community might accommodate this duality while others find the contradiction insupportable.

A different type of metaphor for analyzing ethical issues comes from systems theory. Just as a factory system may be analyzed as the operation of interlinked components, each functioning in response to messages from other components, so an ethical system may be seen as the functioning of interdependent parts. The state, schools, churches, families, and all other social institutions become components linked together. One institution's rules affect the next institution's. For example, the rightness or wrongness of a driver's speed may be determined by speed limits established by the federal government (on interstate highways), or by state and local governments which set speed limits according to weather conditions, congestion, and local conditions (e.g., school zones), or finally by the manner in which police officers interpret these regulations. Thus, local, state, and federal regulations, along with individual interpretations, all play a part in defining whether the driver ought to be arrested and fined, i.e., in defining right and wrong. Further, a rule today might be changed tomorrow depending upon the influences that components of the system have on each other. Systems thinking helps one to understand ethical thought as the dynamic and ongoing result of many factors. But systems thinking has its disadvantages: a person can feel insignificant and removed from the shaping and reshaping of norms and, consequently, lack motivation to internalize existing ethical codes.

Another metaphor for ethical thought comes from the language of structures: the foundation, the framing, the finish work. You may think of the foundation as representing the deepest and broadest dimensions of ethical consciousness, the framing as representing the organization and structure of cultural groups, and the finish work as the individual and idiosyncratic shaping of personal conscience. I prefer this metaphor and shall use it to distinguish relative ethical claims from universal ethical claims.

Foundations for ethical choice

The concept of foundation suggests something fundamental, a base upon which a thing stands. An ethical foundation, then, might represent the sense of "oughtness" that is shared by people of all times and places. This sense defies linguistic form, although people throughout history have tried to express it. One example of a universal moral imperative that forms the foundation of a system of social ethics is what has come to be known as "the golden rule": "Do unto others as you would have them do unto you." Similar concepts are expressed in various ways in many cultures. Confucius said that practicing *jen* (roughly translated as "humanism") is not to do to another person what you yourself don't want done to you. "If there's something that you don't like in the person to your right, don't pass it on to the person on your left. If there's something you don't like in the person to your left, don't pass it on to the person on your right" (Yum 1991). Two basic ethical principles of *dharma*, a Hindu code of conduct, are compassion and the avoiding of unnecessary injury to others. (Koller 1982, 62). The traditional Japanese group ethic has led to what outsiders label the "I am we" formula, having to do with *kou* (filial piety), *giri* (duty), and *on* (obligation)—an ethic leading to considerable sensitivity to one's associates (Haglund 1984). Thus, one can find expressions of this comprehensive social ethic in many languages and in many different versions.

The philosopher Immanuel Kant has placed this sense into what he calls "the categorical imperative":

> Act only on that maxim which you can at the time will to be a universal law. (Greene 1929, 302)

An abstract, philosophical statement of this kind may seem somewhat irrelevant to the practical task of culture learning; however, all of us should think more about basic ethical imperatives. Elvin Hatch, for example, has argued that cultures can indeed be judged and that such assessments may be made on the basis of universal imperatives. To answer the scoffers who say that such a measuring device can't possibly be found, he has tried to identify a universal ethic for all peoples in all places. He calls his formula "humanist principles."

1. It is good to treat people well (or that we should not do one another harm),

2. People ought to enjoy a reasonable level of material existence (or conversely, that poverty, malnutrition, material discomfort, human suffering, and the like are bad) (1983, 134-37).

Hatch's "principles" on first reading seem simple, obvious, and general, and yet they have a prescriptive power concerning how people ought to act and how people ought to be treated. Upon such a foundation of universal morality, then, is built a structure of ethical consciousness. You might wish to think through what you believe the people of your own culture consider the crucial principles of their ethical foundation.

The framing of ethical consciousness within cultures

When you make ethical choices, it is unlikely that you will be able to trace your decision back to the philosophical base on which any given choice rests, though some people in weighing moral alternatives do think through the philosophical principles involved. More typically, people behave without consciously examining the process by which they arrived at the principles on which they are acting. If pressed, they might say they made such and such a choice because they were

- doing what was fun
- doing what was educational
- doing what was safe (or efficient or effective)
- doing what felt right
- doing what was consistent with their values
- doing what was approved by their religion
- doing what their college, travel agent, employer, supervisor wanted them to do
- doing what was American (or Italian or Brazilian or Indonesian)

If you pause to examine the nature of the rationale you give for your choice, you will discover a cultural apparatus encompassing it. If you do what is fun, you are conforming to what your culture has helped you define as fun. If you do what your college wants you to do, you are submitting to the influence of a social institution within the culture. If you make choices in keeping with religious principles, you pay allegiance to a culturally shaped tradition of faith and practice. If you fit your conduct to Brazilian or Indonesian patterns, you are adapting to ethnic or national entities shaped by those cultures. Whatever may be the cultural influence, you can be sure that the ethical norm has resulted from an important process that served some group of people well enough to be deemed significant and useful and right.

What are the special influences that contribute to a culture's shaping of its ethical norms? Many factors, great and small. Consider, for example, how a peoples' worldview supplies a fundamental frame of reference for all of their thinking about right and wrong. A large portion of the planet's population, for instance, sees ultimate good in terms of harmony, a belief that prevails in Eastern religions where life is understood in terms of cyclical patterns, pantheistic and immanent divinities, and quests for meaning through self-discipline. Contrast that with the worldview of an equally large portion of the population that sees ultimate good in transformation, a central belief in Western religions where life is understood in terms of a transcendent deity, a teleological design for history, and liberation through divine grace (Smart 1988). Clearly, cultural groups within each of those two larger world communities would do their ethical framing differently from each other.

But worldviews, important as they are, aren't the only shapers of ethical norms. Marshall R. Singer (1987) describes two other forces that help to form values—*environment* and *history*. Imagine how any of the following environmen-

39

tal factors might affect a culture and eventually help shape its values: a cold rather than a hot climate, arid rather than fertile soil, antagonistic rather than peaceful relations with neighbors

The people of polar and tropical regions have been contrasted not just in the kinds of houses they live in, but in the openness and closedness of their human relationships. One may even build a case that the climate of southern Europe has contributed to the development of values and behaviors different from those in northern Europe. In southern Europe, doors and windows are opened. Language is expressive, gestures expansive. Emotions, ranging from anger to *amor*, are publicly proclaimed and demonstrated. In northern Europe, the colder weather drives people indoors and under wraps. Distance is measured, as are linguistic and emotional expression.

Singer illustrates how environment and history influence culture by comparing the acceptable age for marriage in the nineteenth century in Ireland (about thirty) and in India (about twelve or thirteen) and links those social codes to seemingly unrelated factors: life expectancy, food sources, and population-growth rates. He concludes:

> ...every group is confronted with environmental realities of one sort or another. Every group must deal with those realities in one way or another, or it will perish. (Singer 1987, 169)

It is important to remember that one's sense of what is ethical is framed within a culture through a complex dynamic of philosophical, historical, and environmental forces.

The finish work of ethical development

As we have seen, the foundations for ethical choice may be seen as deep and wide as human consciousness. All over the world and all through history human beings have upheld what they consider to be moral verities. These moral verities are the foundation upon which the construction of ethical consciousness builds, within the context of a culture, by framing up certain local or group understandings. Our fathers and mothers express these understandings in those memorable words, "Now remember who you are." Good character is acknowledged by a communal seal of approval.

The finish work in this construction project is of a more personal nature. An individual lives by a conscience that is shaped by the imprint of genetic makeup, the idiosyncrasies of personality, the reinforcement of personal experience, and the consequence of personal choice.

To locate this personal function within the larger construct, consider an anecdote. Kermit Eby, in an essay on personal integrity (1955), tells of Rabbi Joseph the builder: One day when he was working high on a scaffolding, his opinion was sought on a certain matter. The questioner, standing below, called up to him, "Come down. I want to ask you something." Rabbi Joseph replied, "I cannot come down because I was hired by the day."

In this story, one may see the whole of this ethical structure in relief. First is the foundation work in ethical consciousness—Rabbi Joseph was honoring his belief in what he considered a universal principle, that a good life depends upon hard work. Just as we expect others to do their share of work, so we do ours. Second, one may see what we have been calling the framing work in ethical development—the Jewish communal understanding that makes the rabbi a respected person to ask for counsel and that supports an esteem for conscientious work habits. Third, the rabbi puts his own personal touch upon the matter—taking a work contract so seriously that he single-mindedly works at fulfilling the contract, avoiding all distractions.

Like Rabbi Joseph, we all develop a unique and idiosyncratic conscience. We do it as we try to make sense of life, prove our genuineness, tell the truth, and seek peace. We do it as we try to avoid wrongdoing and the loss of self-respect.

Because of the personal nature of this finish work, people go about it in different ways. To be sure, most of us aren't aware of the ongoing process of making and remaking our ethical commitments. We work with what we've been given and with what we've got. On occasion, we become deliberate about ethical choices; then, we each use a privately held recipe of subjective feelings and beliefs mixed with another powerful ingredient—the real world. Thus we come up with a newly educated personal conscience.

With this perspective on values in mind, it should be clear that intercultural experience and culture learning do not have to lead you into a morass of cultural relativity. Instead, by throwing light on your own values and bringing them into sharper focus, the intercultural experience offers you the opportunity to enhance, elaborate, and strengthen the value system you have inherited and developed over the course of your life.

Applications for culture learners

The study of values can expand the range and the depth of your culture learning. Examining your values calls for intellectual processing—vigorous brain work of the most demanding kind. But there is also the emotional side to the study, because values touch our feelings. Values also govern action and can be understood only when put into practice. Here are seven suggestions to help you process values intellectually, emotionally, and behaviorally. Some of them are keyed to related guides, some of them refer you to other literature.

1. *Reacquaint yourself with your own culture's values while you are in a new cultural setting where values seem to differ from yours.* To help in this, we suggest an exercise having to do with political values, adapted from work by David Bender (1989). Read over the following list of fourteen personal and political values:

Your Values	American Values	Host Culture Values
financial security		
freedom of speech		
equality of opportunity		
self-reliance		
loyalty to country		
tolerance of others		

Your Values	American Values	Host Culture Values
freedom of religion		
individual initiative		
right to private property		
government by law		
concern for the underdog		
fair play		
justice		
social order and stability		

Now, do three things with Bender's list: (1) Rank order each of the items according to how important they are to you personally. In other words, place a 1 after the item you value most highly, a 2 after the next one, and so forth. (2) Rank order each of the values according to how important you think they are to most Americans. (3) Rank order the values the way you suppose the people of your host culture would.

This exercise, limited to just one small group of the ideas we hold dear, can help you retrieve from your subconscious some of the values you take for granted. You might try the same exercise in social, educational, and religious values and the like. In your study journal, record what you consider to be your core values.

An especially potent way to explore comparative values is to do this exercise with one or more members of your host culture, asking them to add values of importance to them which do not appear on the list. Discussing the results with an open mind and nonjudgmentally will result in significant and often surprising discoveries about your host culture's values.

2. *Be aware of how your own value system might constitute a set of blinders that limit or modify how you see the values of others.* To help you in this task, refer to a study made by Geert H. Hofstede (1984) of four selected value dimensions using data from 116,000 respondents in forty countries. He then compared how these values were rank ordered in each country. The comparison is quite revealing for citizens of those countries (in which the United States is included) and can be found in Guide 26.

3. *Find structured ways to identify your host culture's values.* Values, unlike laws, aren't written for all people to read and memorize. They are hidden...until people act. The casual tourist is likely not to be able to determine what a peoples' value system is. To help you intercept the values, I recommend the work of Milton Rokeach (1960, 1968, 1973, 1984). Rokeach developed a scheme by which values can be identified, examined, and better understood. See Guide 27 for ideas on how Rokeach's schema can be used to study both your own values and those of your host family, work colleagues, friends, and neighbors.

4. *Learn about the formation of their values.* This is a difficult task. One way you might approach it is to find examples in your host culture of what Singer (1987) calls the basic influences on perception: (1) physical determinants, (2) environmental determinants, (3) learned determinants, (4)

Singer (1987) calls the basic influences on perception: (1) physical determinants, (2) environmental determinants, (3) learned determinants, (4)
attitudes and values, and (5) belief systems. Then think about whether the
examples you come up with do indeed serve as molders and shapers of
the way your hosts live. To help you do this, Guide 28 provides a list of
culture contrasts developed by Sondra Thiederman (1991) designed to
stimulate your thinking about how and why values differ.

5. *Don't judge your host culture's value system prematurely.* There has been
    considerable discussion about the validity of an outsider evaluating a cul-
    ture. Cultural relativists, such as Melville J. Herskovits (1972), argue that a
    culture's value system is indigenous, arrived at through a historical pro-
    cess that gives it inherent authenticity. It is unlikely that an outsider, mak-
    ing judgments about it, will be able to appreciate fully the context, the
    culture's history, and the fact that it constitutes an integrated and logical
    system. On the other hand, Elvin Hatch (1983), whom we cited earlier,
    thinks the relativists have been too hesitant to use humanistic principles
    in assessing whether a peoples' values ultimately lead to well-being. The
    controversy serves to caution us against quick and ethnocentric judgments
    of others.

    A good place to explore your host culture's values is in a small discussion
    group where you can consider together the wisdom of being a cultural
    evaluator in regard to any given value.

6. *Explore the moral ambiguities in your host's values through the art of the
    culture.* The local framing of morality will surely offer you what seem to
    be inconsistencies and contradictions. Social mores confuse and provoke
    even the people who accept them as part of their culture. Use the culture's
    arts to help you clarify your thoughts about these ambiguities. Make a
    habit of going to the theater to see local plays. I have found that drama
    kneads the moral sense, working it over for an audience to contemplate.
    Theater is a microcosm of life because life is a stage where characters live
    out the consequences of their moral choices. Films and novels deal with
    values in a similar way. See Guide 29 for suggestions of movies, novels,
    and other art and artifacts useful to an inquiry into values.

7. *Use your study journal to refine your thinking about the development of
    your own values and moral perspectives.* Travelers and sojourners who get
    involved in discussions of universal and relative values are forced to think
    about the origins of their own ethical structures and to place under new
    examination the moral health of the community back home. For thought-
    ful people, the clarification of their own values is an ongoing activity,
    sometimes characterized by struggle, sometimes characterized by slow
    percolation. A study journal accommodates both. Begin with the introduc-
    tion to journal keeping on p.165, then use Guides 30 through 36 to ex-
    plain the use of such a journal and give examples of journal entries that
    you might find useful.

    Sojourners know that new experience becomes new knowledge, and new
    knowledge demands disciplined thought and action.

Part B

The Culture-Learning Process

I. Beginning Well

Introduction

Up to this point the essays in this book have taken a bird's-eye view of the cultural terrain, viewing culture in broad terms. Now we begin walking the trails. It is appropriate that direction for taking the trails is cast in a form that we call "guides."

You'll notice that each guide is brief and written in a workbook style: do this, do that, try this exercise, answer these questions. You'll also soon recognize that the guides are down-to-earth and practical, designed to help you deal with new situations and different kinds of people, communicate cross-culturally, and master the process of culture learning.

Each of you will find some of the guides more valuable than others, and some less applicable to your circumstances. If you're living with a host family, Guides 12-19 will be particularly useful. If you're looking for ways to improve your journal writing, you'll find models in Guides 30-36. If you're interested in discussing critical events arising from cross-cultural settings, you'll find case studies beginning with Guide 44. You might want to browse through all of the guides before settling down to work in any one set.

The guides are grouped in sections. The first (Guides 1-4) is entitled "Beginning Well" because it has to do with preparing yourself for the experience, leaving home, arriving abroad, and making initial contacts.

Guide 1

Getting Ready to Go

If you don't like to be told how to get ready for a trip or if you think such instructions seem juvenile, go on to Guide 2, but be careful. There are a number of ideas here you won't find in other getting-ready-to-go lists. At least browse the list quickly, just in case there's a good idea in it you haven't already thought of.

Practical preparations

1. Contact your travel agent early—at least six months before departure. Some ticket prices specify a waiting period.

2. Get your passport early. Verify all facts on the passport after you get it. (We know a person whose passport mislabeled his sex.)

3. Listen to the grapevine—anybody who's been there. Gather nitty-gritty as well as cultural information. How much does film cost? Are your allergy medications available? Does it make sense to take along an umbrella? Are the people really friendly? What's the inside of a typical home like? What is popular among young people? What are the current important local political issues?

4. Begin a "contacts" list of people in the host country. Connections are important in international travel. These connections will take many forms (your cousin's former neighbor, Paul's host family of three years ago, the secretary to the consul, the man who works for Firestone).

5. Assemble the library you plan to carry with you: address book, travel guide, maps, journal, language book, photo album, a novel originating in your host country. (You'll be glad for a book when you have to wait during your trip.) Many of the larger countries and/or popular tourist destinations have information offices that supply useful maps and fact books.

6. Make a list of important names, addresses, and phone numbers at home. Include emergency numbers and addresses for all credit cards, licenses, and documents you are carrying.

7. Do you know how to dial direct from the host country to your home? Will your calling card be accepted? Find out now.

8. Are your eyes in good condition? Have they been checked lately? Take along an extra pair of glasses and contacts (and contact fluid).

9. If electricity is in short supply where you are going, wean yourself from electrical appliances.

10. Get your teeth cleaned and checked. Repair work may be better, more convenient, and less expensive here than there.

11. Check with your physician or travel agent on immunizations. Schedule them in good time. Know your blood type.

12. Be sure to have twelve personal photographs—for example, copies of your passport mug shot.

13. Do you have comfortable walking shoes that are good for five miles a day? Practice walking.

14. During your absence, will you have business and legal transactions? Give power of attorney to a family member or trusted friend.

15. Try to get two good nights of sleep before leaving.

For culture learning

1. Set your agenda: Why are you going? What are your goals? What do you want to see? To do? To be? What do you expect to receive? To give?

2. Read a novel set in the country to which you are going.

3. See films shot in the host country or directed by citizens of the host country. Study the films not just for their story line, but also for cues about how people look, talk, gesture, laugh, play, fight, and eat, and the day-to-day routines that you will eventually make your own.

4. Reserve about twenty hours for browsing at your local library in books about your country of destination that will help you lay the groundwork for culture learning. The more background you can acquire about the country's history, geography, demographics, industry, government, religion, education, and the like, the better.

5. Listen to language tapes. Review grammar. Do as much reading in the language as you can.

6. Inventory your personal talents and interests. You will build bridges across the cultures with the "stuff" you are made of. Should you carry with you anything that reflects these interests (in basketball, biking, classical guitar, knitting, stamp collecting, photography, watercolors, etc.)?

7. Begin keeping your journal. Record what you know of your new home. Jot down your goals. Describe your thoughts and feelings, note your questions.

Packing your bags

1. Find the right luggage. One sturdy case plus a light travel bag or backpack.

2. Take about half of what you originally pack! You won't enjoy lugging around a bunch of heavy suitcases. You'll probably be able to purchase necessities if you leave behind something important.

3. When packing for a trip, if you aren't sure of plans at the end of the journey (such as who will meet you at the airport or where you will be staying the first few days), pack one carry-on handbag for easy access to clothing for a day or two. That way, if your suitcase is delayed in its arrival or inaccessible for some other reason, you can get by for several days.

4. American and European student travelers tend to dress quite informally, sometimes to their own disadvantage. Good grooming and clean clothing help you at customs check-ins. Hosts may be suspicious of long hair, torn jeans, halters, short shorts and bare feet.

5. Take about $100 in cash for arrival costs such as taxi and tipping; put the rest into traveler's checks. Record check numbers and keep them in two different places, one with you, the other in your luggage or with a friend.

6. To guard against travel theft, don't put valuables in exposed pockets of luggage or handbags. Don't put wallets in hip pockets. Carry shoulder bags so that the bag is by your side instead of behind you. Leave expensive jewelry at home and use an inside belt pouch for passport and cash.

7. As you travel, save stubs and receipts. You don't want to throw away a valuable ticket voucher. Later, when you are more relaxed, you can figure out what may be discarded.

8. A wet suitcase is a sorry mess. Carry plastic bags to put wet garments in.

9. Carry a small amount of cash always in the same pocket, so you know where your money is. (Be unobtrusive in counting your money.) Keep your other funds in a safer place.

10. Take a collection of personal and family snapshots. You can use them to make connections with host families and new friends. Pack some local gift items. Favorites include: jacks, playing cards, picture postcards, cosmetics, T-shirts, baseball caps, paperback classics, note cards, M&M's (if you don't travel in high temperatures), coffee mugs, pencils and pens, pillow cases, small flower vases, or other nice but inexpensive things which may be special to your hometown or area. Make copies of (or purchase) your favorite cassettes. Your future friends will happily make exchanges.

Pretesting Your Dispositions

How well will you do on your trip abroad? Are you well suited to traveling? Do you possess the attributes (steadiness under pressure, patience, etc.) necessary to successful adventuring? How will you adapt to the kinds of differences which lie ahead?

It might be useful—now, before you are in the middle of things—to take a look at some of your typical ways of dealing with new situations. The following experiment in self-awareness will help you assess your adaptability.

It may surprise you in its simplicity (and in your responses to it!). The experiment is based upon observations we made of students during their early days overseas in first confrontations with local cuisine. How they behave at the lunch table turns out to be a good indication of their cultural adaptability. Even if you are going to a country where the cuisine is familiar, this exercise will help prepare you for encounters with other aspects of the culture to which it is not so easy to adapt.

Trying new foods

You can engineer this project yourself, or ask somebody else. You need to be presented with a menu of new, strange, and unnamed foods. Perhaps you might go to an ethnic restaurant and take a chance. Or you might ask someone to plan a surprise snack. In orientations for people going abroad, I have given participants a paper plate on which are three items. I don't name the items, just hand them the plate and invite them to eat.

Some recommended foods: a slice of papaya, Chinese *jiaozi* (boiled dumplings filled with meat), Mideast *cous cous* (cracked wheat), Haitian goat, East African *ugali* (white cornmeal mush), a cup of tripe soup, boiled okra. If you do it on your own, simply choose foods that are completely new and to which you cannot predict your reaction when you sit down to eat.

When you are finished, complete this questionnaire with brief answers.

1. Did you taste each item?
2. Did you eat all of it?
3. Which did you like best?
4. Which did you like least?
5. Which, if any, of the following describes your experience of eating these foods?
   - I licked my lips; the food was yummy.
   - I felt nauseated.
   - I wondered whether I'd become ill.
   - I wished the servings had been larger/smaller.
   - I hoped I wouldn't meet up with those foods overseas.
6. (If applicable) Can you identify the items by food group, area of origin, or by some other means?

If you are with others in a formal or informal group, separate into subgroups of two or three (if there are more than just a few of you) and discuss:

1. what you know about the foods you ate
2. what you thought of the foods
3. what your expectations are of the food and drink you will encounter when you are abroad

After the discussion, complete a second questionnaire, again answering briefly.

1. In the discussion, did you learn anything about the foods?
2. Did you feel free to be totally honest with the group? Why?
3. Were you informed at all, or surprised at all, by what others said about their reactions to the food?
4. Are you at this moment more, or less, inclined to have seconds of any of the food?
5. How do you typically react when you encounter foods you don't like?
6. Do you order strange foods when you go to restaurants?
7. In general, does your family at home often try foreign foods other than those common in the United States, i.e., Chinese, Italian, etc ?
8. Do you look forward to international and ethnic food?

Beyond foods

Using this simple exercise, think about your disposition toward anything new or strange or different. Unfamiliar street signs. People standing too close or smelling different. Foreign accents. Bathrooms different from those in the United States. Tools made differently from the ones you now use. Disregard of queuing etiquette (pushing and shoving to get to the head of the line). Long dark nights. Greetings that require shaking hands with everyone in the room. Strange TV programs. Smiles that don't communicate happiness. Personal questions that invade your privacy. Late dinners cooked in olive oil.

As you think, try to answer these questions:

1. Which are you by nature: cautious, conservative, deliberative and protective, or are you experimental, impulsive, innovative, adventurous? How might your personal bearing influence your early days overseas?

2. How do you usually encourage yourself to restructure your thinking when you find evidence that your previous way of thinking was wrong or dysfunctional?

3. When you've had just about enough of the strange and ambiguous and seemingly unpatterned, how do you reestablish your sense of structure and reinforce your feelings of security? How will you come to your own defense overseas? Do you sleep in? Take a walk? Find friends? Cry? Write letters? Sulk? Sing?

4. What in your personality, your experience, your training, or in your companions and/or family (if you are sojourning as a family) will help you in your initial adjustments overseas?

Managing Your Pace

As you leave for your visit abroad, your wristwatch will confound you. Travelers think about new foods, a strange language, a different bed, and perhaps a cold shower, but seldom do they consider the disorientation having to do with time. Preview the trip, imagining what it will be like. Notice the crazy fluctuations in the pacing of activities:

- fast: hurrying to finish packing and saying good-bye
- slow: crawling through traffic to the airport
- fast: hurrying through the lobby to the airline counter
- slow: waiting in slow-moving lines
- fast: hurrying to the boarding area
- slow: waiting as the plane is caught in a backup on the runway
- slow: sitting eight hours on the plane
- slow: waiting for luggage, then customs

As you arrive at your destination, you feel a twinge of panic whether you are traveling with a group and taking up residence with a host family or are alone (or with your real family) settling into your own selected housing. Will things work out according to your schedule?

For the sojourning family, the questions tumble across the clock. Will your transportation be waiting for you at the airport? Is there time to go to the rest room? How long will the bus ride take? Can you move into the house right away? Has the electricity been hooked up already? During which morning and evening hours may you use the rationed water? How long until they install a phone? At what hour will you be able to buy milk? Do you pay rent in advance of, or after, the month? When must you make the first appointment to enroll the children in school?

For those of you who will be hosted by a family, you hope your hosts are on time to meet you at the airport. Yes, there they are. But your time problems aren't over. You are tired, not just from travel, but also from the fact that you arrived at midnight (your time). Your eager host family has met you at 4:00 P.M. (their time), and they want to take you first to see their village, then to eat a special dinner, and then to a party in your honor. Your time troubles have only begun. Some things go too fast, others too slowly. And most things don't happen when you want them to.

If you intend to find your own apartment and to enroll in a foreign university, you won't remove yourself from time problems. You are told to be at a particular corner by 6:40 A.M. to catch the right bus, but there you stand in line thirty minutes because all of the buses are full and pass by. After finally arriving late at the university downtown, you rush into class hoping to catch up, only to discover that your internal clock abruptly stops as you sit through two-hour class periods in tiny rooms that are hot by mid-morning; furthermore, you can't grasp what they are saying. Finally classes are over. Your intentions to buy stationery and postage at noon are frustrated by the closing of stores. Afternoon drags on endlessly in more classes. When you arrive home (after pushing and shoving on the buses) you are too exhausted to enjoy the evening, tired from faulty timing.

For group travelers, you face the experiences of waiting for then rushing through hotel meals, missing hotel meals, waiting for buses, waiting for tour guides, enduring a tour guide's too-long explanations under the hot sun, needing a drink and having to wait, not finding the rest room, getting to the concert forty-five minutes early, going too fast in traffic, going too slow in the line at the money changers, etc.

Unless you've traveled directly north or south, you'll face yet another major time-breaker. Jet lag. You can't, in the wink of an eye, subtract or add eight (or ten or twelve) hours from or to your internal clock without feeling it. For some, it's a headache, an upset stomach, heavy eyes, sleepless nights, a brain that won't function. The physical symptoms may be easier to bear than the emotional and mental ones which also occur.

Especially in the early weeks in your stay abroad, when you must function by an external clock you don't understand and an internal clock that has somehow been violated, you can help yourself by deliberately managing your pace. It's a suggestion you'll value—particularly at those extremes when you either must try to waste time creatively or hurry more deliberately. Here are some ideas to help you manage your pace.

1. Slow down. Move slowly. Talk slowly. Go to sleep slowly and awaken slowly. Indeed, this is a substantial request of travelers who kept up a frenetic pace back home in the final days before the trip.

2. Get a full eight hours of rest daily. Most travelers need more than eight during the first days. Don't feel guilty about your fatigue. Sleep.

3. Find resting places when you are away from home all day. In the city, locate not only several rest rooms, but also places where you can spend thirty minutes relaxing. Learn to enjoy a slow refreshment at a corner shop.

4. If convenient, try to build in a routine midday rest. Some cultures have a siesta. It's a great way to relax and refresh.

5. Reduce your expectations. Give yourself simple goals that you can reach easily in your first days. Each accomplished goal reinforces your confidence.

6. Reduce your agenda. Can you put aside some of the concerns/obligations/commitments that weigh you down? Give your attention to a few of the most basic or important ones.

7. If you get lost, stop. Don't run. Sit down. Relax. Think things through. Plan how you will find out where you are. Then proceed slowly.

8. Take walks, especially in your neighborhood; it will help the orientation process. Find safe streets or parks. Sometimes walk fast for exercise. Sometimes walk slowly for repose.

9. Let your journal keeping be a time for slow reflection. You'll enjoy the journal more if you write in it slowly.

10. Learn to tell time by local standards. See Guide 23. As you blend in with the pace of your surroundings, your disorientation will be replaced with a sense of belonging.

Guide 4

Meeting Your Hosts

The contents of this particular guide anticipate the needs of those travelers who will, upon arriving at their destination overseas, be meeting and living with a host family. This is largely a student population, although many volunteers in international service organizations use such arrangements, and a growing number of professionals and other people who intend to live overseas for an extended period of time choose to live with a local family, at least at the outset, to facilitate authentic and speedy orientation to language and customs.

The statements and suggestions you read in this guide have been shaped especially by experience in Latin American cultures. They nevertheless serve as a model for going to live with a host family in any country.

Before meeting your hosts

1. Remember that your hosts are as excited as you. They've been reading even the fine print of your application, telling their friends about you, planning for this occasion. It is seen also as a kind of celebration. You can almost think of it as a party.

2. Your family wants to please you. They've fixed up the house. They may have made special purchases, such as a bed or a dresser, for you. They are thinking about the foods they will prepare for you. They hope that you will be happy living with them.

3. You may be nervous, but so are they. You are probably anxious about understanding their language and fitting in with their family activities. They may be anxious because they know that your country is richer than theirs, and your own style of living may be far more luxurious than they can offer. Or there may be ambiguities or conflicts in the relationship between your two countries that create uncertainties.

4. It's a bit difficult to predict exactly who will meet you at the airport, because your "family," in many cultures, is likely to be larger than the individuals who live together in one house. Relatives, neighbors, and friends may, at least for this occasion, be included among those who meet you. Don't be surprised if two cars of people are waiting just for you. On the other hand, if you are arriving in Europe or Japan, the number will probably be smaller, limited to the nuclear family, as it is for students arriving in the United States. It may even be your experience to be met at the airport by someone the family has sent, such as a chauffeur or family friend.

Meeting your hosts

1. The very moment of meeting your family will be dramatic and probably awkward. Be yourself. If the language of your host family is difficult for you to understand or converse in, say your hellos in English. Allow the tone of your words and your smile to say it for you.

2. Your hosts may have greeting customs that are different from yours. If you already know their customs (for example, special verbal expressions, handshakes, hand on arm or shoulder, hands together at the breast and bowing, kisses on the cheek, embraces, etc.), greet your hosts using their manner of greeting. If you don't know these customs, you might have a brief opportunity to observe how others are greeting, and then try it. But don't hesitate to fall back on your own familiar way of saying hello. Your hosts will accept your cordiality just as you give it.

3. Say hello to each person in the party meeting you. If it's a large group, it is easy to feel overwhelmed and neglect making eye contact and addressing each one. You'll hear their names, though you will probably not catch them all: Joaquín Guttiérrez Barzona, Satyajit Mazumdar, Yasuhiro Kobayashi. Even if the name gets confused into a clutter of strange sounds and syllables, address each person individually. Ask people how they are. Perhaps you can begin to make conversation, commenting on a ball that a child is carrying, the graphics on a sweatshirt, or an especially pleasant smile one of the greeters is giving you.

4. Physical distance may be important right from the start. Your host family (if from certain Asian cultures) may guard a respectful distance between individuals. In some cultures, the head of the family will be the first to close the distance, and others will then follow. On the other hand, your family (if Mediterranean or Latin American) may crowd close around you. Keep your eyes open, notice their preferences about space, and allow them to set the distance between you.

5. Don't be surprised if your hosts stand around awhile and visit. They might prefer to extend this moment of saying hello before heading home. Let them set the pace.

6. Let them also help you carry your luggage. Don't be suspicious; they are your family.

7. You might use a car or a taxi or public transportation, depending largely upon the family's ability to pay. You might proceed directly home, or you might first visit relatives. Or they might want to show you the town since they are driving through it anyway. Sometimes families go straight to a restaurant for a welcoming meal or to a coffee shop for refreshments. Be ready for anything—and relax and enjoy it.

After meeting your hosts

1. When you arrive at the house, ask for everyone's name again. Go to a table, take out your notepad, and begin writing them down. Your hosts will probably start right out helping you learn them.

2. Some families will show you to your room and leave you to your unpacking. Others will want to help you unpack. Their curiosity is not to be interpreted as snoopiness. They do the same with each other.

3. Your hosts will probably start out explaining their house and their customs, much of which you won't understand. Ask questions. Where is the bathroom? What are breakfast habits? How do you use the key to the front door? Later you will have to ask some things again, especially in clarifying the use of the most complex room of the house—the bathroom. Who showers when? What is to be done with towels? Toilet tissue—some cities don't have a plumbing and sewage system to accommodate any toilet tissue. How do you turn on the hot water? They will explain. Don't be surprised if customs in this sensitive area seem strange at first or are very different from your own.

4. If you have studied the language, you probably know something about the communication styles of your hosts, but there is much to learn—whether you speak your language or theirs with them. In some cultures, families engage in almost continuous verbal interaction; in others, there are long periods of quiet. In some families, everyone is expected to talk. In other families, the father will be the spokesperson. In some cultures, communication is indirect and mildly suggestive, while in other cultures, address is direct and blunt. A Norwegian family will be very different in this regard from a Brazilian family, a Japanese family very different from an Arab family. There will be modes of nonverbal communication to be learned. In your particular context, however, it is important to express yourself, especially where the extension of courtesies is more formalized than it is in the United States. If not inappropriate, greet all family members morning and evening when entering and leaving their presence. Express your appreciation for everything they do on your behalf. Compliment them; put it in words, smiles, and, if it's the custom of the country, hugs. Whether they come from a verbal culture or nonverbal culture, everyone likes to be appreciated.

5. Join in family activities. The family may feel awkward if you sit around waiting for something to happen, or worse, if you retreat to your room. Your family may not know, understand, nor appreciate the individualism and guarded privacy which Americans value so much. Even if they do, they want you to participate in their family events. In some cultures, even when you study, do it with them unless they themselves model some other norm. In some cultures, families share and exchange their private possessions more than is done in the United States. A visiting female should not call it stealing if her host sister wishes to use her cosmetics. The sister probably expects her guest to wear her clothing. If you want something to be kept private and personal, lock it in your suitcase.

6. Since your family's friends are an extension of the family, you will be introduced to many of them in the early days. You honor your family in meeting them, in learning about them, in participating in their lives, and in enjoying them. You offend your family in failing to show interest in them.

7. And of course, be honest. On the evening of your arrival, if you are tired, ask to go to bed. If you are thirsty, ask for a glass of water. Later on, if you are homesick, say it. If a question of family schedule confuses you, mention it politely. Your family wants you to be comfortable and to get off to a good start.

II. Settling In

Introduction

The reaction people have to the first weeks of their overseas experience varies from individual to individual. But culture shock, or cross-cultural adjustment, theory suggests that many, if not most, people go through a honeymoon stage at the beginning of their sojourn. For a period of several days to several weeks they ride on a current of excitement and fascination with all the new things they are seeing and experiences they are having.

This series of guides, called "Settling In," is designed for those first days. Guide 5 enables you to get your bearings in the new city. Guide 6 helps you meet people. And Guide 7 helps you learn how to frame appropriate questions. With these three, you're on the way.

Guide 5

Orienting Yourself to the City Center and Getting Around

Fear or worry about getting lost is the frequent companion of many people when they start to explore on their own a strange new environment. Even if it is not, getting your bearings early on helps speed up the process of culture learning by making accessible to the learner more facets of the culture more rapidly than would otherwise be the case.

This guide offers a systematic way to orient yourself by identifying a center, learning it well, and branching out from there. The center used in this exercise is the center of the town or city in which you live. It is your task to transform it from a busy, confusing unknown—or, in many cases, a noisy, congested metropolitan mess—into the center point of your orientation.

This study is designed to help you experience life in the city, make friends with strangers, adapt yourself to foreign circumstances, put your new language skills to use, do elementary field research, use informants as the means of gaining knowledge about a community, and make decisions about daily survival needs.

Procedures

This is a project well suited to the second or third day after your arrival. If possible, do it with another person, but not in a group.

Part 1

Establish a center point in the city. Using your city map, find the central intersection, park, cathedral, government building, monument, or whatever might be used by residents to mark the center of their city.

Go there equipped with the portion of the map that shows downtown (folded open), a clipboard, paper, pencil, a paperback language dictionary, and enough money for lunch. (Leave your camera, backpack, money belt, and other superfluous items at home.)

Take a walk starting from the center, going several blocks, then returning to the center. Go in a different direction several blocks, then return. A third direction. Then a fourth. You've moved out from the hub in four directions and have returned.

Now take your original trail, but go only one block. Instead of returning to the hub, move in a circumference of that hub. When you finish the first circumference, make a second one, a block more distant from the center.

Go slowly. Stop to rest. Consult the city map. Allow yourself to be diverted. Take notes. Make sketches. Retrace steps to refresh your memory of where you've been. Try to answer any of these questions (many of which you will rephrase to fit your city).

1. Is there a main street? What is it called? What is the name of the principal street that intersects it?

2. By what names are the north-south streets labeled? Is there a systematic naming or numbering scheme as you move south to north?

3. By what names are the east-west streets labeled? Is there a systematic naming or numbering scheme as you move west to east?

4. Identify the buildings/parks/monuments in the immediate central city. Write down their names.

5. Find these:

    *   the municipal town hall: is that the location of the city's chief executive?

    *   a major bank: can you change traveler's checks there?

    *   a department store: is it open during the noon hour?

    *   the post office: how much postage is required for a letter home?

    *   a bookstore: does it sell writing supplies, language-learning materials, foreign (English) language books, city guides and maps?

    *   a hotel: who do you think are the principal occupants?

    *   a major church or religious edifice: do residents physically express devotion as they pass the church?

    *   a museum: what are the categories of exhibits (science and technology? gold? fabrics? paintings?)?

    *   a factory: what is made? Is the product on display somewhere? Is it a specialty of that country or region?

- a medical facility: does this institution offer a medical specialty or a general service? Is it one you would feel comfortable using?

- a school: what can you deduce about the local educational system from watching the students arrive and leave?

- a coffee or soda shop: what do people order for a mid-morning snack?

- a market: how are products organized differently from those in markets at home? Can you buy flowers here for your host mother or to take when you're invited out to dinner?

6. Is there a crowd in the central park? If so, what is drawing it?

7. Where can one get a shoeshine?

8. Which of the buildings has a public rest room?

9. Which streets seem the more congested? Dangerous? Unguarded?

10. Where can one rest?

11. Who do you think would be a good person to ask about directions?

12. Do the buses come into city center? How are they marked? Where are the bus stops? How are they marked?

Find a restaurant downtown that is used by locals rather than tourists. Take a long lunch break. Study the menu. Jot down names and prices of menu items. Consult the waitress or waiter and your dictionary as needed. Order something "native."

As you eat, review your notes from the morning explorations.

After lunch retrace your steps. It will help you establish patterns, a routine. Observe the buildings and life on the street more closely. You may wish to spend a little more time in the museum. Talk with some of the guards.

This is also a perfect opportunity to do some shopping. Make your first purchases without the pressure of needing something specific or being short of time.

Later, in the park, assuming it is warm enough to sit (if not, a coffee shop or other indoor public place can usually be found), you may wish to record notes in your journal about what you've experienced that day, or perhaps make sketches of some of the interesting buildings you've noticed or scenes you've observed.

Part 2

Here's a way to orient yourself further to the urban/town milieu by learning about taxis and the public transportation system before you have to use them for a purpose.

Riding the buses

Get on a bus going in any direction. After a while get off and board a bus returning to where you came from (though check with the driver or look for other signs that it goes back to the same place you got on).

1. How do people queue for a bus—stand in line, take turns, push, shove?

2. Is there a bus fare? How does one pay—a token, a punch card, cash? Who pays?

3. Does one buy a ticket at a booth, pay the driver at the beginning of the trip, during the trip, or at the end? Is payment placed into a box, given to the driver, or collected by a bus runner? Does the bus require exact change? Are transfers accepted? Is there a time restriction?

4. Is there any system to the seating arrangement? Who sits up front? Who moves to the back? Who sits with whom? Does one ask permission to sit beside a person?

5. Does the bus permit standees? If so, how do the standees hold on? How do they carry an armful of packages, yet hold on?

6. How do drivers treat passengers? What things seem to upset drivers?

7. Do people talk with each other? Who chats or doesn't? If so, how loudly do they talk? What do people talk about? Do you hear laughter? boisterousness?

8. Does the style/quality of dress of passengers vary at different times of day? Do people who are poorly dressed tend to get off/on at certain stops?

9. Do beggars get on the bus? Do sellers hawk their wares on the bus?

10. Are seats relinquished for any special incoming passengers? What happens when the bus is crowded—are people more irritable, quiet, friendly, noisy?

11. How are heavy bags accommodated? Where do people put umbrellas?

12. Who determines how far open a window will be? Who opens or closes the windows in the event of rain?

13. Do the riders rest their arms on the window ledge? Do they put their feet onto the seats? Do they lie down on two seats? Do they read newspapers? Do they listen to music?

14. How are the buses decorated? What gives them distinctive characteristics?

15. Observe the give-and-take among vehicles from the perspective of the bus—the priorities, the signals, the courtesies, and the retaliations.

16. How does one signal to get off? Do people push a bell, pull a rope, call out a command? Do passengers getting on or off receive assistance?

17. Do people leave by the same door they entered? Who moves first, those leaving or those entering?

Traveling by taxi

Take a taxi to a familiar destination—then take one back or return on foot or by bus (depending on your preference, knowledge or finances!).

1. What stops a cruising taxi?

2. Are you passed up by some taxis? If so, can you figure out why?

3. Is the fare charge clearly stated in or on the cab? Does one bargain over the fare? Is the functioning of the meter visible and understandable? Are cabs expensive in this country?

4. Is the cab an independent operation or is it one unit in a fleet of cabs owned by the same company? Does the driver have radio contact with a dispatcher?

5. Do riders always sit in the back seat? Who may sit up front?

6. Do cab drivers drive differently from other drivers? Do you feel safe in the cab?

7. Do the drivers want to carry on conversations?

8. Can you make any hypothesis about what kind of people become cab drivers?

As your experience with the city increases, you will discover that much of your culture learning takes place while you are on the move—walking, traveling in a bus, or going by taxi. From your careful observations, you will be able to learn about the ways people interact in a variety of situations, about the routines in the workaday world, about the contrasting sections of town and the classes of people who reside there, about security and crime in the streets and how local people guard against petty thievery, about the relationship of males and females in public, etc. Through this kind of activity, your environment will slowly but surely take coherent shape and become a comfortable setting for your overseas experience. Use the guide as a model for exploring school, college, office, or other places you frequent.

Guide 6

Finding Help

Friends once told us that when they travel (in the United States) with their small children and want to find the restaurant that suits the family mood of the moment, they have good luck when they first drive to the town library and ask the librarian for a recommendation. Our friends said that librarians seemed to understand both the needs of a family and the resources of the community. This modest example illustrates the effective use of informants. In getting acquainted with a new culture, you can spur your progress by finding the right people to assist you. Here are some suggestions on how to go about it.

Finding role models

A culture expresses itself in diverse ways, so many in fact that the stranger is likely to miss just about all of the cues that make life more convenient for the native residents. How do you find a reliable electrician? Which pharmacies are open at night? Which holidays do the public schools observe? Is the faucet water safe to drink?

If you are invited to the home of a new acquaintance, how formally should you dress? When should you arrive? Should you take a gift for your hostess? If you live with a host family, what should you wear when lounging around during evening hours? On a date, how do you communicate that you want to be a casual friend and not a steady and exclusive partner?

One possible answer to all of these questions is "Do as the Romans do." Learn to imitate behaviors. But the motto isn't enough. Sometimes you as an outsider

70

just can't intercept—nor understand—all the signals of the local Romans. For example, you are sure that bargaining is expected at the market in your East African town, and you have tried to watch and listen as local people argue their way to a satisfactory selling price, but when you try it, you get the feeling that the sellers are offended by the way you bargain.

Another reason to hesitate about doing as the Romans do is provided by the number and variety of Romans. Whose Roman behavior will you use as a model?

- Someone you meet in the park?
- A university student?
- The store clerk who is friendly to you?
- A spouse who lives in your apartment building?
- A host brother, sister, or cousin?
- A fellow worker on the job?
- People who share your professional interests?

Each of these persons may model how to live effectively in your host culture, but you should think carefully about the qualifications of each one, especially his or her availability, knowledge, and reliability. Get into the habit of imitating the right people.

Finding cultural interpreters

Another way to get answers to your questions seems simple enough: ask someone. In fact, it is not so simple. There is no guarantee that the right person will be around when you need the answer, nor will it be certain that you will be able to use the right question in the right words and with the right nonverbals to get the answer you need. It makes sense therefore for you as a newcomer to establish a continuing relationship with someone to whom you can refer cultural questions. You might wish to think of this person as your cultural informant, interpreter, and mentor. She or he can tell you about local customs, explain mores, interpret current events, and help you think through important experiences. This person should not only interpret the local culture, but also be willing and able to identify those of your behaviors that are unacceptable in the society and describe the rationale for local behaviors that seem unacceptable to you.

Who is a good choice for cultural interpreter (or mentor, or informant)? Certainly the person should be interested in helping you in this way; should have local ties and be a part of a local network; should have teaching (coaching) ability and not be afraid to be direct, honest, and helpful; should be available; and (in some situations) should be of the same sex.

1. A schoolteacher? Yes, good choice. This person is likely to know youth well. As a teacher, he or she will have learned much about the history and ways of the country and is likely to be a respected member of the community.

2. An experienced host parent? Yes, excellent. This person knows your program and has been through the process of helping previous guests in their learning about culture.

3. A local resident who has been to the United States? This person has the advantage of knowing the contrasts between American culture and his or her own.

4. A culturally sensitive American who has lived there for a long time? Here is a winner if you have already discovered that local people respect this foreign resident. He or she will not have forgotten what it was like to be a newcomer, although he or she might expect you to make a quicker adaptation than they themselves can remember making.

5. A pastor? Possibly, although the church's own religious and moral agenda might skew the interpretations.

6. A representative of the tourist office? You'll find this person friendly and articulate, but probably giving a PR flavor to the response.

7. A youth with an agenda, i.e., seeking employment or looking for a scholarship to study in your country? He or she will be eager to please—perhaps too much to say what you need to hear.

8. A medical doctor? Possibly, but the specialized work of this professional will give you better counsel in the area of the specialty than in general topics.

Let these role models and cultural informants know how much you value their help. At an appropriate time, take them to your favorite restaurant and/or to a play or concert or similar appropriate event in your host culture.

But what kinds of questions are the most fruitful to ask as your pursue your culture learning? The next guide offers some suggestions.

Asking Questions

A healthy curiosity motivates you to get out, snoop around, become involved, and learn. It stimulates questions such as the following:

- How can they possibly pick coffee from bushes on a hill that steep?
- Do you think our State Department and embassies understand this part of the world?
- Why do you think socialistic strategies are not solving East African issues?
- Is it insulting to use the word *pachuco?*
- What is the function of gift exchanges in the negotiations we hope to carry on with this company?
- Is child abuse less frequent here than it is in the United States?
- Will this proposed highway sufficiently benefit the impoverished farmers of the area to offset the ecological damage it will cause?
- In a refugee camp health clinic, what's a nurse's range of work?

Not all people are equally curious, nor equally skilled at asking questions that produce informative answers. It may take some practice. Successful question-asking consists of three parts:

1. finding a topic that offers interesting perplexities, raises doubts, produces contradictions, but nonetheless seems significant;

2. framing the question in ways that will provoke the most revealing and varied responses; and

3. directing the question to the right source of answers.

In this exercise, you'll practice the three parts of question-asking.

If you are with a group, break into subgroups of no more than three. If you're not in a group, find a friend to do this exercise with you, or do it with your spouse or children. Do it on your own if necessary and discuss the process with a friendly source.

Finding a topic

Topics are everywhere, so ubiquitous that you won't see them in front of your eyes. As a way of getting started, choose any subject that will reveal relatively obvious cultural differences. Here are a few obvious ones:

- foods and eating
- roads and transportation
- buying and selling
- sports and recreation

Let's demonstrate the process by developing some questions about foods and eating. The task is to call up twenty aspects of foods and eating which stimulate your curiosity. For now, just list the topics. Here are four possibilities. Add others of your own.

1. my host mother's role in food preparation and consumption

2. quantity of food in servings

3. fat content in frequently used foods

4. communicating that I don't like a food

Framing the question

Next, think up a question about each aspect of the topic of foods and eating. For example, you might create this question about the mother's role in food preparation: "Is it customary for the mother to serve food at the table to the father?"

Before moving on to create a question for the next item, ask your subgroup partners to rephrase the question, not necessarily to improve it, but to show that questions may take on various forms which will provide different responses. For example: "Does my host father actually want my host mother to fill his plate for him?" Practice the framing of questions. The more ways you can find to frame a question, the better.

Here are questions and rephrasings on the topics of foods and eating. Continue the exercise of making and framing questions over the aspects of foods and eating you came up with.

Topic 1 (about homemaker's role)

1. Is it customary for the mother to serve food at the table to the father?
   Rephrased: Does my host father actually want my host mother to fill his plate for him?

2. (your question and rephrasing)
   etc.

Topic 2 (about quantities of food)

1. Why does my host mother ask me to eat so much?
   Rephrased: Is it just my faulty impression that a host feels bad if the guests don't stuff themselves?

2. (your question and rephrasing)
   etc.

Topic 3 (about fat content)

1. Does the use of lots of oil in stir fry raise the cholesterol levels here?
   Rephrased: The food is quite oily. Are those polyunsaturated fats?

2. (your question and rephrasing)
   etc.

Topic 4 (about not liking foods)

1. Is it appropriate for me to tell them that I am vegetarian?
   Rephrased: If I simply leave food on my plate untouched, does that convey to them that I prefer not to have that food served to me again?

2. (your question and rephrasing)
   etc.

Notice that the rephrasings tend to become more complex, introducing values, attitudes, and preferences. Differences in values and attitudes are at the heart of cross-cultural misunderstanding; you can see, therefore, how important good question-asking is to effective culture learning.

Directing your questions

Now review all the questions. Which ought to be asked of someone and to whom should they be directed? Decide, if you're with a friend or in a group, who will ask whom which question. Which form of the question seems most appropriate for the person of whom it will be asked? Next, go out in the real world and ask your questions!

Question-asking is a skill that requires practice. As you get better at it, you'll also be more confident in your discourse with others, and you'll recognize a marked improvement in your ability to delve into and discover things unknown about your host culture. Consider especially the potential for learning the culture in pursuing such issues as disciplining children, attitudes toward authority, and ways of dealing with birth, marriage, and death.

III. Getting Early Glimpses of the Host Culture

Introduction

The label for the next series of four guides—"Getting Early Glimpses of the Host Culture"—refers to a visual process. This reference is not casual. An understanding of the concept of perception or the way in which people see the world around them is vital to the study of cultures.

The guides in this series do not elaborate the theory of perception, but are instead perception activities. Before you begin those activities, however, we'll talk just a little about the perceptual process and how it affects cultural study.

The perceptual system is like a projector and screen. The projector, culturally constructed and then deeply set into our psyche, projects upon our mental screen pictures not only of what physical things are, but also of what appropriate behaviors, values, attitudes, and patterns of thinking and feeling are. It also projects pictures of stereotypes of other peoples and cultures. These internal pictures then become the reference point for dealing with the world outside.

For example, we have mental pictures of trees, flowers, and reeds. When we go out into the world and look around, our attention is called to something. Is it a tree, a flower, or a reed? We unconsciously check this external observation against our internal picture. Through this referral process, we conclude, it's just like our mental picture of a tree, so it must be a tree.

Even though the picture, or pictures, of the world provided to us by our perceptual systems aren't and can't possibly be complete, we construct out of these fragments a whole. This whole does not, and does not need to, conform precisely to reality. What it does is give us a framework for functioning effectively in the world in which we live. It enables us to understand what we see and to predict what will happen next.

Yet, even though it works fairly well with trees, the perceptual system is very fallible, especially when dealing with people. Constructed as it is from fragments of experience and the somewhat haphazard influence of parents, peers, and mentors, it leads us into expectations that are not always met by real-life events, i.e., our predictions don't always pan out. We thought she was joking, but she was dead serious. We thought he would make a right turn, but he made a left one. We thought she would accept the invitation, but she said no.

If these misperceptions occur so often at home—and they do, sometimes with very serious consequences—then how much more frequently must they occur when you're in an unfamiliar cultural setting? To compound the problem, the mental or perceptual framework you have for your host culture is likely to be even less accurate than the one you have for your own. With less information and, in a sense, a greater need to predict with certainty, you are drawn into stereotyping, which means depending for your predictions on a highly oversimplified image of the other culture. To further compound the difficulties, when your expectations are not met or your predictions fail in their accuracy, you blame not your own faulty perceptual system, but the other person.

Finally, your stereotypes—which in the beginning constitute a not wholly illegitimate effort to comprehend the world with inevitably inadequate information—easily turn negative and become invested with all manner of fears and other more or less destructive emotions that close off your ability to perceive accurately no matter what new data presents itself.

One of the principal purposes of cultural study is to flesh out the perceptual framework you have for understanding a culture and its peoples, that is, to expand your knowledge and sharpen your perceptions of them. But even more important is to gain insight into *their* perceptual system or worldview, to be able to see or empathize with where *they* are coming from. Ultimately, the aim is to help you both discard stereotypes and function effectively within the culture, that is, bring your expectations more in line with reality and enable you to make more dependable predictions. One way to do that is to consciously examine cultural differences. Here's a guide with which to begin that process.

Noting Differences

Raymonde Carroll, in *Cultural Misunderstandings: The French/American Experience* (1988), says that although many French and Americans perceive each other as quite similar, there are in fact profound differences which often cause breakdowns in their relationships—issues such as privacy, self-disclosure, and appropriate topics and styles of conversation. French and American perceptions of each other and of social situations lead the participants into faulty predictions. Carroll, like most cultural scholars, urges a careful detection and sorting out of those differences, followed by a revision of how they are perceived.

Instead of leaping blindly over cultural differences—pretending they aren't there or trying to minimize their significance—you need to learn to take a good look at them. *Seeing* cultural differences will lead you to an understanding of them which will foster cross-cultural communication.

Here is an exercise to help you perceive cultural differences more accurately. It leads you through three stages: identifying differences, analyzing them, and enhancing communication through your new understanding of the differences. Modify the exercise to fit your situation.

Select a cultural behavior to observe

We suggest you focus upon a single behavior, so that your observations can be relatively specific. Select a behavior from this list of nineteen, or let the list lead you to another of more interest or relevance to you.

- playing (as in athletics)
- adorning, fixing up one's body
- cooking
- courting, dating
- dancing
- feasting, celebrating
- praying, worshipping
- participating in a funeral or other death rite
- driving
- gesturing
- giving gifts
- competing for attention, for power, etc.
- greeting other people
- maintaining cleanliness (food, house, car, person)
- singing, whistling, making music
- working
- getting medical care
- laughing, joking, playing pranks
- studying

Let us suppose that you select the final one, studying, as the behavior you wish to observe.

Identify the differences

Here is a scheme to use. It is designed for an American student in the People's Republic of China trying to identify the differences between her study habits and the study habits of Chinese youth her age. You, of course, would make the comparison with a student in your host culture.

A scheme for identifying differences in study habits

Lead questions	American student	Chinese student
study where? 　　library, dorm, 　　classroom, home, 　　elsewhere	_____	_____
study when? 　　days of week, 　　time of day, 　　hours at a stretch	_____	_____

Lead questions	American student	Chinese student

study what?
    assignments, books,
    notes, labs, videos,
    projects
	_____	_____

study how?
    desk, chair, lamp,
    bed, phone, radio, food,
    typewriters, computers,
    alone, with others,
    memorizing, writing,
    active, passive
	_____	_____

study why?
    grades, job,
    family expectations,
    personal advancement
	_____	_____

The number of cited differences could grow quite long. But what do the differences add up to? They are not merely curiosities; they are the stuff of culture learning and call for analysis.

Analyze the differences

Here's a work sheet to direct your analysis. We will continue using the hypothetical case of study habits, expecting you to adapt the work sheet to your subject. On the left side of the work sheet are some key assumptions that govern cultural behaviors. How do these kinds of cultural assumptions shape specific behaviors in your own culture and in your host culture? The task is to examine the descriptions you wrote in the above scheme in the context of each of the assumptions listed. Do the study behaviors, American or Chinese, reveal themselves as a manifestation of these assumptions? How? What is the significance or relevance to you as a culture learner, as a guest in the society, as one who must adapt to different cultural norms? As you jot down your notes you will need more space, probably several pages from your journal.

A work sheet on the relationship of behavior and cultural assumptions

Cultural assumptions*	American study habits	Chinese study habits
Perception of oneself: assumptions about how one identifies self in relation to others, in regard to self-concept, self-respect	_____	_____
Personal responsibility: assumptions about the tasks or obligations an individual is expected to do independently	_____	_____

Cultural assumptions*	American study habits	Chinese study habits
Concept of time: assumptions about past, present, future orientations; about time as a commodity; about use and misuse of time	_____	_____
Use of space: assumptions about quantity and quality of space, about exclusive and inclusive space, about maximum and minimum space	_____	_____
Desire for achievement: assumptions about motivation, desire, advancement, obligation	_____	_____
Competition and affiliation: assumptions about cooperative and noncooperative, individualistic and group-oriented actions	_____	_____
Equality, status: assumptions about class, rank, dominance, and nondominance	_____	_____
Work and play: assumptions about the unity or separation of work and play	_____	_____

*The items are adapted from Stewart and Bennett, *American Cultural Patterns: A Cross-Cultural Perspective,* 1991.

Enhancing cross-cultural communication through an awareness of cultural differences

It is easier to identify differences than to detect the subtle cultural assumptions that support them. Even more difficult is understanding the variants well enough to communicate better across cultures. For example, I may discover that my hosts differ from me in how they use their study time, and I may come to the point of seeing a relationship between their study behavior and their larger cultural assumptions about achievement, but I may still have a long way to go before I can fully work out the most desirable relationships between *their* assumptions, perceptions, and behaviors and my own.

Most important, an eyes-open study of differences can help you sharpen your perceptions of strangers, leading you to make more accurate generalizations about them. Second, you can draw mental pictures of them that come closer to who they really are, rather than pictures based on flawed stereotypes. Third, as you consider the differences that distinguish them from you, you may become a better predictor of their conduct, because their behaviors will begin to be more consistent with what you noticed on previous occasions. Fourth, these apparent differences may serve as paths by which to find your way into their culture, where you can discover what is concealed from the outsider. Finally, this rigorous study may help you to shape your behavior to be more compatible with theirs, without compromising who you are.

Reading the Signs

In this series of first glimpses of your host culture, you are being challenged to *see* culture. This is a demanding assignment, because generally cultures don't reveal themselves easily. They comprise internal understandings of life, and they share common perceptions that cannot be easily perceived by outsiders. They exchange meanings through subtleties beyond the range of the human eye.

However, cultures do reveal themselves in part through a system of both verbal and nonverbal cues that recent scholars have come to call signs. Nonverbal cues include how one smiles, gestures, and walks, how one uses time, space, tools, material possessions, etc. In fact, anything that stands for something else is a sign.

The study of signs has, in our century, become a science and spread around the world. Semiology (or semiotics) has affected our ways of perceiving and of thinking in many fields of work, from linguistics to mathematics, from music to theology, from athletics to missions.

Every culture has its own system of signs. To the insiders, the sign system is natural, largely unconscious, almost like breathing. Meanings are given to signs. Signs are coupled with other signs. Signs are modified, sometimes discarded, other times reinforced. But to an outsider, the sign system will likely be impenetrable, because the outsider has had no part in the assigning of its meanings.

For Americans there is an additional issue to be concerned about. Communication scholars point out that the United States and Canada are considered very low-context cultures, which means that in communicating, Americans and Canadians depend heavily on words to carry their meaning and very little on the context of the communication, i.e., relationships, status, location, nonverbal behavior, etc. (Hall 1981; Gudykunst and Kim 1984a). Some of the cultures to which Americans and Canadians travel are similarly low-context—much of northern Europe, for example. But most other cultures of the world are, comparatively, higher-context cultures, where people rely more heavily on unspoken cues, clues, and signs to say what they really mean. Americans focus attention upon words and forget that communication includes a much larger sign system.

In intercultural communication, the person who picks up and uses nonverbal cues will probably have an easier time than the one who speaks the language but fails to pick up the subtleties involved in nonlinguistic sign systems.

Learning to read the signs

Here's a strategy—or better said, a sequence—for learning to read cultural signs.

1. Begin with printed signs. Look around. Locate places where you find a constant or heavy use of printed signs. A road intersection. A school. A shopping strip. Is it a context of play, work, worship, travel, etc.? What forms do the signs take—a printed notice, perhaps, or a drawing? Does the sign use an image or logo? Describe its use of color, texture, lights and darks, lines. Are they strictly local in content or is there something universal in them, as in international road signs, for instance? Can you locate other signs nearby that relate to each other? (For example, a street sign indicating a school crossing. A sign nearby indicating a 20-mph speed limit.) Are they of the same form? Do they give the same message? Do they intensify the first sign through repetition, size, color, etc.? Do they serve to focus the first sign or cause distraction from it? Do they duplicate the first sign? Do they clarify or confuse the sense of the first sign? How do these signs compare with signs of the same general function in the United States?

2. Try to "read" some buildings. For this task, you aren't to give your personal descriptions of the building, but rather attempt to discover what the building represents, what it stands for, what it reveals about its culture. I'll give some illustrations below; you continue the exercise.

Reading the messages of buildings

Building	Message
the chapel	My people are poor, humble, hard-working, yet saintly.
the mansion	Wow! Look at me. My owners not only have power and money, they also have Old-World tastes.
the presidential house	The citizens of this country don't want an imperial president, but rather one of modest means.

Building	Message
the school	_____
the embassy	_____
the airport	_____
police headquarters	_____
others	_____
	_____

3. Select other tangible objects for a reading. What you just completed—the reading of buildings—you might now replicate. For example, read the messages having to do with the ownership or use of:
   - cars, trucks, motorcycles, and other vehicles
   - electrical appliances
   - toys
   - clothing, uniforms

4. Try to read selected contexts. Here are some questions that might help you get started.
   a. At the grocery store as your bill is being calculated, can you find any contextual cues that encourage
      - silent waiting?
      - chatting with other customers?
      - chatting with the clerk?
   b. What are the contextual cues that a party is thirty minutes from being over?
   c. From clues that you notice in the street, how can you decipher whether it is appropriate to wear shorts in this village?
   d. What might be some hints, apart from his words, that tell you what the museum guide really meant when he said, "Come back next week and I'll let you see the special jade exhibit in the storeroom."
   e. By reading the context, discover how loudly one should talk in a bus, in a restaurant, in a classroom, in a religious edifice.

5. Read body language for meanings. Here is a list of meanings one might expect to find in any culture. How does your host culture "say" them nonverbally?
   - "We are modern, up to date."
   - "Oh no, not another foreigner."
   - "I demand that you wait on me now."
   - "At this moment I wish to be alone."
   - "Hey, let's have some fun."
   - "We are in deep, deep trouble."

6. Read people reading signs. Observe your cultural consultants as they interpret contexts, as they respond to nonverbal messages, and as they put their own expressiveness into signs. Ask them to interpret the signs you see and hear but don't understand. Ask them to demonstrate how to convey particular meanings. With their help discover the latent (hidden) meanings in what you see and hear.

This guide isn't complete unless it reminds you to think about signing in your own culture. Pick up an American magazine. What signs have the editors chosen to use on the cover to attract you and then to make you want to turn the page? Move through the magazine, studying only the full-page ads. Look for signs that define your country, your people, your places and pleasures. How does signing in your country compare with that in your host country? How does the signing in each serve as a visual outcropping of cultural bedrock? Use your journal to continue your study of signing.

The following guide considers further the topic of nonverbal communication.

Interpreting Nonverbal Cues

As you have seen in Guide 9, we use gesture, posture, space, time, and many other subtle nonverbal cues to convey meaning. This guide explores in greater detail the ways in which people communicate through their use of body language.

Carey Quan Gelernter, a newspaper columnist for the *Seattle Times,* writes, "If you are Americans chatting in a coffee shop, you probably touch each other twice an hour. If you are English, you probably don't touch each other at all. If you're French, you touch 110 times an hour." This is a humorous example of the relevance of body language. The person who frequently crosses cultural boundaries must learn to intercept, interpret, and use this type of nonverbal cue if communication is to be efficient and effective.

Observing nonverbal actions

Stop, look, listen, and then try to answer these questions about nonverbal actions in your host country.

1. Direct your attention to how family members in your host country give nonverbal cues to each other. How does a parent beckon a child? How does a child beg for others' attention? How does a child tell a sibling to "stop it!" How does a teenager show the wish for independence? How does a parent indicate that the fooling around has gone far enough? Which of these cues are used in the same way you use them at home? Which are different?

2. Consider basic life functions. What are some of the nonverbal ways people refer to eating? to sleeping? to drinking? to having to use a rest room? to bathing? to primping? Think about the faculties they employ in making these cues: the face and eyes, the hands, the shoulders and back, the hips and legs.

3. Find examples of how people describe other people, for example:

   - "The child is big for his age...maybe this big." (In some cultures, for animals, hand extended, palm down; for children, hand extended, palm down but wrist crooked upward)

   - "She is very wealthy, and she wants you to know it." (A slight, quick twitting of nose or a thumb quickly rubbing two fingers)

   - "He is very lazy" (Head resting on palm) or "He's a go-getter." (Snap, snap of fingers)

   - "She is devious" (Raised eyebrows, tilt of head or a quick sway of hips) or "She is a saint." (Hands folded in prayer or a cross traced across the heart)

   - "That child is stupid" (A twirling finger pointed to side of forehead) or "She is terribly bright." (Eyebrows up, eyes open wide)

   - "He takes to the bottle a lot." (Thumb and little finger raised, thumb pointed to mouth, wrist wriggled back and forth)

As you observe these nonverbal cues, can you also detect the ways that the people add nonverbal emphases to what they are conveying, such as making the gesture twice, or using two gestures that reinforce each other, or using both non-verbal and verbal means to say it?

4. Look for nonverbal communication in public. If a person is waiting in a long line in a bank, how does he or she express displeasure at the waiting? How does one hail a taxi? How do fans at a ball game tell the referee that a call was wrong? If you have traveled in more than one foreign country, indicate the similarities and differences in the nonverbal cues.

5. As people pass on a sidewalk, is there eye contact? Do both men and women make eye contact? at what distance? for how long? In the United States would you answer those questions similarly in (a) your hometown, (b) a Southern city, (c) downtown New York?

6. Cultural observers would say that the use of and the functions and sanctions related to staring vary greatly from culture to culture. Is staring acceptable? by whom? toward what? Is staring ever considered an illness? a manner of admiring? a way to attract attention? Do parents scold children for staring? You may have to chat with a cultural informant or interpreter to help you understand local staring customs.

I like, I dislike—nonverbally

Now try a more focused study. Recall only the nonverbal cues that convey that people in your host culture like or dislike something. For each of those two meanings, find at least one nonverbal cue, and write it down.

categories of nonverbal cues	host culture cues of liking	host culture cues of disliking
eyes	_____	_____
eyebrows	_____	_____
face	_____	_____
tilt of head	_____	_____
hands	_____	_____
posture	_____	_____
space	_____	_____
time	_____	_____
pitch of voice	_____	_____
tone of voice	_____	_____

Here's an exercise that is normally done in a group, though one could do it informally with a friend or two, with one's own family (if you're abroad together), or even with the host family if you have established a very trusting relationship. In fact, it would be especially enlightening to do this exercise with a bi- or multicultural group.

With whatever group you have assembled, take turns in role playing one of the nonverbal communication acts listed above. It may be a facial expression, a gesture, a use of space, an expression of speed or tone or punctuation. The performer should indicate when and where the act was observed. As time permits, interpret the possible nuances of "I like" or "I dislike" found in each nonverbal act.

On the basis of what you learn from these nonverbal cues, you may try to construct a larger system about liking and disliking that could not be understood only from words. What do they like? Whom do they like? What do they dislike? Whom do they dislike?

While this exercise focuses on *like-dislike,* you might wish to study other messages coded nonverbally by your host culture. Examples:

- I am intelligent; I am stupid.
- I am submissive; I am powerful.
- I am wealthy; I am poor.
- I am a follower; I am a leader.
- I am conservative; I am progressive.

This guide should be a reminder that you, too, engage in nonverbal communication. Some of the cues you give off are American-made; some are of your own making. People in your host country are reading them, sometimes correctly and sometimes incorrectly. In your journal you might wish to inventory your more obvious and frequently used nonverbal cues and assess how accurately they are being interpreted by your hosts. Should you change some of your nonverbal signing in order to be a better intercultural communicator? Should you try to modify or use additional ways to reinforce your nonverbal communication so that people will understand you better?

Identifying Agendas

This guide is designed to help you examine your overseas study experience from a perspective you probably haven't thought too much about—the personal and educational agendas which people bring to a sojourn abroad. We typically associate agendas with committee meetings. The agenda lists those issues that someone feels deserve the attention of the group. The items may be ranked or placed in order of priority. But agendas are not limited to meetings of committees and other groups. Organizations, large and small, have their own agendas, as do individuals.

An individual has personal commitments. A professional has his/her specialty. A nonprofit organization has its mission statement. A legal entity has its charter. An insurance company has its policies. A government has its interests.

In the case of travel and intercultural transactions, there are multiple parties involved, each of which has an agenda. Intercultural transactions have frequently been unsuccessful because one of the parties realizes its own agenda at the expense of the other or simply doesn't recognize the legitimacy of other agendas.

Hidden agendas

Many agendas, particularly those guiding the routines of our lives, are not consciously known, much less articulated. Agendas are like icebergs: more is hidden than is apparent. Some are stated openly; many more remain unspoken, not necessarily out of a desire to conceal or mislead, but as a result of our innocence, our lack of awareness of our own cultural assumptions, our inability to understand our motivations or even our own identity. We might travel with purposes altogether concealed from ourselves, covert motivations that may even conflict with our carefully constructed statement of goals.

So it is useful to ask some basic questions. Why are you sojourning in another country? Can you identify your agenda? Can you articulate your motivations accurately and openly?

This guide helps you with those questions, then urges you to consider related questions. Why do the people of this country welcome you? Why does your host family open their home to you? What do they have in mind? The questions lead you to look most carefully for evidence—from their perspective—of their motivations and their wishes. An understanding of their agenda may help you in two ways: (1) in adjusting to their cultural norms, behaviors, and routines and (2) in culture learning.

A look at some agendas

In this guide we will illustrate agenda setting as it relates to one particular kind of traveler—the student. If you are not a student, adapt the materials to your own purposes.

There are many agendas in operation when American colleges run international programs, but the participants don't always know what they are. I have on occasion asked students newly arrived abroad to write down the goals they have in coming overseas. Usually I find the lists to be general, imprecise, and rather removed from what one would expect of a collegian. But if the students aren't too perceptive about their own goals, they are even less aware of the agendas of other people involved in the program.

Here are some illustrative agendas that might figure in an international program, though not every item will be present in any given institution or individual involved.

The U.S. college or university wants to

- internationalize its curriculum
- keep up with competitors' programs
- fulfill its own stated mission
- foster global citizenship
- strengthen on-campus programs such as foreign language study
- facilitate small-group, faculty-student interaction
- teach, on-site, such topics as political science, history, and literature
- have students experience and transcend culture shock
- have students know the experience of being a minority
- instill or strengthen ethical/religious values
- impress accrediting agencies
- attract new students
- increase endowment funds

The parents want their son or daughter to
- learn about another country and about the world
- travel under supervision
- complete college requirements
- clarify vocational plans
- develop positive values
- provide them (the parents) with a vicarious international experience

The student wants to
- escape from campus
- complete graduation requirements
- see the world
- study with a particular prof
- practice a foreign language
- enjoy adventures
- see if he/she wants to major in the language or history of the country
- learn about possible international careers
- get away from rules and be independent
- study without books
- try out a new skill

The hosts want to
- establish friendship with a foreign visitor
- strengthen country-to-country ties
- earn some money
- gain prestige in town
- have someone to stay with Grandma
- introduce a role model for the children
- establish a contact in the United States
- get access to foreign products
- discuss current events
- practice English
- get a job done

Your agendas and theirs

As a first task in a difficult assignment, write down your agenda for traveling to a foreign culture. Be as thorough and specific as you can. Try to list at least one item in each of these categories of goals: (1) physical, (2) social, (3) intellectual, (4) emotional, (5) spiritual or philosophical, (6) interpersonal, (7) vocational, and (8) economic.

Your second task is to write down what you think might be the agendas of your host family (to show off a foreign guest to relatives), fellow students (to argue American political theory), faculty (to provide comparison-contrasts with American authors), or work-camp director (to contribute muscle to the project).

Now use your journal to work through the following questions that are designed to help you see the implication of the respective agendas of, let's say, you and your host family. (As you have time, you might apply the same questions to the agendas of other participants.) This is not a quick or easy task. You will likely process this material over a long period of time.

1. Identify five agenda items pertaining to your host family and you that are *apparent* goals, clear to you and to your family. On what occasions are those goals explicitly shared?

2. Similarly, identify five that are probably *concealed* in small part from your host family or from you. Why are they hidden? Are the causes of the concealment personal? What would be the consequences if they were uncovered?

3. Which of the goals—yours or theirs—do you think are culturally shaped or even biased? Are you able to find the linkage between the agenda item and the cultural determinant?

4. Identify two or three items on the several lists that are highly compatible with each other (such as the goal of discussing current events). Identify an agenda item on your own list and one on your host family's list that could be completed by the same effort.

5. Identify two or three items that are in obvious conflict with each other (such as your desire for privacy and their interest in having you more fully involved with the family). List agenda items from their list you are not comfortable with. In which might you slight or offend another person (such as your wanting to sunbathe on the back patio)? Can you find a gracious way to disassociate yourself from an agenda item you are personally opposed to?

6. Which agenda items throw a lot of responsibility upon you (being a model for their teenager)? Which items demand a lot of someone's time (keeping Grandma company)? Which ones require financial resources?

7. In which items are you being used by someone else? In which are you using someone?

8. Which ones reward only you? Which of the goals will reward the most people for the longest period of time?

9. Which of your agenda items are so personal that you'd prefer no one else to know of them?

Understanding agendas and motivations—yours and those of your hosts—is a good way to explore cultural differences and to improve your skills in managing the cross-cultural experience. It helps you see relationships from clearer perspectives and comprehend better their dynamics. In a situation where agendas are not only personally different but may be culturally different as well, major misunderstandings can be avoided or at least dealt with more productively.

IV. Living with a Host Family

Introduction

Although we recognize that only a fraction of sojourners choose to live with a host family, a family-living arrangement constitutes such an ideal setting for culture learning that we feel it deserves its own section of guides.

Some people find the host family option unattractive. The pressures, tensions, complications, and lack of privacy seem burdensome. You don't know their language or their customs, their food is different, their schedules and routines odd, and their expectations of you tiresome.

Why not live in a dorm, hostel, apartment, or pension where you don't have to bump up against this foreign culture quite so constantly and intensively? Which, of course, is precisely why you *should* take advantage of a host family arrangement if it is available. Living with a host family contributes significantly to a rapid orientation to the culture that, despite the discomforts of the sudden immersion, can be much less painful than is sometimes the case with persons living alone or with compatriots from home. A family is one of the best settings imaginable for culture learning. In the midst of this core cultural institution, the foreigner benefits from daily encounters with basic cultural characteristics. In the secure atmosphere of the home, one goes through cultural adjustments, experiences personal growth, and expands one's perspectives—all key aspects of culture learning—more rapidly and satisfyingly than in any other environment. From the years of experience I have had in placing American students with host fa lies and watching the results, I've come to the conclusion that a sojourner can learn in six weeks with a family more than someone living in a dorm, pension, or hostel can learn in a year. Furthermore, the family setting is a wonderful place to expand linguistic skills. Trying to master a new language can leave you feeling so helpless, vulnerable, embarrassed, and exhausted that the supportive atmosphere of the family is welcome indeed.

These guides are designed to help you make the most of your family stay. Browsing through them, you may at first wonder how lists of questions can be of much help. But students who have used them have concluded that the questions not only assist them in becoming more aware of what is going on around them, but also focus their attention on topics and issues that are central to understanding and learning a culture. In a sense, the questions provide an agenda, giving order to the cultural impressions with which one is barraged.

The space allowed in this book is inadequate for a recording of your answers, comments, and reactions. Do that in your journal. (See Guides 30-36 for more on journal keeping.)

The People

Frequently I have come across people living with host families who can't name the family members, mainly because they didn't catch the names upon first introduction and later, already having asked a number of times, were embarrassed to ask yet again. Give yourself a break. Make it one of your first tasks *to write down all the names of family members* and memorize them. If you can't spell or pronounce a name, ask your host to write it down or help you practice saying it. Go to extreme efforts at the beginning to learn all the names.

Here are some guidelines for beginning, immediately upon arrival, the process of "learning" your host family.

1. Get the full name and age of each family member living in the home.

2. Get not only formal names but nicknames or other informal names by which they are called and find out which names they prefer *you* to use in addressing them.

3. Do nonfamily members live in your house? Who are they? Why do they live there?

4. Characterize each person living in your home, using four or five adjectives describing personality, appearance, and behavior. Review this list later and see how accurate it is; you will probably find some surprises.

5. Are there family members living away from home? Who are they? Where do they live?

6. Make a listing of extended-family members. Indicate their relationship to your core family. Do you get to see any of them? When? Draw a family tree of the extended family.

7. Are there deceased members of the family who continue to be remembered by the others?

8. Are there photographs of family members or of other people exhibited in the home? Who are they? When were the pictures taken? Why are they valued?

9. Show your hosts snapshots of your family. This may be one of the first points at which you begin truly to bridge cultures. Note how your hosts respond to your family. What cues might you take from their responses as to their regard for family, and what do these say concerning their feelings about the nature of families and family life? Do their responses give you any cues as to their expectations of you as a quasi member of their family?

The House

If you observe carefully the layout of your host family's house, you should be able to make some inferences about them as individuals, as a family, and even about the culture in which they live.

Think of each room as a theater stage. What scenes are played out in each? What actors play the most important roles? How do their behaviors reflect their culture?

Can generalizations be made about the culture from those behaviors? (Review these answers later to see how accurate they were.) Also, see Guide 15 for more on the use of the bathroom.

1. Draw a diagram of the house and the lot it sits on. Show pertinent details, identify rooms, place furniture, appliances, and equipment in it.

2. When was it built? By whom? Who owns it?

3. Describe the construction style and materials.

4. How is the house furnished?

5. Comment on the decoration. What is on the walls? Is the front door plain or fancy? How is color used?

6. Describe a possession that the family values highly. How do you know they prize it?

7. Where in the house does your family eat breakfast? Watch television? Entertain guests? Retreat for privacy? Place wastepaper and garbage? Store tools?

8. How is the house guarded or protected? Are there locks? Bars? Grids? Broken glass on outside walls? Alarms?

9. If your family were typical of the entire culture, what are two or three inferences you could make about the culture, based strictly upon this house and these possessions?

10. Do a brief comparison of your house at home and your hosts'. What are the similarities and differences in physical facilities? What are the similarities and differences in how your natural family and the host family use their respective houses and possessions? What are the similarities in values having to do with home and possessions? The differences? How do your own family, house, and possessions express your culture?

Roles

Spend several days observing the roles of family members. As you did with the rooms of the house, think of "role" in terms of the theater: the part each family member plays in the drama of family living.

Observing roles

1. Who in your household
    - prepares meals?
    - gasses up the car?
    - handles the cash?
    - mows, rakes, tidies the lawn?
    - sweeps or washes floors?
    - answers the phone?
    - makes beds?
    - repairs an appliance?
    - plays tapes in the house?
    - goes shopping for groceries?
    - answers the door?
    - corrects, disciplines the children?

- plans religious or holiday activities?
- contributes art and artifacts to the house?
- irons clothing?

2. Who in your household is the
   - chief source of humor?
   - main comforter?
   - authority figure?
   - religious center?
   - athlete?
   - provider of money?
   - romantic?
   - inventor?
   - debater?
   - partier?
   - reader?
   - spoiled baby?
   - visionary?
   - politician?
   - bully?

3. Describe the roles of the following people:
   - father
   - mother
   - child #1, #2, #3, etc.
   - grandparent #1, #2, etc.
   - boarder
   - uncle
   - aunt
   - maid
   - gardener

Making some generalizations about roles

1. Explore the origin of the roles. Are they acquired by birth? Social status? Are they assigned? If so, who assigned them? Is any one role an outcome of an individual's personality? Do the schools, churches, or government impose roles? Can you identify any other possible sources of the roles?

2. What evidence can you find that your family differs from other families in that culture in the way they assign and carry out roles? What are the specific differences? Why do these differences arise? Do they affect your

family's relationships with other families? Are these different ways of doing things the specific cause for particular pleasures or tensions in the home?

3. Are roles shifting or evolving in that culture? Talk with your family about it. Can you pick up any cues that times are changing, that behaviors are now different from what they were in the past, that the expectations of people in certain roles have been revised? Explore the reason for any changes you identify. Try to imagine or estimate what will be the eventual consequences in the society of these role changes.

4. Compare the roles played by your host family with those of your own family and ask all the above questions about your natural family. Finally, examine your role in your natural family as it compares to the role you are playing or are expected to play in your host family.

Routines

People behave according to established routines, conforming to them rather unthinkingly. So will your hosts. In the midst of all the adjustments you have to make to the differences encountered in your host's home, determining what the routines are and concentrating first on adapting to (or, indeed, adopting) them, is a way to quickly find solid ground in the uncertain footing of your new environment. But routines are, in a sense, more than just routines. They reflect personal and cultural preferences and they differ not only from family to family but from culture to culture. Adapting to family routines is a significant step in knowing and adapting to the culture. It can be an important phase in the culture-learning process.

This guide offers you a way to begin systematically learning your host family's routines by picking out a number of daily aspects of family life to observe. While you can also ask the family about their routines, many routines are followed so automatically and unconsciously that people are often at a loss to respond when asked to identify or describe them.

The early morning

1. In what order do family members rise?
2. At what time?
3. Who prepares breakfast?
4. Who eats breakfast? With whom? Do they talk during breakfast?
5. What are the morning activities prior to the "day"?

- plans religious or holiday activities?
- contributes art and artifacts to the house?
- irons clothing?

2. Who in your household is the
   - chief source of humor?
   - main comforter?
   - authority figure?
   - religious center?
   - athlete?
   - provider of money?
   - romantic?
   - inventor?
   - debater?
   - partier?
   - reader?
   - spoiled baby?
   - visionary?
   - politician?
   - bully?

3. Describe the roles of the following people:
   - father
   - mother
   - child #1, #2, #3, etc.
   - grandparent #1, #2, etc.
   - boarder
   - uncle
   - aunt
   - maid
   - gardener

Making some generalizations about roles

1. Explore the origin of the roles. Are they acquired by birth? Social status? Are they assigned? If so, who assigned them? Is any one role an outcome of an individual's personality? Do the schools, churches, or government impose roles? Can you identify any other possible sources of the roles?

2. What evidence can you find that your family differs from other families in that culture in the way they assign and carry out roles? What are the specific differences? Why do these differences arise? Do they affect your

Guide 14

Roles

Spend several days observing the roles of family members. As you did with the rooms of the house, think of "role" in terms of the theater: the part each family member plays in the drama of family living.

Observing roles

1. Who in your household
   - prepares meals?
   - gasses up the car?
   - handles the cash?
   - mows, rakes, tidies the lawn?
   - sweeps or washes floors?
   - answers the phone?
   - makes beds?
   - repairs an appliance?
   - plays tapes in the house?
   - goes shopping for groceries?
   - answers the door?
   - corrects, disciplines the children?

Routines

People behave according to established routines, conforming to them rather un-thinkingly. So will your hosts. In the midst of all the adjustments you have to make to the differences encountered in your host's home, determining what the routines are and concentrating first on adapting to (or, indeed, adopting) them, is a way to quickly find solid ground in the uncertain footing of your new environment. But routines are, in a sense, more than just routines. They reflect personal and cultural preferences and they differ not only from family to family but from culture to culture. Adapting to family routines is a significant step in knowing and adapting to the culture. It can be an important phase in the culture-learning process.

This guide offers you a way to begin systematically learning your host family's routines by picking out a number of daily aspects of family life to observe. While you can also ask the family about their routines, many routines are followed so automatically and unconsciously that people are often at a loss to respond when asked to identify or describe them.

The early morning

1. In what order do family members rise?
2. At what time?
3. Who prepares breakfast?
4. Who eats breakfast? With whom? Do they talk during breakfast?
5. What are the morning activities prior to the "day"?

The bathroom and bathing

(See Guide 13 for suggestions on how to view the use of other specific rooms.)

1. How often and at what time of day do family members bathe?
2. What do they wear to and from the bathroom?
3. Is there hot water in the bathroom? How is it obtained?
4. How long is a typical shower?
5. What is done with wet towels? Who does it?
6. What does the bathroom look like when they finish?

Clothing

1. How do family members dress when they are simply at home and comfortable?
2. Do they ever go barefoot?
3. How do they dress for work?
4. What are dress-up occasions?
5. What toiletries and cosmetics do they use?
6. Do they spend much money on shoes? Haircuts or hairstyling? Perfume? Accessories?
7. Are there status symbols related to particular garments?

Food and dining

1. Keep a record of everything you eat for three consecutive days. Indicate if you eat at home or out. If outside the home, tell where.

day	breakfast	noon meal	evening meal	other
1	_____	_____	_____	_____
2	_____	_____	_____	_____
3	_____	_____	_____	_____

2. In your host home, who buys the food? Prepares it? Serves it?
3. From hearing them talk, which foods do they value more, which less?
4. What are the alleged foods of rich people? Of poor people?
5. What foods, if any, would one give as a gift?
6. How does one communicate liking a food? Disliking a food?
7. By the standards of nutrition you've learned, evaluate the family's diet.

The evening

1. Who works in the house all day? Who comes home from work? When?
2. Until dinner, what does each person do?
3. Who prepares dinner? Who eats when? With whom?

4. What activity takes place at the table besides eating?
5. Describe the activities following dinner.
6. Who goes out in the evening? When? Where? When do they return?
7. When do people go to bed?

Expectations

The close observation of your host family began with specific and tangible items such as house furnishings. Roles and routines, the topics of Guides 14 and 15, represented less tangible aspects of family life. Here you try gently to uncover several seemingly hidden realities—your host family's agenda, their preferred routines and habits, their house rules and opinions. All of these topics not only define who they are, but also indicate what might be expected of you if you indeed wish to be a participating member in the family.

Their agenda

Review Guide 11 on agenda setting and use it as a framework for exploring further the motivations of your family in having invited you to live with them. What do they want from the experience? If you are perceptive enough to make an accurate and comprehensive listing, then you can turn to the next task of noting which of those agenda items you think you can help them fulfill and which you can't, those you've already addressed in your relationship with them, and those that still need attention. Your journal is an appropriate place to mull these questions over.

Their routines and habits

You want to define and become more aware of routine family behavior patterns. The family members themselves will hardly be conscious of them, so that except for a few of the most salient they will not be explained to you. To help you identify these routines, a few suggestions are given below. There are many, many more, so expand the list according to the routines that are most apparent, important, or unique in your family. Describe their behavior in each of these and then assess the degree to which you should participate in them and how.

- watching television
- visiting the next-door neighbor
- washing windows
- entertaining guests
- buying milk each morning at the corner grocery
- attending Sunday afternoon games at the club
- conversing together
- suggesting movies to see together
- locking the gate and house at night
- disciplining the children
- going to Saturday night mass
- preparing the garbage for Tuesday pickup

Their rules

Few families have a written rule book, but most family members know the rules. You will be told some rules and discover others only after unknowingly breaking them. Guests living in host homes report mixed success in their attempts to learn the rules by asking the host parents what they are. There often seem to be discrepancies between what the parents *say* and what is ultimately enforced. Why the problem? Well, as we've already noted, the family is probably not conscious of all or even most of their rules. It is also probably assumed that everyone knows them whatever they are. Perhaps the family is a little embarrassed about their rules or never before was asked to put the rules into words. Perhaps they hesitate to impose the rules upon a guest. Whatever the case, it is fair to suppose that this inarticulateness is the experience of families worldwide. It does not give license to a guest, however, to be cavalier about rules; families aren't.

You can expect to discover rules in the following territories:

- table and house etiquette
- bathroom use, house tidiness
- appropriate clothing and grooming
- association patterns outside the house
- dating
- acceptable and unacceptable language
- curfews
- school, church, club, work obligations
- use of money
- public and formal codes of courtesy

Examine carefully the behavior patterns of your family in each area. They will provide reliable guidelines as to what their rules and expectations of you are.

Another indicator lies in the opinions expressed by family members. Even in cases where the family does not openly talk about their rules, they will express opinions. For the most part, these opinions aren't random, haphazard, or disconnected. Rather, they reflect and are reflected by the routines and rules—and, indeed, values—that the people live by. If you listen carefully to the full range of a family's opinions—even about the way the garbage collectors throw the empty cans back onto the lawn—you will have access to a "text" that may help you understand the kinds of behaviors they regard as proper or on which they frown. That text will also help you to intercept some of the assumptions that they have made about you and their expectations of you.

Here are some further questions to pursue.

1. What do you think the family most appreciates about having you in their home?

2. What may be the most difficult aspect for them in your being with them?

3. What do you think is their impression of your country, your family, your education, your career plans, your personality, your culture and customs?

4. What is one specific way that you, in the next week, can anticipate their wishes or needs in your behavior? How might you respond to them in a creative and compassionate manner?

5. To bring into even sharper focus this picture of your family, try to compare your host family and your natural family in regard to agendas, routines, rules, and opinions. Where the two families are similar, you are likely to function comfortably. Where the two families are different, you may need to give more attention to your own attitudinal and behavioral adjustments.

Interactions

This guide will help you sharpen your observation skills as you attempt to understand better the nature of personal interaction and patterns of communication among your hosts. Interactions take place constantly, providing a wealth of social and cultural information. Although you may still be a beginner in speaking the language, you can learn a great deal about styles of interaction simply by watching people in conversation, listening for volume, tone and stress in their speech, and noticing their gestures and the social distance they maintain. You should also be ready to begin making some inferences about the motivations and attitudes behind the interactions—a light cross-cultural dose of social psychology. This is one of the most important guides in this section. Understanding how people interact is critical to getting beneath the surface in cross-cultural relationships and to the effective pursuit of culture learning.

Who interacts with whom? When? How?

1. What is typically the happiest part of the day in the house? The most tense?

2. When does the family spend time together? Doing what? Is anyone excluded?

3. Do all members interact in equal freedom with father? Mother?

4. How do they react to grandparents? Uncles and aunts? Cousins?

5. Within the family setting, who touches whom? Where? On what occasions?

6. Do all members interact with the maid? The gardener? The driver? Are these workers treated as family members or employees?

7. Do neighborhood children play in your host's house? If not, where do they play?

8. Do relatives drop in unannounced? Does your family meet relatives elsewhere? Where do they live? How often do they meet? Describe the events.

9. Do friends stop in after school?

10. During the day, do neighbor women get together? Where? When?

11. Do neighbor men interact? When? Where?

12. Does your family have dinner parties? Sunday guests? Who do the guests tend to be? What do they talk about? What do they do?

13. Is your family a member of an intimate small group?

14. Does your family regularly socialize at a club? Does your family ever eat out? Go to movies? Attend athletic contests? Who goes? With whom?

Inside the house

Describe in detail the words and gestures used by your family upon

- seeing each other in the morning
- leaving for work or school
- going to bed
- saying good-byes (for an extended absence)
- showing approval
- indicating displeasure
- apologizing
- getting angry

Behavior toward the outsider

1. How does your host family answer the phone?

2. If a wrong number is called, how do they respond?

3. When there is a knock at the door, how do they react when it's a food huckster? A bill collector? A beggar?

4. To whom would your family give a gift? On what occasions?

5. Whom in the family or neighborhood do they tease?

6. Are there feelings against some residents of your immediate neighborhood? Why?

7. How does at-home behavior change when the people are in a car? At an athletic event? At the market? At a family gathering?

Making some generalizations

1. As you think about the interactions of your host family, you might profitably compare and contrast them with your own family. On the scales below, place an x at the appropriate place on each continuum to describe your host family, and an o at the appropriate place to describe your own family.

private	public
active	passive
formal	informal
authoritarian	democratic
extended	nuclear
hospitable	reserved
driven	casual
class-conscious	egalitarian
tolerant	prejudiced
political	apolitical
communal	private
generous	tightfisted
gossipy	tight-lipped

Are there other characteristics that should be added to this list?

2. In your journal write out a profile of your host culture using this exercise and other exercises, experiences, and readings. Cover such things as customary behaviors, values and assumptions, expectations, and patterns of communication and interaction. Compare and contrast them with your own cultural characteristics and then record how you feel about the similarities and differences.

Neighborhood

To continue the metaphor of the theater, you might wish to enlarge the stage upon which you observe your host family performing to include not only the rooms of the house and the immediate property but also the neighborhood. This extension of the stage greatly complicates the drama—and, of course, makes it more interesting.

By calling attention to its names, institutions, population, activities, and attitudes, this guide will enable you to understand better the neighborhood's scene and setting. It will then ask some questions about your family's role within the community.

Place

1. Does your neighborhood have a name?
2. What is the name of the county, district, and/or province in which your city is located?

Institutions

1. Five major businesses in your neighborhood.

   a.   d.

   b.   e.

   c.

2. Five government-sponsored institutions in your neighborhood.
    a.
    b.
    c.
    d.
    e.

3. Five religious and/or educational institutions in your neighborhood.
    a.
    b.
    c.
    d.
    e.

The people

1. Number of people in your neighborhood.
2. The percentage of inhabitants in your neighborhood who are between ages
    a. 1 - 10
    b. 11 - 20
    c. 21 - 30
    d. 31 - 40
    e. 41 - 50
    f. 51 - 60
    g. 61 - 70
    h. 71 - above
3. Name one of the neighborhood's most influential persons? What qualifies him/her to be influential?
4. Who serves as the butt of jokes? How did he or she come to be teased?

Activity

1. Describe the neighborhood's activity
    a. at 11:00 A.M. Monday
    b. at 11:00 A.M. Saturday
    c. at 11:00 A.M. Sunday
2. How do the residents earn a living?
    a. as blue-collar workers
    b. operating small businesses out of the home
    c. in the service professions

    d. in agriculture and related industries

    e. in domestic service

    f. in the trades

    g. in government

    h. in business or finance

    i. other

3. What sports do the residents play? Where? When? Who plays? Who is the neighborhood's soccer rival? How did that particular team become a rival?

4. Which are the neighborhood's biggest festivals? Describe the festivities.

Opinions and attitudes

1. Of what is the neighborhood particularly proud?

2. What does the neighborhood consider to be its biggest scandal during the past year?

3. What has been the neighborhood's biggest tragedy during the past year?

4. What do youth complain about?

5. If the neighborhood had access to one million dollars, how do you suppose the people would spend it?

Your family and the neighborhood

1. Is your family native to this neighborhood? If not, when and why did they move here? Are they are proud of it? Defensive? Critical?

2. With which institutions (business, government, religious, educational) do they interact regularly? From which of the institutions do they consciously distance themselves?

3. Who are the local residents your family looks up to? Fears? Socializes with? Scorns?

4. How do your family's activities at 11:00 A.M. on Monday, Saturday, and Sunday conform to, or contrast with, the prevailing neighborhood activities?

5. Would you conclude that your family plays a major, supporting, or minor role in the drama of your community? Does your family function behind the scenes? Are its members leading actors in the neighborhood drama? Does your family direct the play? Are your family members the play's resident critics?

As a final project in this exercise, draw a map of the neighborhood, showing streets, buildings, parks, including your host's home and any other special sites.

Guide 19

Evaluation

This evaluation form is not designed just to help you make an appraisal of your host family, but rather to help you review your own integration into it and to spur you to further culture learning. It's a tool to be used from time to time during your stay so that you can fine-tune your cross-cultural adjustment. You might use it about a third of the way through your visit, again about two-thirds through, and, finally, at the end.

1. Is the house adequate for its inhabitants? Is the house within easy reach of the bus stop? Do you find the house and the community safe?

2. Can the family afford to keep a guest? Is your diet healthy and sufficient? Are you able to have privacy when you need it? In what ways might you take fuller advantage of what the family has to offer you? In what ways might you better accommodate its limitations?

3. Do you respond positively to the atmosphere of the place? Is the family a happy one? Is there love and laughter? Are there unresolved and damaging conflicts in the home? What has been your contribution (positive or negative) to the atmosphere?

4. Do you think that the role of each family member at home is constructive? The role in the neighborhood?

5. Has the family taken you in as one of its own members? Which family routines include you? Exclude you? To what extent do you take initiative

to include yourself or make decisions to exclude yourself from family activities? Would you like to be closer to your family? Do you see any specific opportunities to further your own integration into the family?

6. Are you able to interact comfortably with all members? Are you able to communicate about your wishes? Do they understand you? Do you understand them? What are the circumstances in which you find communication most difficult?

7 Which part of the day or week do you most enjoy in your home? Least enjoy? Is there sufficient family activity of interest to you? What are some of the interests you have introduced into the home?

8. Do you enjoy the family's contacts outside the home? Are you free to invite your friends to your house? Have you facilitated the comfortable meeting of your friends and your host family?

9. Can you affirm the family's attitudes toward money? Politics? Moral values? People of other races? Do they appreciate your country? Have you been successful as a listener when they express their opinions?

10. Can you live by their rules? In what ways are you able to honor their rules? Which, if any, expectations of you by the family are unrealistic? How do you deal with the rules that you don't like?

11. Are your values, by and large, compatible with the family's? Which of their values are challenging to your own philosophy of life? Which of your values are you clarifying as you live with them?

12. Can you describe your family's motives for having hosted you? Do you think you are satisfying those?

13. Does the family understand the goals of the program you are in? Is the family supportive of program activities (such as field trips) that take you away from your home? Are you aware of any dissatisfaction with program policies?

14. Under what circumstances would you recommend that this family be assigned another international guest? Is this home more appropriate for a male or female guest? Can you think of other qualifications in fitting a guest to this home?

15. Summarize the culture learning you have gained largely through living with a host family. As you review your agenda of culture learning, how might your family help you achieve your goals?

V. Moving into the Cultural Milieu

Introduction

Earlier in this book we referred to what theorists call the honeymoon stage of the typical cross-cultural sojourn, when a person is caught up in the excitement and fascination of new experiences. The honeymoon doesn't last forever. Soon reality sets in. Cultures are more than something to be fascinated by, they are to be lived in. The way of life of strangers must be dealt with in one way or another. Gradually—sometimes abruptly—the elevated emotion levels off and begins to drop. At this point sojourners can opt to retreat, become isolated, or even go home. Or they can choose to enter into what the authors of *On Being Foreign* call "the increasing participation phase" of cross-cultural adaptation (Lewis and Jungman 1986).

The next series of guides assumes that you will opt for increased participation. If you use each of the guides well, you can't help propelling yourself further into the cultural milieu. But be warned; knocking at and entering the gates of a new culture might also give you a jolt of culture shock. Guides 24 and 25 are specifically designed to help you deal with that.

As you work your way through this series of guides, I hope it will become clear that cultural adaptation is not something you have to endure, but rather something to be actively managed by your own culture learning.

Naming Your *Cucarachas*

At the beginning of a stay overseas, especially if you are located in or near the tropical zones, you may make a quick acquaintance with *cucarachas* (cockroaches). So startling may this encounter be—in kitchen, bedroom, bathroom, or shoe—that your conversations, letters, and memories of the term abroad may be populated, even infested, by cucarachas.

But international living is more than a cucaracha. Away from home there are worlds to explore, not the least of which is the grandeur of the human spirit of people in other cultures. Isn't it curious that so many of our thoughts and words have to do with the creepies and the crawlies of our international environments?

A project

Here is a little exercise to help you transcend your preoccupation with your own cucarachas. Throughout the first weeks of your term, set aside some time to identify the petty irritants and pestilences you've encountered. Name each one. Refine its shape and size and place in your universe. Then release it, while releasing yourself from its domination.

To help you get started, I'm listing here some cucarachas that travelers and new residents overseas have named in group sessions:

- cockroaches, of course
- spiders, bats, snakes, and slugs
- mondongo soup (stomach and intestine pieces), vertebra soup, rice soup

- cold showers
- macho men, holy men, overbearing men
- toilet paper that's not to be thrown in the toilet
- squatter toilets
- wet shoes, wet clothes, broken umbrellas
- local time (late as usual); hyperpunctuality
- littered streets, littered parks, littered lots
- fussy mothers, demanding fathers, 9:30 P.M. curfews
- crowded, broken, noisy buses
- beggars, street urchins, thieves
- indefinite street directions, unclear street signs
- males' unbuttoned shirts, females' tight dresses
- potholes, rude drivers, bicycle congestion
- smiling faces, bows, unresponsiveness
- spoiled children, doting parents
- evening TV serials, loud tapes
- theft of clothing and personal items
- tight spaces, small restaurants, crowded alleys
- rigid social rules, formalized courtesies, excessive rituals
- absence of wastebaskets
- rudeness toward maids, migrants, or Gypsies
- diesel smoke, air horns, motorcycle noise
- rules on footwear, skirts, slacks, and jackets
- treatment of animals on the street
- teasing of retarded or handicapped people
- soccer fervor (violence), bullbaiting
- formalities of the educational system

Questions for discussion

1. Which of your cucarachas are frightening? Life-threatening? Disgusting? Pathetic? Humorous?

2. What characterizes your cucarachas? Are they natural phenomena, such as flora and fauna? Are they manufactured? Are their customs alien to you? Are they results of economic situations? Political or religious orientations?

3. In what way is your list different from your traveling companions' lists? Does your own personality help to determine what you consider to be a cucaracha?

4. Which of the cucarachas can be removed from your presence? Which of them will you have to put up with?

5. To survive in the presence of those cucarachas that won't go away, what preparations or precautions or dispositions would help you?

There is another angle from which to consider cucarachas. One day as a group of my students were recovering from cucarachas, someone wondered about the experience of foreign residents and students in the United States. Do they too face cucarachas? What are the bugs or beasts that break the confidence of Asians or Africans who find our culture strange? Are these sojourners assisted in any way to name their cucarachas and to transcend them? What might we native sons and daughters learn about ourselves from their lists? We bring the subject up in all our groups now.

If you're by yourself rather than with a group, mull it over and jot down some notes in your journal if so inspired. This is also a good subject for discussion with a friend or even a host culture informant you've gotten close to. Later, if you are in a group of local residents who have lived in the United States, bring up the question of what their cucarachas were.

Reviewing Critical Events

Earlier in this book (chapter 3) we discussed action-reflection-response learning, which can be seen as a kind of university of hard knocks. Experience can be a good teacher—if you are a good student. A particularly valuable procedure in action-reflection-response learning consists of reviewing critical events (or critical incidents, as they are called by cross-cultural trainers). We outlined four distinct steps in that process:

1. learning to recognize a critical event
2. stopping to reconstruct the event
3. getting more information about it
4. making new interpretations or shaping new behaviors

As we noted in the earlier discussion (feel free to stop here and go back and read chapter 3 again), the systematic reviewing of critical events can serve two very important functions: (1) to help you get through crises and (2) to spur culture learning. This guide will aid you in putting into practice this learning technique.

Look at category I below. It includes examples of critical events or the likely circumstances out of which critical events arise. Do any of them bring to mind critical events you've experienced? Go on to category II, which suggests ways to reconstruct the events. Which of those have you used in the past in dealing with a crisis? Category III identifies possible sources of information that can provide you with more factual data you can use in analyzing and interpreting what happened to you. Finally, category IV suggests some possible changes that you might need to make as a result of your reviewing the event.

After you browse through these lists, reviewing your own recent experiences as you do so, you might wish to reread them more carefully, noting specific items for future use. You will undoubtedly be caught in critical events again and again. While they will continue to surprise and even shock you, having a strategy for reviewing them will serve as a kind of life jacket to keep you afloat. But even before you encounter the big crises, use the items on these lists to think through the smaller provocations, annoyances, disappointments, and surprises that come your way. Use your journal as your workplace; allow these lists to be your plan; call upon your mind and heart as your tools. With such a strategy, critical events need not rule you; rather, you will transform them into occasions of learning.

I. Recognize critical events

1. A man makes advances on you in a crowded bus in a way that frightens and angers you.

2. You go to a party and once there, don't know what to do.

3. You have an accident in which a traveling partner is injured.

4. There is a contradiction between what a person tells you and what he or she does.

5. You have a crying spell in the youth hostel, brought on by homesickness.

6. Someone promises you a trip to see Chartres Cathedral, and you end up bar-hopping instead.

7. You engage in a conversation about Eastern European ethnicity that turns a bit nasty, apparently because of something you said.

8. You are assigned as a volunteer or service learner to a "job" where there seems to be no work to do.

9. You get lost as you try to walk back to the center of the city from the royal palace.

10. You experience an event (let's say a Madrid bullfight) that makes no sense and annoys or even sickens you.

11. You are stood up by the person who was so friendly with you at the crafts shop (and who promised to take you to the pottery cooperative).

12. The pension owner is angered when you knock at the door at 11:30 P.M.

13. You lose your wallet to a pickpocket.

14. You are described in a group as having learned Arabic less well than the other three team members.

II. Learn to reconstruct the event

1. Suspend immediately your mental and emotional reactions and review slowly and deliberately what is happening.

2. Pull back from the action, pausing to relax, and then think carefully about the experience.
3. Replay the event in your mind, in slow motion.
4. List objectively in chronological order what happened first, second, third, etc.
5. Establish clearly what the setting and context were: where it took place, when, under what circumstances, etc.
6. Compile a list of words you thought you heard.
7. Recreate the dialogue as you recall it: she said, then I said, etc.
8. Sketch on a pad all of the pictorial elements of the event.
9. Identify all of the actors in the event, the minor characters as well as the principals.
10. Determine the reasons for doing what you did.
11. Look for cause-and-effect relationships: this caused that.
12. Relate this event to other events, comparing and contrasting.
13. Recognize and accept how you feel.
14. Record it all in your journal.
15. Resolve to get more information.

III. Get more information

1. Is there (was there) a person at the scene who can (could) help you?
2. Is there a host family member who can assist?
3. If the event constituted news, watch for mention of it on television or in the newspaper.
4. Seek out a knowledgeable and sympathetic (empathetic) friend who may be able to help analyze the event and/or may have experienced a similar one. If so, what was the end result?
5. Ask your cultural interpreter about it. (See Guide 6.)
6. Look through your books (and those you might borrow or buy) on the host culture. Think back through your academic and other experiences: are there principles that can serve as guides in this situation?
7. Revisit the "scene of the crime" and see what it looks like in a more dispassionate light. Recreate the event in your mind as you observe the setting in which it took place.

IV. Change your perceptions, attitudes, and behaviors

1. Apologize.
2. Reestablish a broken relationship or establish a new one.
3. Modify an opinion or discard an old prejudice.
4. Rekindle your sense of humor and let the event pass.

5. Tend to dressing and curing emotional wounds.

6. Empathize or identify anew with somebody else's experience.

7. Understand the cause-and-effect relationships at work in the event.

8. Accept, in the extreme, the terrible realities of injury and death.

9. Recognize that you got through this one, and you'll get through the next one too.

Learning the isms

A lecturer, upon learning that a group of us had just arrived in his country, gave us a gracious welcome and then said, "If you want to become acquainted with this country quickly and significantly, learn our 'isms'."

His counsel has proven to be wise. Ism words, it turns out, begin as private conditions or individual actions which ultimately become a broad social phenomenon or movement or a widely held belief. An idea becomes an ideology, an inspiration, a religion, a personal problem, a social blight, a method, a way of being, a personal preference, a corporate mentality. In other words, an ism is a personal entity that has spread out and become institutionalized by society. According to the lecturer, the isms can be a window through which to view people defining their world and their role in it.

Consider a relatively recent ism: feminism. I do not know when the word was first used; the *Oxford English Dictionary* documents citings of the terms "feminism" and "feminist" in the 1890s. But feminism was not in common (that is, popular) usage when Betty Friedan published *The Feminine Mystique* in 1963. She and a minority of other women were keeping alive a sensibility about what it meant to be female. The book enjoyed a wide readership. Its ideas stimulated the thinking and emotions of Americans and contributed significantly to feminism becoming a social movement, a critical perspective, a political persuasion, and an expanded concept of the meaning of the word "woman." To understand contemporary society in the United States, Canada, and Western Europe, one needs to comprehend the nature of feminism.

Most of the isms we are familiar with are far older than feminism, and more universal. (Perhaps in time, feminism as an ism will be universal.) Name five of the most important isms in your life and thought. Look at the list below. Are your isms on it? Does the list include isms which hadn't come to mind but which you might want to substitute for ones on your list? How many on the list can you define without retreating to the dictionary? Are there isms you've encountered in your host country that are unique to it and/or that you've never heard of before?

A list of isms

name	definition
agnosticism	_____
alcoholism	_____
Buddhism	_____
capitalism	_____
Catholicism	_____
chauvinism	_____
collectivism	_____
colonialism	_____
commercialism	_____
Confucianism	_____
conservatism	_____
consumerism	_____
feminism	_____
hedonism	_____
individualism	_____
industrialism	_____
institutionalism	_____
intellectualism	_____
internationalism	_____
isolationism	_____
Judaism	_____
machismo (macho-ism)	_____
parochialism	_____
professionalism	_____
progressivism	_____
Protestantism	_____
Puritanism	_____
racism	_____
regionalism	_____
sexism	_____
socialism	_____
spiritualism	_____

Now use the isms as instruments in defining and exploring culture, that is, as part of the process of culture learning.

1. Identify five isms that are crucial to defining your home culture.

2. Identify five isms that would be considered contrary or antagonistic to the dominant ism of your home culture.

3. Identify (ask a cultural interpreter if necessary) five isms that are an integral part of the host culture. Take care to define the terms fully. Try to discover how these terms represent subconscious understandings, collective thinking, political and economic movements, or philosophical persuasions. How does the force of these isms affect the way you will live in this country?

4. Identify five isms you feel would be contrary or antagonistic to your host culture.

5. Compare the isms you've identified for home and host cultures. Which are similar, which divergent? What are the implications for intercultural communication and cross-cultural interaction? How can you use this knowledge to facilitate your ability to communicate and adapt?

Dancing Their Rhythms, Telling Their Time

Several students from India came to class at my college one day to talk to us and help us understand the long-standing and complex love-hate relationship between the Indians and the British, illustrated so vividly in E. M. Forster's novel (and film) *A Passage to India.* When the Indian students were asked to identify sources of the tension, one of them replied almost without thinking, "IST—India Standard Time." She went on to explain that the sense of time that Indians live by is totally perplexing to the British.

If the British had come to terms with India's sense of time, enough to regard it as an authentic expression of what it means to be Indian instead of stereotyping Indians as an ignorant people for whom time didn't matter, the history of their relationship might have been different. That, of course, is a gross generalization, but there is a kernel of truth in it.

In your new home, the cultural clocks will confound you at least to some degree—more so in some cultures than others. There are cultures in which time seems almost irrelevant or, at least, its management haphazard. Don't be fooled, however. No matter how it appears, every culture has a clearly defined and understood sense of time which, despite your frustration (if that's what you feel), offers a fruitful context for culture learning.

Time frames

All cultures have time frames—that is, the units that define the time limits of a function. Always keep in mind that those frames differ from culture to culture.

Begin by identifying some time frames that you regularly use:

- a second ("just a sec"); a minute ("I'll be ready in a minute")
- a commercial break, a coffee break
- being on time
- mealtime, a good night's sleep
- the 40-hour week, sick days, vacation
- the holiday season
- the school year, the fiscal year, the decade

The time frames of your host culture might be strange to you. In many Asian cultures, the time frames tend to be larger or longer, centuries in size, and slower moving. In Latin America and among some Native American cultures, you will probably encounter time frames that aren't clock units: an event begins "when the time is right."

You may also become aware of large time dividers—before or after Jesus Christ, before or after Mohammed, before or after a regime, before or after an economic or a natural disaster.

To get you started in your study of time frames, try to identify your host culture's time frames in the life span. American time frames are suggested on the left side; complete the right side for your host culture. You might want to consult your cultural informant in doing this exercise. Some of the categories on the left won't appear on the right. The right side may have categories not found on the left.

Time frames in the life span

in the United States	in my host culture
a baby (birth-3 years)	_____
preschooler (4-5 years)	_____
child (6-10 or 11 years)	_____
early adolescent (11-13 years)	_____
teenager (14-18)	_____
driving age (16 ff.)	_____
"R" rated movie age (18 ff.)	_____
drinking age (18 or 21 ff.)	_____
legal adult (21 ff.)	_____
marriageable (ambiguous)	_____
young adult (21-35)	_____
middle adult (36-55)	_____
older adult (56-65)	_____
senior citizen (66 ff.)	_____

Rhythms

All cultures have rhythms. Fast and slow. Back and forth. On and off. Ebb and flow. Up and down. Begin to study rhythms by identifying some of the rhythms in your home culture. Can you define those rhythms in terms of moods, energy levels, clothing styles, activities? Day and night? Workweek and weekend? School year and vacation? Cold months and hot months?

In your host culture, the source of the rhythms may have to do with phenomena you aren't tuned in to. Is there a rhythm suggested by rainy and dry seasons or some other weather pattern? By Holy Week or some other religious calendar? By planting and harvesting, or some other factor of subsistence? By Independence Day or some other event of history? By the sports season? Or the season when fishing is good? Or the season of concerts, ballets, opera, and plays?

With the help of friends, cultural interpreters, or your host family, try to identify an activity or a set of activities that can be described in terms of the rhythms listed below. For example, at the beginning of the week as people arrive at work, the activities tend to be at the "flow" end of the first continuum. On Friday afternoons, the activities ebb. In most cultures, a wedding begins at the formal end of the second continuum and, as the day progresses, moves toward the informal. "On" and "off" may be illustrated in the performing arts. Plays, concerts, and films are showing or they aren't—they're on tonight or off. Farmer's market is an activity of the day, usually the morning, whereas the town's soccer games (now that there are lights) may be played at night.

Rhythms and events

ebb	flow
formal	informal
on	off
day	night
loud	quiet
wet	dry
sad	happy
profane	sacred
fast	slow
work	play

Time contexts

Time is manifest in situations. You can begin examining the contexts of time by thinking of events in your own culture—let's say at home, at school, and at work—when it is appropriate to go slowly or when activities are expected to speed up. The context helps to define the characteristic time takes on.

Turn now to your host culture. Try to recall the places you've been downtown, in the countryside, the doctor's office, or at sporting events. Locate places where people of your host culture

- can expect to wait five minutes

- can expect to wait twenty minutes

- won't be surprised if they have to wait an hour

- will protest if they have to wait at all

Can you find occasions when most people want the clock to move fast? When they want time to stand still?

Compare two contexts and the activities and sense of time that characterize each:

135

Monday morning at 6:30 with Sunday morning at 9:30

Saturday night at 8:30 with Tuesday noon

List the differences. Which has a quicker pace? Why? How do the different contexts affect behavior? Would the differences be the same at home? Can you make your own internal clock tick to the context you find yourself in?

Time manipulations

You come from a culture that believes in controlling nature and manipulating time. It defies the seasons with central heating and air conditioning. It erases time and distance with high-speed transportation. It invented "high technology" out of a need and thirst for labor- and time-saving devices like washing machines, vacuum cleaners, and a whole array of common appliances. It created fast foods and drive-up windows to save time and employs electronic gadgets to manipulate time in reverse and produce slow motion.

Not all people manage time in this way. Even other high-tech societies vary in some degree from the United States. And in still other cultures where modern technology has not yet become ascendant, people are able to blend into contrasting slow and fast flows of time without trying to modify them. Accounts are told of commercial fishermen who may wait for days, seemingly doing nothing but passing the time. But when the schools of fish approach, these same people might work three or four days without a break. I recall hosts who laughed at American students who ran through the rain so that they wouldn't get so wet; in contrast, the hosts stopped their activities and waited for the rain to pass.

To help you perceive and understand the presence of time manipulation, you might wish to identify examples for each of the following:

natural time	artificial time
using the sun	using the clock
showing one's age	concealing one's age
going at a comfortable pace	going fast or slow
living in the present	living for the future
being unaware of clocks	watching the clock
accommodating circumstances	manipulating circumstances

Time and values

Begin to search for connections between time and values. A variety of questions may open this door. When is it good to be speedy? When is it bad? Can you find an occasion when a person offends by staying too long? In contrast, what about the person who gives some extended time to a neighbor in need?

How does development theory prejudice the discussion about time by expecting people to be manipulators of time? Does an individual's "time of life" (age) imply certain restrictions or privileges? Is God (or divine sanction) associated in any way with time?

Identify occasions when a person's use of time is considered to be

- reckless
- wasteful
- compassionate

- prudent
- cunning
- thoughtless

Would they be judged the same in your host culture as in your home culture? Become aware of how people who manipulate time and people who accommodate time make negative judgments about each other. Monitor your own attitudes: are you more critical of the person who manipulates time or the person who lives by natural time?

Dealing with Culture Shock (Part I)

Kalvero Oberg's presentation to the Women's Club of Rio de Janeiro on August 3, 1954, was probably not the first time that the words "culture shock" were used. But that lecture (see Oberg 1960) has become a classic beginning to the formal investigations into this "occupational disease of people who have been transplanted abroad."

Culture shock is a term widely known and a condition widely feared. It involves emotional and physical responses to "the accumulated stresses and strains which stem from being forced to meet one's everyday needs in unfamiliar ways" (Brislin 1981, 13).

But culture shock isn't all bad, as you will discover.

This guide and the one to follow introduce this important topic in outline form, based in part on Richard W. Brislin's *Cross-Cultural Encounters* (1981). As you read, we encourage you to jot down your own personal experiences and observations in your journal. Note whether you've had the experiences described or if a friend has—or, indeed, speculate on why you haven't, if such is the case. Have they affected you? How? If they've had a negative effect, what can you do to counteract or help a friend counteract it?

Stages to cultural adjustment

Oberg suggested that culture shock and cross-cultural adjustment progress through four stages that I am expressing in the metaphor of terrain:

1. the honeymoon on the mountain, elevated emotion from lots of unusual stimuli, exhilaration from novel activities, a heady sense of having done yourself proud in getting to another culture, early fascination with all the sights and sounds

2. loneliness in the valley, the plummet into harsh reality, confusion and frustration, fatigue, emotions turning from buoyancy to heaviness, hostile and aggressive attitude toward the hosts and assertion of cultural superiority, or undiscriminating approval of hosts and denigration of yourself and your own culture

3. the slow climb, getting yourself activated, searching for solutions to maladjustments, meeting people, becoming involved, learning new procedures, establishing new patterns, adapting to new ways

4. the integration partway up the mountains from the valley—putting things together, accepting the highs and the lows of the new culture, redefining your own cultural borders, becoming a part of the host culture and comfortably traversing its various terrains

This is essentially a linear progression and is somewhat oversimplified. Culture shock, culture fascination, culture fatigue, and cultural integration often occur in haphazard order—sometimes in cycles, sometimes in conjunction with each other. Some of my own more painful regressions and depressions occurred in my fifth year abroad. Nonetheless, Oberg did us a service in showing how one might deal with cultural maladjustments in a systematic way.

Take a moment to answer the following questions in your journal: How do your experiences fit into the above stages? How do they differ? Can you think of specific examples for each stage? What stage are you at right now?

Symptoms of culture shock

Oberg listed a number of the symptoms of culture shock. Other writers and researchers have added to the list. Here are some of the most commonly identified symptoms. Have you or anyone you know experienced any of them?

- fatigue, discomfort, generalized frustration
- a feeling of helplessness, the inability to cope with the demands of the day
- excessive preoccupation with personal cleanliness, manifested in worries about food, drinking water, bedding, and dirt in one's surroundings; excessive washing of hands; preoccupation with personal health, minor pains, skin rashes, etc.
- fear of physical contact with attendants or servants; excessive fear of being cheated, robbed, or injured resulting in negative feelings toward hosts; and a refusal to learn their language or practice their common courtesies
- irritability at slight provocations, criticisms; fits of anger over delays and other minor frustrations
- loneliness; a need to meet others, but a reluctance to let them see your sorry emotional state

- a strong desire to interact with, and be dependent upon, long-term residents of your own nationality
- a terrible longing for home, for letters, for home cooking; staring absent-mindedly; being disengaged from the present; in some cases, the active desire to return home
- loss of inventiveness, spontaneity and flexibility, so that work declines in quality
- difficulty in communicating feelings to others

Undoubtedly you will feel some jolts as you try to get along in a strange culture, but you might not experience any of the above feelings with any severity. Your telltale signs of stress may be evidenced in milder ways: a preoccupation with sending and receiving letters, a fear of getting lost, anxiety over language demands, wanting to spend evenings and weekends with other Americans, recurrence of nagging emotional distress, changes in appetite, and, of course, simple homesickness.

Identify symptoms of culture shock you have observed in yourself or others and describe, interpret, and evaluate them in your journal.

Causes of culture shock

A person experiencing culture shock will rarely be able to state the exact cause of the problem. Objective researchers who have explored the phenomenon refer most often to these causes:

- situational factors such as food, housing, climate, transportation, neighbors, etc. and the degree to which they are different from similar situations at home or from what you expected they would be
- the presence of structure where you don't want it and the lack of structure where you need it
- similarly, the presence or absence of time constraints (not enough time for some things, too much time for others)
- the lack of a niche (no place where you fit just right)
- the absence of role models
- the lack of meaningful work (an unclear job assignment, too many employees to do the job or not enough employees)
- increased ambiguity and uncertainty that makes it impossible to predict what is likely to happen next
- questions about your personal competence (self-doubt)
- deprivation of identity reinforcements

This guide has covered briefly the stages, indicators, and causes of culture shock. Guide 25 will aid you in dealing with and overcoming it.

Dealing with Culture Shock (Part II)

The positive results of culture shock

From the perspective of cross-cultural adjustment and adaptation, culture shock urges you to come to grips with its causes and to develop more effective ways of coping and accomplishing your aims in being abroad. It pushes you in the direction of culture learning and cross-cultural adjustment. Recall Milton J. Bennett's developmental model of intercultural sensitivity. Culture shock is a stimulus to move along the culture-learning continuum from ethnocentrism to multiculturalism. Finally, and perhaps most significant, culture shock plays a crucial role in the critical dynamic of intercultural—or what Peter Adler calls "transitional"—experience. According to Adler, this dynamic embodies a "positive disintegration" of one's cultural identity in a dialectic of thesis, antithesis, and synthesis. First, the person moves from dependence on traditional identity reinforcements (thesis) through the crisis of culture shock, in which identity is threatened (antithesis), to an independent reaffirmation of self (synthesis)—and, in terms of the culture-learning continuum, from monoculturalism to multiculturalism (Adler 1975).

The dialectic may seem somewhat abstract until you consider these seven ways in which culture shock can contribute to personal growth (Adler 1977):

1. The new situation demands a response. Those responses are built upon a person's making changes in him- or herself. That process of change leads to learning and growth.

2. Strong feelings can be provocative and energizing, especially if the individual tries to understand the origin of the feelings.

3. If levels of anxiety are low, people put up with it. A strong case of culture shock and high anxiety serves as a trigger to do something about the problem.

4. Culture shock is likely to force the individual to learn about other people and their world, why things are the way they are. That is culture learning.

5. New ideas lead to experimentation with behaviors. You try something out and, if it works, you've gained a new coping skill.

6. Culture shock has to do with a sense of contrasts between cultures. As one works through the problems, one can eventually make a fresh confrontation with one's own culture, coming to terms in a new way with one's cultural roots.

7. One's own cultural identity may be threatened, but the experience opens up new avenues of self-realization and self-affirmation.

Overcoming the negative aspects of culture shock

There is no cultural aspirin, though talk is a good antidote to homesickness. Talk with people who are experiencing it at the same time you are, but don't let the discussion degenerate into mere griping. Name your cucarachas, but then explore ways to overcome them productively. Try also to find a willing ear in someone who has been through the cross-cultural adaptation process in the past. Here are some questions to ask:

- What are the paramount needs you have when experiencing culture shock? What do you long for most?
- What triggers culture shock or your homesickness?
- When do you feel the loneliest, the most down?
- Have you had the experience before?
- How do you get over it?

One of the problems in dealing with homesickness and/or culture shock is that frequently people don't realize (or deny) they are experiencing it. The feelings are ascribed to other causes. It is difficult to counteract something you don't believe is affecting you, but once you do recognize what is happening, there are a number of things to do.

1. Find people to interact with. Give them a smile or a little gift. Ask them questions. As you take an interest in them, your feelings will have a focal point outside of yourself.

2. Surround yourself with some familiar things—a favorite jacket, a photo, a cassette. Make your near environment pleasant and reinforcing.

3. Slow down. Simplify your daily tasks. Relax. Let your emotions catch up with the newness all about you.

4. Develop patterns. Follow the same routine each day so that you get a sense of returning to the familiar.

5. Cry. Laugh. Sing. Pray. Draw a picture. Give expression to your feelings.

6. Revise your goals to accommodate a detour instead of scolding yourself for failures.

7. Give new energy to language study, and use it on simple occasions. It is amazing what language success can do for you.

8. Find times and places to get physical exercise.

9. Confide to friends, and even your host family, that you are sad. Their support will warm you.

10. Make a few small decisions and carry them out. Again, your resolve in small things will pay big confidence dividends.

Be assured that, however stressful, culture shock passes if you are willing to let the process of culture learning and cross-cultural adaptation take its course.

VI. Exploring Value Systems

Introduction

Chapter 5, "Culture Learning, Values, and Ethical Choices," closed with a number of suggestions for the culture learner.

1. Reacquaint yourself with your own culture's values while you are in a new cultural setting where values seem to differ from yours.

2. Be aware of how your own value system might constitute a set of blinders that limit or modify how you see the values of others.

3. Find structured ways to identify your host culture's values.

4. Learn about the formation of their values.

5. Don't judge your host culture's value system prematurely.

6. Explore the moral ambiguities in your host's values through the art of the culture.

7. Use your study journal to refine your thinking about the development of your own values and moral perspectives.

Several of these suggestions are elaborated in this series of guides. The opening paragraphs of each guide will identify the exact linkage with chapter 5. You will likely be referring back and forth between the two sections as you work your way through this section.

The nature of the study of values calls for long-range investment. You won't be finished with the task merely by reading these guides. In fact, this series, more than any of the others, will be useful after you are no longer a newcomer to your host culture.

Identifying American Value Orientations

"Research into values cannot be value-free," wrote Geert H. Hofstede in *Culture's Consequences: International Differences in Work-Related Values* (1984). "This book reflects not only the values of...participants, but between the lines the values of its authors.... I try as best I can to be explicit about my own value system."

Before you embark on the study of values across cultures, it is important to know your own personal value system as well as the value system, to the degree that it differs, of the culture that has helped to shape you into the social being you are.

In this guide we will use data from Hofstede's research to help you consider your culture's values. Hofstede identified four value dimensions, as follows:

1. power distance, the degree to which people believe that institutional and organizational power should be distributed unequally

2. uncertainty avoidance, the degree to which people feel threatened by ambiguity and try to clarify uncertainties by establishing new structures

3. individualism, the degree to which people rely upon and have allegiance to the self

4. masculinity, the degree to which people esteem assertiveness, acquisition of wealth, performance, achievement, and ambition (Hofstede's choice of

the word "masculinity" was unfortunate since it raises and confuses gender issues)

In his report he describes the "connotations" of each value dimension, a few of which are reproduced here.

In high power-distance countries

- Parents put high value on children's obedience.
- Students put high value on conformity.
- Managers are seen as making decisions autocratically and paternalistically.
- Employees fear to disagree with their boss.

In high uncertainty-avoidance countries

- There is more emotional resistance to change.
- People fear failure and take fewer risks.
- Hierarchical structures of organizations are expected to be clear and respected; employees prefer clear requirements and instructions.
- There is suspicion toward foreigners as managers, and fewer people are prepared to live abroad.

In high individualism countries

- An employee maintains emotional independence from the company.
- More importance is attached to freedom and challenge in jobs.
- Students consider it socially acceptable to pursue their own ends without minding others.
- Individual decisions are considered better than group decisions.
- Individual initiative is socially encouraged.

In high masculinity countries

- The independent decision maker is honored.
- Students aspire to recognition, admire the strong.
- Achievement is defined in terms of recognition and wealth.
- The company's interference in private life is accepted.
- There is higher job stress.
- Managers are relatively less attracted by service roles.
- One finds greater value differences between men and women in the same jobs.

You should be able to define readily the contrasting characteristics of the countries which are "low" in each dimension by moving toward the other end of the continuum. In a low power-distance country, for example, parents put less value on children's obedience (see the first item on the list).

Hofstede compared forty countries in regard to the four values. By asking a variety of questions of 116,000 respondents he was able to come up with a score and a ranking for each country in each value dimension. In your search to locate your own value orientation, it is instructive to see the relative position of the United States in these results. Now that you have a general idea of the four value dimensions, where do you suppose the United States ranks on each—low, middle, or high—among the forty countries? Take a guess. Write down your rankings. Why did you choose those rankings?

Now take a look at the Hofstede figures—01 is high, 40 is low.

The ranking of forty countries in regard to four value systems

Country	Power-Distance Index	Uncertainty-Avoidance Index	Individualism Index	Masculinity Index
Argentina	25	10	23	19
Australia	29	27	02	14
Austria	40	19	18	02
Belgium	12	03	08	20
Brazil	07	16	25	23
Canada	27	31	05	21
Chile	16	10	33	34
Colombia	10	14	39	11
Denmark	38	39	09	37
Finland	33	24	17	35
France	09	10	11	29
Great Britain	31	36	03	09
Germany (West)	31	21	15	09
Greece	17	01	27	17
Hong Kong	09	38	32	17
India	04	34	21	19
Iran	19	24	24	29
Ireland	36	36	12	07
Israel	39	13	19	25
Italy	23	17	07	05
Japan	22	04	23	01
Mexico	03	12	29	06
Netherlands	28	26	05	38
Norway	35	28	13	39
New Zealand	37	30	06	15
Pakistan	21	19	38	22
Peru	14	06	37	31
Philippines	01	33	28	11
Portugal	16	02	31	33
South Africa	25	30	16	12
Singapore	06	40	35	24
Spain	20	10	20	31
Sweden	35	38	11	40
Switzerland	32	25	14	05

Country	Power-Distance Index	Uncertainty-Avoidance Index	Individualism Index	Masculinity Index
Taiwan	19	20	36	27
Thailand	14	22	35	32
Turkey	11	11	26	27
USA	26	32	01	13
Venezuela	03	16	40	03
Yugoslavia	05	05	31	36

The results can be made a little more visual on a bar graph. The four scores of the United States are shown below.

The ranking of the United States in regard to four value dimensions

	Power-Distance Index	Uncertainty-Avoidance Index	Individualism Index	Masculinity Index
high rank (01)			(01)	
(04)			XX	
(08)			XX	
(12)			XX	(13)
(16)			XX	XX
(20)			XX	XX
(24)	(26)		XX	XX
(28)	XX		XX	XX
(32)	XX	(32)	XX	XX
(36)	XX	XX	XX	XX
low rank (40)	XX	XX	XX	XX

The United States had the highest score on the Individualism Index, a relatively high score on the Masculinity Index, a middle-range score on the Power-Distance Index and a relatively low score on the Uncertainty-Avoidance Index.

Are you surprised at these results? Explain your answer. Perhaps you hadn't thought of your own culture in this way. Perhaps you think of yourself as somewhat different from the mainstream.

Clearly the most dramatic results of the Hofstede study concern the Individualism Index. What are the implications of coming from an individualistic culture? To start out, respond to the following statements quoted from a number of experts on the subject. Do you agree? Disagree? How do they compare? Would you like to elaborate on or restate them?

Statement #1 (Peter Andersen)

> "People in the United States are individualists for better or worse. We take individualism for granted and are blind to its impact until travel brings us in contact with less individualistic, more collectivistic cultures." (1991, 289)

Statement #2 (Edward T. Hall)

> "Western man has created chaos by denying that part of his self that integrates while enshrining the parts that fragment experience." (1976, 9)

Statement #3 (Robert N. Bellah et al.)

> "Individualism lies at the very core of American culture.... Anything that would violate our right to think for ourselves, judge for ourselves, make our own decisions, live our lives as we see fit, is not only morally wrong, it is sacrilegious." (1985, 142)

Statement #4 (John C. Condon and Fathi S. Yousef)

> "The fusion of individualism and equality is so valued and so basic that many Americans find it most difficult to relate to contrasting values in other cultures where interdependence greatly determines a person's sense of self." (1983, 65)

How do you suppose that your own attitudes and behaviors are shaped by individualism? What are the situations most difficult for you to accept "where interdependence greatly determines a person's sense of self"?

Observing Host Values

As a culture learner you want to be a keen observer of values, but it is easier said than done. Values often remain unarticulated, yet they play an important role in guiding conduct. Values are dynamic, changing. To complicate matters, multiple values compete for priority in the grey zones of our behavior. And if that isn't enough, there is always the possibility of conflict with other people's values, which, even though they may seem to be the same, differ slightly but significantly. In the end, you can't always be sure which values of your own or others are being honored—or violated.

Within a culture, the study of values is demanding. Across cultures, it seems impossible. The novice, especially, needs help in learning to do it well.

Milton Rokeach, who was mentioned briefly in chapter 5, offers a useful schema for that purpose. This schema uses a set of typologies (described in his book, *The Nature of Human Values* 1973) which serve well in providing a system for observing value systems.

Through years of testing Rokeach has come to delineate two kinds of values, instrumental and terminal. He defines an instrumental value simply as an enduring belief that a specific mode of conduct is preferable to a different, opposite, or converse mode. There is a sense of oughtness in instrumental values, since they pertain to morals and to competence.

Rokeach defines a terminal value as an enduring belief that one end state of existence is preferable to an opposite or converse end state. Here you don't sense oughtness so much as you do orientation. Terminal values, says Rokeach, lead us to positions on social issues; predispose us to one particular political or religious ideology over another; prompt us in our presentation of ourselves to others; give us criteria for judging, blaming, or praising others; become a basis for comparing ourselves with others; suggest how we should try to influence others in their beliefs, values, attitudes, and action; and offer us structures for rationalizing conduct that is seemingly not acceptable.

Using this two-part schema for delineating the territory of values, he identifies eighteen instrumental values and eighteen terminal values that stake out claims in that territory. You can use the thirty-six as you survey the values of your host family, work colleagues, students at the national university, residents in your apartment complex, acquaintances at the club, etc.

The thirty-six values are presented here in the form of questions. To answer each question you may have to observe behaviors over a long period of time. Jot your answers and observations in your journal and use them to construct a definition of their values.

Instrumental values

Are your work colleagues or host family members (or some other selected group)

1. ambitious? (hardworking, aspiring)
2. broad-minded? (open-minded)
3. capable? (competent, effective)
4. cheerful? (lighthearted, joyful)
5. clean? (neat, tidy)
6. courageous? (willing to stand up for their beliefs)
7. forgiving? (willing to pardon others)
8. helpful? (working for the welfare of others)
9. honest? (sincere, truthful)
10. imaginative? (daring, creative)
11. independent? (self-reliant, self-sufficient)
12. intellectual? (intelligent, reflective)
13. logical? (consistent, rational)
14. loving? (affectionate, tender)
15. obedient? (dutiful, respectful)
16. polite? (courteous, well-mannered)
17. responsible? (dependable, reliable)
18. self-controlled? (restrained, self-disciplined)

Terminal values

Do your work colleagues (or members of your other selected group) value

19. a comfortable life? (a prosperous life)
20. an exciting life? (a stimulating, active life)
21. a sense of accomplishment? (lasting contribution)
22. a world at peace? (free from war and conflict)
23. a world of beauty? (beauty of nature and the arts)
24. equality? (brotherhood, equal opportunity for all)
25. family security? (taking care of loved ones)
26. freedom? (independence, free choice)
27. happiness? (contentedness)
28. inner harmony? (freedom from inner conflict)
29. mature love? (sexual and spiritual intimacy)
30. national security? (protection from attack)
31. pleasure? (an enjoyable, leisurely life)
32. salvation? (saved, eternal life)
33. self-respect? (self-esteem)
34. social recognition? (respect, admiration)
35. true friendship? (close companionship)
36. wisdom? (a mature understanding of life)

The Rokeach typology helps you to scan the valuescape and to collect observations. If you use it well, you will have accumulated enough units of observation for each of the thirty-six items to begin to make tentative descriptive statements about the values the host nationals seem to hold (and, conversely, the values they seem not to esteem.)

For example, the students from India on our campus, for whom I have the highest regard, have impressed me with the high value they place on a cluster of qualities that I can best describe by three words: open-mindedness, tolerance, and accommodation. This cluster lends itself well to a more careful study using Rokeach. I think many of the Indian students would place a high value on being broad-minded, forgiving, helpful, obedient, polite, and self-controlled. Conversely I would expect many of them to place a lower value on being independent, standing up for their beliefs, daring, logical, or ambitious. Among the terminal values, I see them as valuing harmony over social recognition, and self-respect and friendship over pleasure and accomplishment. India is complex; one can never rely on easy categories to define its heterogeneity, yet the Rokeach typology helps one to identify the relatedness of value-oriented behaviors.

Studying Influences on Values

Where do values come from? How are values shaped? Who or what does the shaping? Values are neither absolute nor eternal. On the contrary, values, like people, are born. They grow up and sometimes become powerful; sometimes they are pale ideals, honored mainly in the breach. Values grow old. Sometimes they die. Values are not fixed.

You were asked in chapter 5 to explore the relationship of values and formative influences such as worldviews. The implication, of course, is that values are made and molded by other cultural elements. Values, in a sense, reflect other lights. Keeping in mind, then, that values are made and molded, we encourage you in this guide to think some more about their origin and development.

To help you in this task we will adapt work done by Sondra Thiederman (1991, 225-31). She identified a series of value contrasts (forty-two of them) and then compared the United States and other cultures in regard to each one. We will select ten from the list to use in this exercise. Later we will give you two assignments, one of which relates to the blank column, "influences." For now, direct your attention in the configuration below to the value contrast in italics, Thiederman's descriptions of U.S. culture, and her descriptions of each "Contrast culture."

Ten culture contrasts

values	culture descriptions	influences
1. *Change versus tradition*		
U.S. culture:	Change is usually good.	_____
Contrast culture:	Change should be resisted unless there is an obvious good to be gained from abandoning tradition.	_____
Your host culture:		_____
2. *Materialism versus spirituality*		
U.S. culture:	Acquiring material wealth is a sign of success.	_____
Contrast culture:	Spiritual growth is more important than amassing wealth. Material possessions can sometimes be a sign of poor spiritual health and can be disruptive of society.	_____
Your host culture:		_____
3. *Rational versus intuitive thinking*		
U.S. culture:	The most productive thinking is linear, cause and effect, and rational in nature; it is based on concrete evidence and facts.	_____
Contrast culture:	Intuitive, creative thinking is most highly valued.	_____
Your host culture:		_____
4. *Youth versus age*		
U.S. culture:	Young people are valued and the elderly discarded.	_____
Contrast culture:	Age is to be respected.	_____
Your host culture:		_____
5. *Independence versus dependence*		
U.S. culture:	It is unhealthy to be dependent on family and the group.	_____
Contrast culture:	It is proper to remain dependent on the family and group into and throughout adulthood.	_____
Your host culture:		_____

values	culture descriptions	influences
6. *Equality versus hierarchy and rank*		
U.S. culture:	Equality is to be honored.	_____
Contrast culture:	Society is better organized if there is rank, status, and hierarchy.	_____
Your host culture:		_____
7. *Boasting versus modesty*		
U.S. culture:	It is appropriate to speak of one's own achievements.	__ _____
Contrast culture:	It is disruptive of harmony and social balance to praise oneself.	_____
Your host culture:		_____
8. *Informality versus formality*		
U.S. culture:	Informality and casual appearance are signs of warmth and equality.	_____
Contrast culture:	Informality can be intrusive and can result in loss of respect for a superior.	_____
Your host culture:		_____
9. *Direct versus indirect questioning*		
U.S. culture:	Direct questioning is the best way to get information.	_____
Contrast culture:	Direct questioning is rude and intrusive.	_____
Your host culture:		_____
10. *Confrontation versus avoidance*		
U.S. culture:	Interpersonal conflicts should be discussed directly.	_____
Contrast culture:	Interpersonal conflicts should be glossed over.	_____
Your host culture:		_____

Before moving into the two assignments in this guide, you may wish to respond to Thiederman's descriptions by adding to them, disagreeing with and rewriting them, or by illustrating them. Putting those descriptions into your own words or thinking of specific behaviors to illustrate each one will help you grasp the point she is making—that cultures differ greatly in their value orientations.

Now for the first assignment. For each of those value contrasts, try to describe your host culture. In some cases your host culture may be nearly identical to the U.S. culture or possibly similar to the contrast culture. Chances are that your host culture will be slightly different from both. You will probably discover that it's difficult to write the descriptions, partly because you haven't been in the culture long enough to know it, and partly because a few phrases and clauses just aren't adequate to cover the many ways that your culture expresses itself. But try, and promise yourself to return to rewrite them after you learn your new culture better.

The second assignment is even more difficult and may turn into an exercise in conjecture, but the exercise will profitably focus your attention on the subject of value formation. To the right of each description of U.S culture you'll find a blank line. It's an invitation for you to speculate on some of the influences that may have shaped each of those cultural expressions in the United States and your host culture as well as to suggest the kinds of influences that might give rise to the values identified in the hypothetical contrast culture.

Although the kinds of influences are likely great in number, you may wish to think particularly about the following questions:

1. How do the understandings of your host culture regarding the origins of life affect their values? Does life evolve from something? From what or whom? Is it created ex nihilo (out of nothing)? By whom?

2. How does their view of nature affect what they hold in high regard and how they behave toward those things? More specifically, do they see nature as something to be controlled and used for their benefit, as something to be feared, or as something to be revered and accommodated?

3. Do they see history as something with a beginning, a linear development, and an eventual culmination, or do they see history as an unending series of cycles? How does their view of history influence their values?

4. What is their understanding of the nature of human beings—that they are essentially good? Fallen and sinful? Or neither? Are humans perfectible? How? Do these understandings contribute to the values that they honor?

5. How have specific events in their history, geography, politics, and economics affected what they hold in high esteem or conversely what they hold in low esteem?

In using this guide, as in using the others of this series about values, you may be assured that a person, especially a newcomer to a culture, can't answer such questions definitively. Values are too complex for easy labeling. However, the exercise is justified by the agenda you've set for yourself. Your inquiry into your host culture's values may yield more than almost any other kind of investigation you might undertake.

Guide 29

Using the Arts in the Study of Values

If you are a student of the arts, this guide won't be a surprise. You know that the arts are value-intensive and have already used them in processing your own values. Literature, painting, music, sculpture, photography—these and other art forms find a ready and enduring content in human values.

'One illustration. Chinua Achebe's novel, *Things Fall Apart* (1969), tells the story of a powerful West African tribal leader Okonkwo. The timing of Okonkwo's rise to leadership coincides with the arrival of the European colonialists. The plot, in brief, follows the consequences of the meeting of European and African cultures. From the first page until the last, one encounters values. First, the values of Okonkwo's people—standards that emerged from tribal worldviews and the wisdom of their experience passed from generation to generation in story, legend, and rule. Then, a challenge to those values by outsiders who violated what had seemed to be inviolable, sacred standards. In reading the graphic account of values falling apart, one thinks about one's own values and the consequences of their role in life. One comes away from the novel feeling horrified yet informed, instructed and purged.

This guide, then, is (1) a reminder to use the arts of your host culture in your study of values, (2) an illustration of resources in one art form, and (3) a discussion of how to use other art forms in the study of values.

Films and values

You can use films not only to give you a preview of the strangers you will be living with but also to examine their values. The ability to give visual image to concealed thought and emotion is film's specialty.

How does one find the films which do that best? If you are reading this guide prior to your departure from the States, you may have time to check catalogues that not only identify but also describe films from your host culture. For example, *The Video Source Book* identifies over 40,000 titles. If you have time, get a catalogue from a large mail-order house such as Facets Multimedia of Chicago (800-331-6197). Overseas, those sources won't be accessible, but others will be. Public libraries, university libraries or audiovisual departments, movie reviews and ads in local newspapers, and theaters that specialize in alternative, documentary, historical, and/or classical films are all channels for finding useful films. Especially helpful is a guide written by Ellen Summerfield entitled *Crossing Cultures through Film* (1993).

Just to emphasize the range of releases now available in film or video, here's a short sampling of cross-cultural works.

Argentina: *The Official Story* (1985)
Australia: *My Brilliant Career* (1980)
Brazil: *Black Orpheus* (1958)
China: *The Great Wall* (1986)
Czechoslovakia: *Shop on Main Street* (1966)
Denmark: *Babette's Feast* (1987)
England: *84 Charing Cross Road* (1987)
Germany: *The Boat* (1982)
Hispanic America: *Ballad of Gregorio Cortez* (1982)
India: *World of Apu* (1959)
Italy: *Umberto D* (1952)
Japan: *Ikiru* (1952)
Russia: *Alexander Nevsky* (1938)
El Salvador: *Dateline: San Salvador* (1987)
South Africa: *Country Lovers, City Lovers* (1982)
Sweden: *Autumn Sonata* (1978)
Turkey: *The Horse* (1982)

In exploring values through film, look for behaviors that reflect assumptions, values, and beliefs. See if these values and beliefs are challenged and note how they change—for better or worse. Films frequently present the principal characters with a value dilemma. Consider alternate ways the dilemma might have been resolved from the one presented in the film.

Other art forms

Film is not the only art form that addresses values. The so-called legitimate theater is older and, arguably, more accomplished than film in its depiction of values. It has been putting characters and their moral choices on the stage for hundreds of years. Become acquainted with your host country's theater and drama groups, not only the big companies who produce plays for large auditoriums but small community groups whose audiences may number in the twenties or thirties.

Explore these art forms and crafts to learn about values:

> architecture
> ceramics
> costume and fashion design
> cuisine
> dance
> drama
> essays
> glass (leaded, for example)
> graphic design
> homemaking (as an art form)
> interior decorating
> jewelry
> journalism (magazine journalism included)
> murals
> music (vocal and instrumental)
> opera
> pageants
> painting
> photography
> poetry
> radio
> sculpture
> short stories
> television

As you use the arts to study values, you will continually face the task of making cultural inferences based on your study of artifacts. You will be trying, in other words, to move from the particular to the general. To help you grasp this crucial linkage, note the following sets, each of which contain a particular and a general.

> the fiddle : Appalachian culture
> patchwork quilts : Amish culture
> the Kentucky rifle : American pioneer culture
> the baseball Hall of Fame : American culture
> drums : West African culture
> breakfast pastries : French culture
> opera : Italian culture
> the Great Wall : Chinese culture
> Flemish painting : Dutch culture
> Arch of Triumph : French culture
> royal palace : Thai culture
> El Prado : Spanish culture
> woven rugs : Guatemalan indigenous culture
> mosques : Moslem culture
> Taj Mahal : Indian culture
> *War and Peace* : Russian culture
> the British Museum : British culture

But don't let these simple juxtapositions foster stereotypes. They are only a beginning. Your further study of the particular will be accompanied by questions such as these: What artistic purpose motivated the making of...? How does the artifact reveal the natural resources of the country? Its social history? How did this artifact modify the course of development of the country? In what way is this artifact used to shape the national identity? How does this artifact express the aesthetic sensibility of this culture? The questions will propel your investigation considerably beyond the artifact itself.

Part C

Techniques for Culture Learning

I. Journal Keeping

Introduction

Travel notes, logs, and diaries—there are many ways to record a trip. At one extreme you find the lean listings of what happened hour by hour, with a naming of the hotels, restaurants, and museums visited. At the other extreme you find extended essays that report and then go on to analyze, interpret, and even evaluate the "contents" of a journey—and sometimes end up as published books.

Cameras, too, have proven themselves useful tools in documenting travel. In the hands of skilled practitioners they can interpret as well as report. Cameras are handy, quick, and, with today's technology, reliable. They seem to have replaced pen and paper in popularity.

I carry a camera, but there is no way I would give up on journaling. Nor can I cease and desist from urging people who venture abroad to write, write, write. To be sure, the ballpoint doesn't offer the ease of an aim-and-shoot instrument, but its range of capacities, even for a beginning writer, cannot be equaled.

You'll meet in the following pages a number of guides having to do with journals. You may have come across many different kinds of journals: day journals, meditation journals, project journals, and report journals. What follows are descriptions of what I call "study journals," along with descriptions of the kinds of entries found in them.

The study journal, by the way, is becoming a more widely used instructional device, where emphasis is placed on action-reflection-response modes of inquiry.

The learners are put into real-life situations, then go to their journals to complete the "homework" of reflection. Clearly the technique is accessible to anyone, whether part of a formal instructional process or not. An international assignment provides a perfect setting for journaling, inasmuch as learning is heavily tilted toward the experiential. Each day, almost from beginning to end, you are involved in new, different, or, in some way, intense experiences. Keeping a journal enables you to process systematically the data from those experiences in the culture-learning context.

One of my colleagues has written, "The best travelers have been journalists." Let's test that assertion!

The purposes of a study journal

Journal writing as an academic discipline doesn't carry a universally accepted definition of what it is or of how it should be done. Here are some ideas which help define the purpose of writing a journal.

1. A journal is a record of what you experience and learn.

2. A journal provides an opportunity to sharpen your skills for clear, precise written communication. Further, the journal accommodates a variety of forms of self-expression, any one of which may contribute to the range and depth of personal vision.

3. A journal can facilitate cross-cultural adjustment by enabling you to register your inevitable frustrations, to document the trials you experience, to follow the course of experiments you make in cross-cultural adaptation, to record the insights you gain and the new appreciations you come to, and to describe in detail your new acquaintances and your interactions with them.

4. A journal facilitates active learning, helping you improve skills of observation, reflection, and evaluation—which are the components of creative thinking.

5. In the journal you can work through the lectures you hear, articles you read, field trips you take—summarizing, analyzing, interpreting, and evaluating them as learning resources.

6. A journal helps you clarify your personal agenda—the issues you brought with you; the shape of your attitudes; your social relationships; your intellectual, ethical, and spiritual development; the responsibilities you face in world citizenship; your family and career plans.

For students there may be a seventh purpose: the journal offers evidence that you deserve academic credit for your study or cultural experience.

The form and style of the study journal

The journal, by its nature, allows you the liberty to express a personal style. It is not a stuffy genre of writing, although it insists upon accuracy in fact, precision in detail, candor in attitude, and clarity in style.

Effective writing uses tangible and specific nouns, active verbs, and only those modifiers that truly shape the nouns and verbs. The student writer, especially, pays attention to spelling and uses handwriting one can comfortably read.

As a reader of journals, I find that my interest perks up when the writer

- names things, using their specific nouns
- writes to express, not to impress
- puts ideas into comfortable, natural language
- quotes people—tells stories—makes connections ("this relates to that")

I prefer the use of three-ring binder notebooks. You can add or delete pages. You can submit your journal to a friend or peer or the prof for review and continue writing more entries that can be added later. You can return to an unfinished entry, develop your ideas, edit, and replace the original notes. If you are on a rough hike, you need not carry (and endanger) the entire journal, but merely stuff some blank pages into your backpack.

In the guides that follow there are more suggestions about procedures and content, as well as examples from selected journals. Take a look, but then make your journal your own. Here's how Janet Kraybill and Korla Miller defined their journal, which incidentally was later published as *Two Voices: A China Journal* (1981).

> ...these entries involve constant dialogue between a "Chinese voice" and an "American voice." As friends and teachers of the Chinese students at Sechuan Teacher's College, we had a unique chance to share their daily experience. They are a generation that has witnessed great changes. Through their eyes, we glimpsed the spirit and growth of the new China. The people we write about are real; the names are not. Our book makes no claim to be authoritative or complete. Instead it is simply a four-month "conversation" between two very different cultures. (vii)

Contents

A study journal is a research paper that is not organized. In it are recorded notes on what one observes, hears, thinks, and reads—notes that are put into a careful first draft. A good study journal should contain the facts and the experience, but journal writing stops short of organizing and polishing the material into a finished form. It does analyze, however. It processes connections and relationships; makes interpretations, comparisons, and contrasts; explores causes and effects; and with great care it evaluates and, finally, comes to conclusions.

The subjective and the objective

A good journal maintains a balance between the personal and the impersonal. Entries that focus only on subjective materials—me, my feelings, my activities, my opinions—lead to a self-centered notebook. There is value in writing about one's own inner journey, one's own personal growth—some of the time. Similarly it's good to write carefully and intelligently about the family with whom you live and about the community. But you also need to take a larger view—examining issues that are national or regional in scope or indeed which affect whole continents or whole peoples or the entire globe. Journal writers often find it difficult to take up issues without coming irrepressibly back to how the issues affect them personally. While it is not wrong to want to tie large observations and reflections to specific, personal experiences, it is important also to be able to transcend self, to put yourself into someone else's shoes and observe the world from the viewpoint of other people, especially people from other cultures.

Four traditional modes

In your journal you can deal with the raw materials in any one (or a combination) of four traditional modes of discourse:

description—to describe, define, delineate, reveal, picture, show, list, trace, outline

narration—to narrate, tell a story, give an account, report an action

exposition—to analyze, detail, explain, explicate, interpret

argumentation—to argue, test, evaluate

Typical prose forms

Within the framework of these four traditional modes you have the option of including a wide range of entries, such as informal jottings, sketches and drawings, photos, clippings, quotes, lists, graphs, charts, lecture notes, and summaries. On other occasions, particularly when you have time, you may wish to shape the compositions into standard prose forms. A few are described below.

enumerations—a listing of observations, perhaps in single-word fashion, maybe in phrases or clauses

vignettes—a kind of verbal sketch without distinct beginning or ending that reveals a moment in time or an impression

critical reviews—a summary or description of an event, a work of art, or, indeed, any human artifact, followed by a critical response to it

narratives—an account of an event, often using a chronological sequence of reporting

topical essays—a study focused upon a selected topic and presented in expository mode

character profiles—a verbal photograph of a person, not biographical in scope, but rather immediate and intimate

personal essays—a first-person account of an event or circumstance for the purpose of revealing the event's significance upon the writer

Narratives and topical essays are the forms especially suited to exploring values and value contrasts and undertaking substantial cross-cultural analyses (though such may occur in the format of the personal essay as well). While the other forms enable you to capture and comment on the data, the narrative and the topical essay give you the elbowroom to put them together and explore their significance for culture learning and cross-cultural adaptation.

In the pages that follow, these prose forms are defined further and illustrated from actual journals.

Enumerations

When you decide to write a journal, the first thought that comes to mind, as it does with many writers, may be: "I don't know what to write."

Don't despair. Some of the bewilderment over what to write can be cleared away by seeing examples of what other people have written. Let's begin with an extremely simple kind of entry: the list. The list is nothing other than an enumeration.

Just because the list seems naively simple, don't conclude that it isn't significant. Indeed, some of the most accomplished writers have used listing to great effect. Here's William Faulkner, describing a rural store:

> ...the old smells of cheese and salt meat and kerosene and harness, the ranked shelves of tobacco and overalls and bottled medicine and thread and plow-bolts, the barrels and kegs of flour and meal and molasses and nails, the wall pegs dependent with plowlines and the shelf above it on which rested the ledgers in which McCaslin recorded the slow outward trickle of food and supplies and equipment which returned each fall as cotton made and ginned and sold....

> (from "The Bear" 1961, 246)

What good is an enumeration?

I like the list for two simple reasons. Once an item is recorded, it is remembered. The list preserves your observations. And second, if you are on the lookout for items that fit into a list, your skills in observation are quickened. Doesn't a photographer see better because she is looking for a potential shot? So it is that list makers benefit from a sensitivity to what is going on around them.

Samples of enumerations

Sample 1

Thursday, September 20

At the market I see

- pigeons strung up on a cord
- a merchant waiting on five customers at a time
- mandarins, grapes, grapefruit
- a mother pointing the boy's penis toward the drain in the aisle
- port, aged two years
- new white potatoes, maintaining a generation gap from the shriveled stack in the next bin

(from Hess 1975, 4)

Sample 2

September 1

I stare out the window as our bus weaves through the streets of Peking. We arrived in China at noon today.

Bicycle bells and truck horns compete for attention in the crowded streets. Mao jackets and baggy pants blur in a sea of blue and green. Women hold hands with women, men walk arm in arm. Rows of wooden stores and teahouses line the streets. Fresh meat hangs from metal hooks, cabbages sit on sidewalks. Old women wash clothes in enamel basins. Men squat in the street, smoking pipes and spitting sunflower seeds.

Everywhere there are hundreds of faces. They stare openly as we pass. One man runs his bicycle into a tree as he cranes his neck to look at us.

I look around the bus. Heads pivot left and right trying to record every image. We hang out windows snapping pictures. Several earnestly attempt to speak Chinese with our hosts. I grab a friend's sweating hand, wondering how long it will take to feel at home here.

(from Kraybill and Miller 1981,1)

170

Sample 3

Music

The American presence in Costa Rica has, in the words of one clerk, "always been here." For the young people in particular (below age thirty) this presence has names and faces, landmarks that mark the passage of the ages: from Elvis to los Beatles to los Who and Alice Cooper, and finally to los Bee Gees, Olivia Newton-John, and John Travolta. With the names come the music, from roc-an-rol to roc fuerte (acid rock) and on to the disco wave then in vogue.

(from Fike 1981, 15)

Getting started

To get you started on an enumeration, make a list of twenty-five single-word items—nouns that your five senses have encountered since you woke today. Play fair. Only nouns such as gate, gutter, puddle, bougainvillea, cart, rain, and smile. Tomorrow try phrases of actions that you participated in during one day. Today I...grumbled when the alarm sounded, shivered through a 26-second shower, started a conversation at the bus stop with the old man in the black beret, tried to genuflect—the first time in my life—when I passed the cathedral, bought bread and cheese for lunch and ate by the fountains.

You'll soon discover the utility, as well as the fun, of the enumeration.

Vignettes

Earlier, I defined the vignette as "a kind of verbal sketch without distinct beginning or ending that reveals a moment in time or an impression." The vignette effectively focuses our attention upon the central image, not on the background.

Journals hold well those short, somewhat intimate or close-up "snapshots" that may or may not have a distinct historical, geographic, or philosophic context, and yet they impress. You are there, you are struck, you record your impression.

The vignette as reality, the vignette as image

You might wish to think of the vignette in two slightly different forms. In the first case, you write the vignette as though you were making a quick sketch, just to get it down. You go no further to fill in details, to give it color and editorial flavor. You simply let it be itself—an image captured by words.

> Thursday, October 11
>
> The fisherman's wooden, algae-bottomed boat contains a net, two red baskets, rope, two plastic buckets, a wine flask, and the man's crutches. He sits on the wharf, the net draped over his leg. He sends the shuttle of plastic thread flying back and forth, quickly closing the holes that dolphins cut as they tried to get the captured fish.

The entry does a fair amount of enumerating—the list of objects in the boat. The entry also illustrates the vignette, because it is a picture of a crippled fisherman at work. The edges are blurred: we don't know his history, nothing of his family or community, how much money he makes. But we are drawn to the fisherman and take the literary snapshot. It stands for nothing, just a man at work.

In contrast, you may wish, upon encountering especially vivid sights and sounds, to allow your imagination to turn the object that attracts you into an image. This reminds you of that. This is similar to, or a metaphor for, that.

Saturday, October 6

Wooden poles prop up the stone wall which wants to lie down and die.

The subject of the vignette—a stone wall—is made to be like an old person supported by crutches.

Monday, November 26

The pounding of seals stamping documents at each desk marks Madrid's persistent heartbeat.

The subject of the vignette—the sound of the bureaucrats at their work, hitting the official government seals as they authenticate documents—is made to suggest a physical, albeit authoritarian, body at central headquarters.

Saturday, February 16

The city holds its skirts in tightly, so that the peeping campo can't see much.

The subject of the vignette—the walled city—is compared to a person with clothes closely wrapped.

There is good reason to use either form. In defense of the first, many memorable moments represent nothing but themselves and thus deserve only the close naming of all the parts. In defense of the second form, the use of images extends our understanding and appreciation; there is no thinking, nor is there poetry, without image.

How long should a vignette be?

As you can see from the examples above, a vignette might be no more than a sentence. Those are the hardest to write, because of your having to reduce a rather large impression into a few words. But you can go the other way, as in photography; you can enlarge the vignette so as to be able to show more details. Here is an example of a simple picture, slightly enlarged.

Monday, February 4

Her territory lies in the half-block zone where buses stop. Dirty leather moccasins, black dress, and soiled bandanna emphasize the severity of her face. She squints to left and to right, like an animal wanting out, but she stays, holding the lottery tickets up as though they were a bouquet of flowers. We have seen her there at 9 in the morning and 9 at night, calling, calling, with only the words *"de España."* Once we saw her make a sale—to a man even older than she.

(The journal entries in this guide come from Hess 1975).

173

Critical Reviews

"Wasn't Herr Bechtold's speech a stunner?" exclaims Mary to her friends. "He is as articulate as our secretary of state, but he makes a whole lot more sense to me. I like what he said about time—that Eastern Europe is the product of centuries, that won't or can't be rebuilt in a five-year plan."

Mary is beginning a critical review. Her initial responses are verbal, informal, intended for her friends, immediate, largely impressionistic, and as yet undeveloped. At the same time, she has made a statement about a speaker and a speech, pointing to an interest in the topic of time. She alludes to another person, a secretary of state, who seems not to measure up to Herr Bechtold, presumably because the two men have a different time frame.

It's informative to go to speeches and lectures with Mary. She helps you grasp what you might have missed. She may even have had the courage to raise a question at the end of the speech that extends the audience's understanding of the subject.

Mary may wish to do some journaling. She's got a good topic for it. Her entry will likely fit into what we call the critical mode, a mode used often in critical reviews.

Which kind of criticism?

When I invite you to be a critic in your journal, I want you to understand what I mean and don't mean. I'm not talking about faultfinding. Effective criticism is not the work of neurotic complainers, nor of negative personalities. Rather, it involves the efforts of a creative, compassionate, disciplined person to confirm what is excellent and to discard what is inferior. The critical mode has to do with finding and honoring quality.

A critical thinker...

- surveys his/her cultural environment with a mind open to finding the full range of its offerings.

- examines this data with a dispassionate mind, questioning what doesn't make sense, getting more information, learning new vocabulary, discovering techniques, investigating new concepts.

- analyzes the cultural offerings using a variety of tools to compare and contrast, classify, dissect, identify the relationship of their parts, trace origins, examine effects.

- interprets the results of the study, explaining it in his/her own words and in the new vocabulary that critical thinking often leads to.

- evaluates, being careful to separate emotional thinking from logical thinking; distinguishes what might be true from what must be true; reveals why one thing is better than the next; shows the purpose, function, and effects of the subject; and indicates a pathway for further critical thinking.

Critical thinking about what?

You can apply the critical mode to lectures, plays, concerts, field trips, dinners, athletic events, or to any number of other cultural and social phenomena. Ideas, habits, worldviews, trends, and fashions—all of these lend themselves to the person who has cultivated critical thinking. Think of your host culture as the continuing producer of many verbal and nonverbal "texts" which invite your critical response.

Samples of critical thinking in journals

July 10

I see the domination and degradation of the women here in the refugee camp every day. I see it when a 19-year-old woman with three kids tells me she can't use birth control, her eyes full of fear for the man she calls her husband. I see it when the cook brings don Santiago his food; she is scared to even look him in the face. I feel it when the 10 men in this house sit around smoking and playing poker and telling jokes not meant for women to hear. I feel it when the men are sent to paint, and I am left with nothing to do, because I am a woman. I feel it when the men leave to unload the truck, jokingly telling me to "go wash some dishes." Being here has taught me that we all have a long way to go in creating a society that values all people, regardless of race, sex, creed or color.

(Hostetler 1989)

Haiti has been called "the dumping ground for North American relief." For all the tremendous amounts of money and relief materials sent to Haiti annually, the quality of life of the Haitian people has improved very little. Some of this is due, of course, to human error. Some is due to "mischanneling." ...But most is due to what some groups term "inappropriate relief": relief material distributed as handouts in nonemergency situations.

That type of giving by missionaries has created a "beggar mentality" in places like Grande Riviere. The fact that in an isolated location like Mombin Crochu, where missionaries haven't followed the traditional line of giving and where tourists are never seen, there is almost no begging, helps prove this....

Far more serious is the fact that inappropriate relief diminishes the recipient's motivation to do for himself. When people are given what they need, very often their lives do improve as long as the source is available and active. But when that source dries up, they are as badly off as they were before unless they are shown how, and motivated, to obtain what they need themselves. And in most cases, this doesn't happen.

(Zuercher 1981, 29)

The journal writer who limits his or her entries to descriptions, always shy of making analyses, interpretations, and judgments, loses a valued opportunity that journals are made for. To be sure, the judgments might better be kept private for the time being and be submitted to subsequent testing. But the journaling process gets the brain into gear for what may result in first-class critical thinking.

176

Narratives

In a diary, you record the events of the day. Period. Diaries, like truckers' logs, have their place; who wouldn't value the diaries written by a grandparent? But you can enhance the value of your memory of the events of the day in two ways: by placing the events into a narrative and by reflecting upon their significance.

A narrative is a story. Something happens in some context, and you are some-how involved. Stories about what has happened to us are powerful, because they call us back into participation all over again in the original events.

A reflection is an examination, a thoughtful review. Something happens in some context, you are somehow involved, and later you think about it and reflect upon its meaning. Narration plus reflection yields understanding.

Let's take a look at one written by Chris Sauder. The entry is long. I don't know how he found time to write in such detail. What you read here is an ex-cerpted version. Be aware of the function of details—from placards to candy wrap-pers—in the turning of Chris's thoughts.

A day with the Mobile Unit

Carlos downshifts the jeep off the highway and onto a rocky road that meanders senselessly into the untamed mountains.

It's 8:30 A.M. and I'm crammed against the wooden cases of medi-cine on my right, and on my left the pharmacist Rodrigo who is mumbling to the doctor and nurse up front. We are the Pérez Zeledón Ministry of Health Mobile Unit #1.

177

After jolting over the first hill, the central valley disappears. The red road gouges into the green carpet of the ridges. Occasional cattle and sheep graze the mountainsides. We pass a farmer, muddy rubber boots, unshaven face, machete on his belt, leading a horse. Several limp strands of barbed wire guard a hill planted in wide-leafed banana trees and coffee bushes. I hold my breath as the suspension bridge sags and groans.

Pueblos bounce past as we forge deeper into the mountains— San Rafael, San Ramón Sur, San Ramón Norte. In each, a church, a school, a decrepit soccer field and a general store denoted by a half-dozen Delta and Derby cigarette placards.

An hour and a half from the highway, we arrive at the clinic. A cluster of people wait on the porch for us: pregnant women, young women who have come for birth control pills, older women worried about cancer of the uterus, babies, small children, a man in a Washington Globe t-shirt.

How do these people live? What do they wish for? How do they spend free time? What do they value?

I look around. The nicest building is a church despite its broken plaster and gaping windows. Strange, a large mural is painted on its wall, showing a rural scene, the uncultivated fields of a fertile mountain valley. A jetliner encroaches upon the valley through a break in the mountains. In the background, Bauhaus-style buildings line the runway. A dawning sun brings development. In the sky two benign cherubs trumpet their blessing.

What do these people know of the larger world?

I catch an answer later in the day. A youth, about my age, offers to take me to the generator that supplies electricity for his house. Walking down the road, dusty now in the heat of day, he suddenly asks, "Did you see the MTV music awards last night?"

"No," I stammered in disbelief. He did!

What is going on? Why are these people putting airplanes and apartment buildings in their art? Why do they want to discuss the MTV music awards?

I recall one of the then seemingly pointless abstractions from Communication Theories class—Marshall McLuhan's notion that communication technologies are shrinking the world into a common culture in a global village.

The people here welcome us and our penicillin and condoms and nutrition charts. They bear no resentment toward our altering their way of life. They dream of Sears, Hitachi, and True-Value. They chase after the images of Hollywood and dream of Disneyland.

The dissolution of rural cultures bothers no one. The capital-

ists see development opportunities, the activists are more concerned about saving the forests than saving the culture of the people
who live in them. Everyone seems to think that all cultures develop
in a straight line and that by giving these "lower" cultures a hand
we can yank them further up the technological tower.

The day ends. The long shadows of the village bounce away as
we drive toward our civilization. I notice only the spine of a TV
antenna stabbing the hillside and a purple candy bar wrapper, discarded like an orange rind, in the grass beside the road.

(Sauder 1991)

The narrative consists of a trip by jeep to a rural village. In the original entry,
Chris includes lots more details of the journey, of the medical tasks, of his exploring the town and talking with people. In writing his narrative, Chris fills the account with vivid nouns. List some of them. How do those specific and tangible
nouns contribute to his memory of the day?

The same details that make the trip vivid also lead Chris to thoughtfulness.
Trace, if you can, the thread of thought about cultural intrusions back to the
initial image-stimulus. What subsequent images and words intensify Chris's disquiet about cultural integrity, cultural influence, and cultural change? For a moment, take the other side of the argument: what images or events might have
contributed to a visitor's enthusiasm for cultural change? In your own sojourn, do
you find yourself affirming regional and local culture as it is, or wanting the
predictability and comfort of what Chris calls the "common culture in a global
village"?

Review some of your own recent activities. How might they look in your
journal if you recorded them in diary form? How would they survive if you recorded them as narratives? Would they be enhanced if you also included your
reflections on the events?

Topical Essays

Well within the exposition mode, the topical essay limits itself to an exploration of one particular subject. Let's say you select your subject early and take notes daily on it—or at least every time you encounter new experiences or materials related to it. You are constantly on the lookout for facts, and your questions to the people you encounter in your daily affairs or in an instructional capacity are oriented to learning more about the subject. Gradually you assemble a mass of notes. Later, you bring the notes together into a single, longer journal entry, using a convenient system in ordering the materials.

Keep in mind the function of the topical essay: it introduces, defines, delineates, explores, explains, compares, contrasts, and interprets. You may assume, even in writing the journal entry, that the reader (who may be none other than yourself) is seeking to be informed rather than to be entertained.

The topical essay is just right for exploring complex cultural issues. The following essay, reprinted from the Goshen College *Record* (Nov. 18, 1988), is the result of my own year-long curiosity about corruption.

> We heard the word *chorizo* first in the market and second at the table of a friend. The second time, it didn't mean sausage. Chorizo is a public word, a national scandal these days. It means corruption. Note how I enjoyed and played on the double meaning of the word chorizo.

The cash picked from a pocket by a street urchin isn't chorizo. A house ransacked by thieves isn't chorizada. A peon who over-charges for cutting the lawn with his machete isn't a chorizero.

Rather, chorizo is middle- and upper-class crime.

When you bribe a customs official to get a thousand boxes of American jeans into the country while paying for only a hundred boxes, that's chorizo. When you misrepresent what you paid for the BMW in order to pay less tax on it, that's chorizo. When you carry a suitcase of dollar bills into the country—hot bills—in order to launder them in a local bank account, that's chorizo.

Corruption is so widespread that people call their government buildings "the local sausage factory." According to a recent poll, more than 50 percent of Costa Ricans no longer have confidence in the integrity of their public officials.

What has happened to Costa Rica?

According to Eduardo Ulibarri, a young Niemann Fellow who now edits the leading daily *La Nación,* at least a half-dozen sources contribute to the moral plague.

First, because Costa Rica has nationalized its banking, insur-ance, health care, and many other services, the government has become by far the largest employer. Employees for the impersonal government can easily lose a sense of personal initiative as well as personal responsibility.

Second, Costa Rica has many agencies with outdated and inef-ficient operations. People have learned that a simple procedure—at the license bureau, the migration office, or the police station—can be an impossibly long procedure, but quickly solved by a gift of money.

Third, one political party—Liberación Nacional, which is roughly equivalent to our Democratic Party—has dominated government since 1948. Its largely unchallenged internal structures have encour-aged a networking of colleagues who know the power of favors.

Fourth, in the midst of Costa Rica's horrendous economic pres-sure, the temptation to get rich quick in narcotics traffic is more than some people can withstand, especially when a nice house, several servants, and a Mercedes Benz speak so loudly of personal worth.

Fifth, the Latin American peoples have never developed a re-gard for public authority as have Anglo-Saxon nations. Be it a red light, an income tax code, or a required school uniform, Costa Ricans haven't internalized rule books.

And finally, Mr. Ulibarri says that traditional sources of moral orientation are breaking down—particularly the family and the fam-ily friend. No new institution is filling the void.

At the table where we first heard of this chorizo, our friend said, "Chorizo is no compliment to our pueblo. It is a menace that threatens our entire way of life."

This particular topical study furthered my own culture learning in a variety of ways. Initially I was fascinated by the strange use of a Spanish noun and the variety of linguistic forms the noun could be changed into. The intensity of the scorn when my friends talked about chorizo led me quickly to the object of their scorn—corruption. Soon the discussions introduced me to various governmental agencies and how they were implicated in corruption. All the while I was able to compare how various people from different parts of the country and from different social and economic levels reacted to the topic. (Incidentally, when I made an appointment to chat with Editor Ulibarri, I gave him a list of five topics from which to choose for our discussion together. He responded that he wanted to talk about corruption.)

The study allowed me to see how this particular culture would shape its own corruption—who would do what, when, how, and with what effect.

Finally, and for me quite significantly, this topical study revealed how my host culture was impacted by outside agencies, governments, and cultures, including the United States. From nearby and also from far away, I discovered, one could get a whiff of sausage.

Character Profiles

The character profile, sometimes called the biographical sketch, is a favorite prose form for aspiring writers. Over the years, enduring portraits of many grandpas and grandmas, neighbors, and football coaches have arisen from the essays of my students.

The profile is not a biography. Because of its length and approach, it makes no attempt to report all of the important facts of a person's life—birth, childhood, baptism, marriage, career, activities, family, death. Rather, the profile focuses upon what a person *is* at this moment, or *was* at a particular moment in the past. It is somewhat intimate, a literary close-up that not only introduces us, but helps us to *know* the person, or at least how the person came to impress the writer.

Think of the character profile as having, in photographer's lingo, a short depth of field. Because of the limited and intimate revelation, your task is to reveal the person in a context of people, things, or actions that quickly brings him or her into focus.

The writing of character profiles can be crucial to your culture learning. How? The very rigors of having to write something on paper about a person demands that you will have done some careful observing, disciplined listening, and even some empathetic living. Those efforts in bringing a human being into clearer focus then reward you with information that goes far beyond your subject. The attributes you notice, the roles your subject plays, even some of the behaviors that you at first thought were personal idiosyncrasies turn out to be linked to larger cultural patterns. The individual, in a sense, becomes a microcosm of the larger culture. You, as a writer of character profiles, catch the cultural nuances.

The brief sketch

Begin modestly. Take a lesson from Myles J. Schrag's journal. Upon arriving in (formerly East) Germany to work in a hospital, he described some people.

> *Marcos*—Poor guy, his eyes are swollen from something so he's missed a couple days of work. He was a riot Thursday nite playing drinking games with sober Germans at Christiane's party.
>
> *Christiane*—She lives near the Ost See and seems to miss home a lot. She thinks Halle people aren't too friendly and has trouble meeting people. She has beautiful dark eyes.
>
> *Evi*—I've worked with her mostly in room 13. She told me how the Stassi kept her friend's husband for three days for no reason.
>
> *Thea*—The cook, who will forever be trying, along with us, to solve the mystery behind what differentiates omelette, Eier Kuchen, and pancakes.
>
> *Karolla*—The center of attention for dying her hair red just this week. She took us three to the Handel House yesterday on an absolutely miserable cold, wet, windy day during her break.
>
> *Sister Barbara*—Truly the head of Station 2. She's sweet, level-headed, stern, and fully respected. The epitome of a leader. But she still asks too much of us when we clean.
>
> (Schrag 1991)

Even in the writing of brief sketches, Myles was noticing not only personal traits but also cultural patterns. Can you identify examples of both elements?

As he learned to know these people better, he was able to describe them more fully and he was able to continue to think about culture. For example, he returned many times to write about the old political system in (East) Germany and the emotions of people as they remembered their recent history.

A description of "tia"

Here is a longer character profile from the journal of Felicia Rohrer that begins in description and ends in reflection not just about *tia* (aunt) but about cultural understandings of family. Follow the transition.

> Presently my host mother's tia is at our house. It seems she is always dropping in every other evening or so, and snoops around to see what is going on. She usually intrudes right when we're in the middle of eating supper. Then she comes in and somehow expects to be fed. She's very easy to please—just give her the rest of the *arroz* in the pan, along with about five cups of *café*. But she never offers to help do the dishes—she just plops down in front of the tv and jabbers while everyone else is trying to do their work.
>
> To me she seems a nuisance. She is so nosy! I think she is more

interested in going through my belongings than is my host mother. It would seem to me that she would be a nuisance to my mother also, because she never knows if she should cook more food or what tv station to have on. Right now she is jabbering with my mother while she is doing the ironing. Doesn't tia have any work to do?

In conversation with doña Margareta (my host mother) I found out that tia is single and lives with Cilia (doña Margareta's sister) down the block. She somehow feels a tie to her because tia took care of Cilia and her while they were young. She can't read or write and for some reason she doesn't seem to want to try either. But nevertheless it seems there is this family bond. Even though she is unmarried and unwanted they are obligated and very happy about it—to take care of tia.

In the United States I don't think this would happen. It would be very inconsiderate of any person to drop in during suppertime and expect to be fed. Let alone if this happened practically every day—my mother would get quite irritated, especially when it is obvious that she can cook and take care of herself.

But I think this family bond here is very admirable. The family really takes care of each other. It must eliminate many of the elderly from having to go to nursing homes—because here the family would take care of them.

(Rohrer 1990)

What are some of the traits and behaviors of tia that Felicia immediately notices? Which of those particulars annoy Felicia? Why? How do you suppose Felicia and tia are similar to each other? different from each other? In what ways might Felicia have been culturally conditioned not to be attracted to tia? Would there be people like tia in Felicia's culture?

What do you suppose helped Felicia to begin probing for cultural explanations of tia's behavior? How does she get more information about tia? What does that additional information reveal about the host culture's attitudes toward family interdependence? Do you think Felicia understands her own culture's attitudes toward family relationships? How would you contrast the two cultures in this regard?

A profile of Mme. Fortuney

The second example is excerpted from a longer profile written by Melanie Zuercher. Since Mme. Fortuney became so crucial to Melanie's entree into Haitian culture, she became a central topic for journaling.

Along with grandchildren, I seem to make life exciting for Mme. Fortuney, too. Every week she reads and comments on the schedule of activities I bring her. A trip to the Citadel! *"C'est magnifique!"* her hands wave. *"J'aime l'histoire beaucoup, beaucoup, beaucoup!"* A new phone book has arrived with a picture of King Henri Christophe on the cover. She launches into a long discourse.

During the morning, she keeps busy scolding and supervising Maria, the maid, and Monjoli, the yard boy. In the hot afternoon, she naps and talks on the phone. But lunch, the big meal of the day, would be an empty affair had she no one to talk to.

Often she talks about food. She is a health nut in her own way. She uses very little grease in cooking, she tells me proudly, unlike most Haitians. She believes in vegetables—carrots and spinach and beans fresh from Kenscoff, in the mountains above Port-au-Prince. And I do get fruit for breakfast—every morning she declaims *"la belle fig"*—rather than cold spaghetti or pumpkin soup.

(Zuercher 1981, 22)

In Melanie's view, even Mme. Fortuney's language is interesting, so Melanie includes the very exclamations. At the same time as the words reveal Mme. Fortuney, they identify people and places, products and activities of the host country.

Myles's friends at work, Felicia's tia, and Mme. Fortuney are not presented to us as completed biographies, yet the glimpses have given us an introduction to interesting people and the cultures they live in.

Personal Essays

Intercultural travel, study, and service all contribute wonderful resources for personal essays. This prose form typically builds upon anecdotal materials and is narrated by a persona by the name of "I," who moves through events. "This is what happened to me." Because the action is made vivid by tangible and sensory details, the reader can be there, with the narrator, experiencing it too. The meaning of the events emerges through the narration, providing fresh insights, evoking emotions, and even effecting attitudinal changes. Because the reader participates in the events with the narrator, he or she experiences them more vividly than if they were narrated by a dispassionate third person.

The personal essay is just that—personal. One spills one's gut in this prose form. It takes courage to write a personal essay, and even more courage to allow one's own vulnerability to be published for others to read. Thanks to Bruce Leininger for the following personal essay.

The mountains of Yunan

China. Have you ever thought of going there? Sounds exciting doesn't it? A whole new world to experience. I've been there: traveled, studied, met people, saw lots of countryside. But to be honest, at the time I wasn't too impressed with the grandness of this strange land. "Big deal. So this is China. It's just another place to fail." I had a habit of getting down on myself. "It seems like no matter what I do 'I can't get no satisfaction'." Secretly, I'd hoped that this mystic land of the East would pull me out of the rut I was in and give me a life that I could enjoy.

My hopes began to fade after I'd visited China's greatest monuments. "I've seen Tiananmen Square, the Great Wall, and the Forbidden City, and still I feel my life slipping away." I mustered up "I'm the luckiest guy I know" feelings whenever I could, but the life-quenching fears always won the upper hand. "Oh God, countless customs that I can't even begin to understand or recognize. I hope I don't offend anyone. I know I feel different from any of the other students in this group. We've spent days together in the same train car, but no one seems interested in knowing who I really am. I don't think anyone will ever understand me. My real feelings will only drive people further away. In any case I'm going to sit here and say as little as possible."

But one afternoon, under the clear, bracing skies of Kunming, the creature I'd hidden inside crawled forth. Kunming lies 26 train-hours distant from Chengdu Normal University where my SST unit was based. As the train tunneled through the mountain ranges of Yunan Province, I began to gather a sense of strength and excitement. I grew up in a land of gently rolling hills, so an encounter with these huge, misty forms rising out of the earth sparked a sense of majesty and mystery in me. Their lure became irresistible, breaking through my self-defeating attitudes and whispering to me, "Give up some of your safety. Sometimes you must follow your desire and surrender to situations beyond your control."

After a lonely week of touring Kunming I found myself sitting in the sun on the patio of the Red Peacock Hotel gazing longingly at the mountains in the distance. I imagined myself perched on their crowns or roving along their backs. "Perhaps their boundlessness, their wildness will let me cast my cares aside for a bit and be free...Oh! But when will I go there and how? Hmmm...No car. No bike. No free ride. Hmmm...I've got legs! I'm going now!"

I, equipped only with basic supplies stuffed into the generous pockets of my travel shorts, skipped down the front steps of the hotel and took my first few strides past farms in the Kunming valley. "Those mountains could be miles away. Chances are that an afternoon's walk will bring them no closer. And once I do reach them I might get lost in this giant web of pathways. The train's leaving for Chengdu tomorrow and I could be left behind, lost in a country where I can't even ask for a bathroom. Hmmm...thinking this way will never get me to the mountains. I'll worry about that later."

The footpath I set off on soon became a road that led to a duck farm by a marsh and ended at a low stone dike/walkway that bounded a lake beyond. In the fields to my right a woman, head wrapped in blue cotton, swung her hoe high, sinking the blade into the soil, turning it over for a new crop. Along the lake fishermen tended nets from rickety wooden piers that extended a stone's throw from the dike/walkway. They sat chatting with their backs turned to me. Every few minutes they stirred to lift their square nets. One of them turned and shared a smile with me. His friendliness touched something deep inside me and softened the worried lump in my throat.

An hour later I left the dike and entered a small town. School had just let out and the street was filled with children playing and fighting. After sighting me they let out with a volley of "hellos." Several of them followed me as the road dipped into a tunnel. Their voices echoed around me as I sang back a "hello" in reply. They caught right on and soon we were doing a blues call and response that would have made B. B. King smile. Two boys walked with me for a stretch while we exchanged token phrases in Chinese and English. "You are Chinese. I am American. Have a good day." If I met such friendly people on my return trip, they'd surely guide me back.

After passing through the town I followed a pipeline and a highway for a while. But time after time I was forced to abandon the thoroughfares and weave my way through a mess of footpaths before finding another main path. The last of these brought me to the foot of the mountains I'd longed for.

I bounded up the path that led up the side of a hill. In my haste I blundered into fields and had to retrace my steps. The grade grew steeper as I fit my hiking shoes into the hand-cut steps. My breath was sharp in my chest as I crossed the last piece of farmland and entered the open meadow. I sprinted to the crest and stood there filled with the excitement that had been growing step by step. Across the plain below I could see the places I'd passed on the way. The whole route was clear now that it was behind me.

I lingered for a moment then started back down.

(Leininger 1990)

At the beginning of the event, what is the person's sense of himself? Of others' dispositions toward him? How does his cultural isolation in China mirror the personal sense of isolation he carries within him? Is his personal sense of isolation intensified or ameliorated by being in a foreign culture? In light of this low self-esteem, what is his initial strategy for coping in China?

The mountain ranges of Yunan Province call to him. Why? How does this phenomenon of nature in China connect with his own person and his cultural heritage? What is the influence of nature upon his thoughts and emotions? What is it about the hills that calls him out of himself?

What does he notice during his hike? That is, the journal entry reveals to us at a second level what he himself did not screen out. What are the particular sights and sounds that entice responses from him?

189

Of the range of items you have listed, which of them have to do with human connections? Of what does the communication consist? When connections are made across cultures, what are the simple carriers of meaning? To what extent can he participate in this cross-cultural exchange?

What is the function of the height of the mountains and the author's climb up them in the progression of the essay? More specifically, trace the progression from self-centeredness to other-centeredness. And the progression of his spirits? In what part of the narrative does he use the verb *mustered up? Sprinted?*

What might be implied in the second-to-final statement? Answer in geographical terms. Next, try to give your answer cultural content. Finally, answer in terms of the voyage of his persona. How has he changed?

Do you think the final sentence is triumphant or foreboding?

We hope that the selection of journal entries in this series of guides is sufficient to inspire you to get started in your own journal writing.

II. Explorations

Introduction

Up to now the guides have offered ideas on how to settle down in your host culture and on how to deal with, respond to, and learn from both your immediate living situation and the larger cultural environment. In this set of guides we want to outline ways in which you can *systematically* study the culture, dig more deeply into it, and flesh out more fully your understanding of it.

One thing that motivates the writing of this series of guides on "Explorations" is an awareness—from having been through it myself—that newcomers can rather quickly become isolated from the society they have come to experience and from the people they want to meet. This isolation is partly a consequence of timidity and partly a result of settling into a pattern of survival behaviors in which you hide from the uncertainties around you. It also results from inertia. The host culture simply doesn't open its arms to welcome you and show you its secrets and treasures. It goes on its own way, and you have to figure out how to jump in, to put yourself into the flow. The projects recommended in this section are designed to help you do just that. They are practical, and they have been done by others. You will find them do-able.

A Plaza Study

In a new culture, among strangers, it is important to stop, look, and listen. Yet there is a tendency—especially during those first days of anxiety—to accelerate your pace of living as you move about and to do things more rapidly in order to surmount the uncertainties and sort out the ambiguities you are experiencing. Here's a project to slow you down. And when you get to that slow pace—almost a stop—you'll be able to learn as much as when you hurried through the day.

The plan is simple: pick a plaza (or park) preferably in a smaller town outside the capital city. Or if your host culture doesn't center its life around plazas, choose a central point in your own neighborhood or area where there is a confluence of people and a variety of social and economic activity. Take a friend (or your children) if you wish. Be sure also to take your journal and, if you are so inclined, your sketchbook. Spend the morning there, three or four hours. Then before you leave, grab lunch nearby.

Select a plaza you don't now know. After you arrive, make yourself comfortable. Sit awhile, get up and walk around, sit somewhere else. Observe what is going on around you. But don't just "look" at it, absorb it, stare at it until the details sort themselves out. Since this is an observation project, you need not feel obligated to initiate conversations with strangers, but of course you want to be courteous.

Questions to open your eyes

1. What is in the plaza itself? List contents, draw sketches if you wish.

193

2. What surrounds the plaza? List buildings by name or function.

3. Make a simple diagram of the area, showing streets, park, buildings, etc.

4. Is the architecture distinct? Do any of the buildings stand out from the others?

5. Who is in the plaza? Who passes through it?

6. What are the people in the plaza doing?

7. What flora and fauna can you see?

8. Who takes care of the place?

Questions to stimulate your thinking

The questions to this point have asked you to identify and describe. Now you are invited to do some inductive thinking. Using the evidence you see, try to build some tentative generalizations about the people and their cultural patterns.

1. Why do the people come to or pass through this area?

2. What is acceptable pedestrian behavior and etiquette?

3. How do they respond to authorities such as traffic officers?

4. How do they give a morning greeting? When do they not greet each other?

5. How would you describe their treatment of older people?

6. How do they discipline their children?

7. What is considered proper street attire? Who is in uniform? Does attire distinguish the people of specific occupations? Identify an individual's economic level?

8. What is their attitude toward littering?

9. How do they treat their pets?

10. Is this a highly technological society? What is the evidence?

11. Are the people deeply religious? Why do you say so?

12. What, if anything, can you conclude about their schools?

13. What conclusions can you draw about their pace of life?

14. How do the people use/guard/share space?

15. What clues do you have about their employment?

Analyses and journal writing

1. Use your journal to record your thoughts about the plaza and its neighborhood.

   a. Why does the town have a plaza?

   b. What functions is it fulfilling now? What other functions does it serve at other times of the day or week?

   c. Do the people like their plaza?

    d. What are some of the chief ways that the plaza tells about and reveals the cultural characteristics of the people who live near it and use it? Would you like to live near this plaza?

    e. If you were a resident of the town, how would you use the plaza?

2. Now that you have thought about this particular place, its people and culture, try to make comparisons with plazas elsewhere. How (in design, atmosphere, function) is this plaza similar to or different from other plazas in your host country and city? How might the similarities strengthen your understanding of your host country's culture as a whole? How might the differences highlight the uniqueness of this particular community within your host country?

3. Compare the plaza with parks in your hometown. This comparison will surely call your attention to the function of public places and the nature of human intersections in America.

As you come to the end of this project, allow yourself to review your thoughts and activities of the morning. Did you have to crank up confidence to get started? Was it difficult for you to slow down for a morning? If so, are you now moving internally and externally at a fast pace? Should you use more activities of this kind to slow down your pace?

Are you a disciplined observer? Do you enjoy looking for the telltale clues that contribute to your understanding of cultural patterns? Do you feel comfortable using the details of your observation to construct tentative conclusions about the people and their community?

Did your presence in the plaza attract attention? From whom? How did you respond?

What have you learned this morning about your host culture? About your home culture? About yourself?

Studying Institutions

This guide proposes to do two things: (1) to call your attention to the wide range of institutions available for study and (2) to provide a scheme that defines what an institution is and gives you a framework for examining any institution you might select to study.

Institutions

An institution is any agency or organization structured to provide a service or product to a constituency. Some are private, some public. Some are old, solidly built to last for years, others come and go and, at the moment you happen to study them, are likely to be in a state of change. Their size, complexity, and ambiance vary greatly. But they have something in common—they reveal their cultural context.

While some institutions don't even have a front door to knock on, many others welcome visitors and scholars. Identifying the purpose of your visit will usually reward you with a generous welcome.

Here is a generic list of institutions. It is your job to look for suitable examples that are accessible to you and that, in the examination, will further your learning goals.

agriculture: a coffee, banana, cocoa, or palm oil plantation; a dairy, poultry farm, beef ranch; sugar, flower, or nut farm

art: a theater company, a community theater, an art gallery, a museum of art, the national or state orchestra, a professional music ensemble, an artists' league, an art or textile coop

retailing: central market, department store, shopping center, corner grocery, drugstore, bookstore, an organization of street hucksters

communications: radio or TV station, newspaper plant, magazine publisher, an advertising agency, a movie theater, a record/disc distributor

education: a nursery, a kindergarten, a primary school, a middle school, a high school, a vo-tech school, an ag school, a college, a textbook supplier

history and archeology: a museum of history, a gold or jade museum, an archaeological dig, a library

government: the presidential house, the court building, the legislative assembly building, a ministry office, the housing authority, the office of tourism, the military organization

health and welfare: a hospital, a clinic, a home for the aged, a children's shelter, a drug rehab center, a detention center, a nutrition center

manufacturing: a mineral processor, a car-assembly plant, a fabrics manufacturer, a tire company, a foods processor, a utility, a petroleum refinery, a furniture factory

recreation: a central park program, a professional athletic team, the national stadium, a private club

religion: a temple, mosque, cathedral, monastery or convent, parish school, seminary, church-run community center, bazaar

A scheme for studying institutions

After you make arrangements to visit an institution, especially if you are going alone or if you are in charge of a small group, you might be anxious: "But what shall I be looking at? How should I spend my time during the visit? What shall I ask questions about?"

Think of an institution as a structure with many interlinking components, each of which varies in function, size, and shape. Although every institution is different, many are made up of the components shown in this wheel. The spokes are used to represent the interrelatedness of the components.

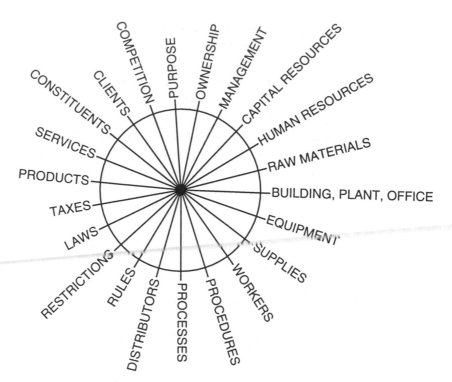

Now that you have in mind a general picture of the many components of an institution, try to describe the institution you are visiting. To do this, use the outline shown on p. 199.

To describe the institution's PURPOSE you may have to ask a tour guide, manager, or other informant to explain why the institution was begun and what it hopes to accomplish. Jot down a few of the key words that you hear. Move on to the next component, OWNERSHIP. Is the institution owned by an individual, a partnership, a family, or possibly a number of shareholders? Who are they? Why are they interested in owning the institution? What impact does their ownership have on the product or service? Proceed to the following components.

People typically want to show their institutions in the best light. Allow them to do this. If you have opportunity, however, try to discover some of the challenges and problems that attend the day-to-day operations. Ask politely about the limitations (such as the capital resources), the restrictions (maybe something having to do with product codes), the odds they have to work against (possibly time or weather or the difficulty of finding good employees). From what you learn, record notes in the outline.

As you become informed about the institution you will discover the linkage among the components. For example, EQUIPMENT and PROCESSES are likely related. So you might ask how changes in equipment (such as computers) have changed the way the institution has done its work. You may assume that DISTRIBUTORS are in some way related to CLIENTS. So your question can anticipate that relationship by asking which of the clients voluntarily come to the institution? Which of them must it find? Which are the hardest ones for the distributors to reach? In such a manner, allow two or more components to inform each other.

components   **your observations and comments**

PURPOSE _____

OWNERSHIP _____

MANAGEMENT _____

CAPITAL RESOURCES _____

HUMAN RESOURCES _____

RAW MATERIALS _____

BUILDING, PLANT, OFFICE _____

EQUIPMENT _____

SUPPLIES _____

WORKERS _____

PROCEDURES _____

PROCESSES _____

DISTRIBUTORS _____

RULES _____

RESTRICTIONS _____

LAWS _____

TAXES _____

PRODUCT _____

SERVICES _____

CONSTITUENTS _____

CLIENTS _____

COMPETITION _____

Once you have a pretty good understanding of the institution itself, try to learn about its relationship to the neighborhood, the government, the region, and—you guessed it—the culture.

You may wish to try to answer questions such as these: How do cultural values affect the operation of this institution? For example, is the institution affected by the culture's general preference for affiliation over productivity? Or, how does the culture's authoritarian style show up in this institution? What is the institution contributing to the current social, economic, political, or educational dynamic?

What are/were your expectations when you started your institutional study? Were those expectations based on your knowledge of your own culture, stereotypes of the host culture? How has the institution met or diverged from your expectations? What are the implications of that for the overall process of culture learning in which you are engaged? How are the values and cultural norms of the society reflected in the institution you studied? How might they be improved? How do your criteria for improvement reflect your cultural outlook or the outlook of a knowledgeable host national?

This guide introduced you to the study of institutions in general. The following guide will pertain to a selected institution. After using the two guides, you should have good tools for the study of your institutions of choice.

Guide 39

A Study of Religious Institutions

Religion constitutes a central motivation for the people of any culture. Consequently a study of religion can be a profitable unit in your curriculum. This guide suggests three ways you might study religion and elaborates on a selected religious institution: (1) through philosophical inquiry, (2) through a religious ritual or event, and (3) through a religious institution such as a temple, mosque, or church.

Philosophical inquiry

You may want to approach your study of religion with a philosophical frame of mind and think in a slightly more abstract way about worldview, mythos, and religious perception. Your inquiry is likely to be question- and concept-oriented. You will want to use questions such as these:

1. Identify the gods of the culture. Has the concept of god changed or evolved in the past fifty years?

2. Is God transcendent, out beyond, the Holy Other, controlling the universe from a distance; or is God immanent, here and now, inside of humans and an integral part of life?

3. Is the earth considered to be animate—alive with an identity and feelings almost like those of a human, an animal, or plant?

4. If a child is trampled by a wild animal, do people say that it was the will of God? That it was human error? That it was a matter of chance?

5. Are good health, good fortune, good spirit seen as gifts of God? Is aesthetic beauty attributed to God? Is order considered to be a manifestation of God? Is harmony thought to be rooted in God?

6. Do people curse God? Lay curses upon each other?

7. Do people believe in Satan, devils, or evil spirits? In magic?

8. What would you say the majority of people would consider sacred? Are there sacred places? Sacred objects? Sacred times? Sacred creeds? Sacred people? What endows a place, an object, a time, a creed, or a person with the quality of being sacred?

9. Do the majority of people suppose that an individual has a spirit? A soul? What do people think happens to a human being after death?

10. Are people considered to be basically good but needing discipline or basically bad and needing salvation, or neither good nor bad?

11. When considering the broad subject of knowing, do people think that the deepest knowing comes from personal and disciplined reflection? From hunch? From empirical data? From divine revelation?

12. Is nature considered to be good, bad, or nonmoral? Is God seen as working through nature? Is nature an extension of God? Is God an extension of nature?

Your philosophical inquiry into the cultural meaning of religion can be quickened and informed by myth studies. (This is not myth in the sense of untruth, but myth in the sense of the origin and development of shared meaning.) See chapter 5 again for its reference to people such as Joseph Campbell for whom an understanding of myth is basic to an understanding of life.

Religious ritual or event

While some cultural inquirers know how to use the abstractions of philosophical inquiry, others prefer to use more tangible tools. You might prefer to begin your study of religion by using things you can hear and see, deriving from these experiences a new understanding of the subject.

Among the religious resources you might give attention to are a saint's day, a religious pageant, a festival in a holy week, sacred garb, religious publications, a pilgrimage, religious sanctions, and sacred music.

For example, if you are sojourning in the Moslem world, learning all you can about Ramadan (the fast from sunrise to sunset during the ninth month of the Moslem year) can help you understand Islam. By observing who fasts, how and why they fast, how they behave after sundown (it differs greatly from individual to individual and from culture to culture), and what the effect of the fast is on the society and on individuals, you can extend your appreciation of the power of the Koran, define various kinds or degrees of devotedness, identify crucial markers that distinguish Islamic groups from each other, and understand the reasons for the growth of Islam in the world today.

Religious institution, edifice, or holy place

You may wish to undertake study using the outline suggested in Guide 38. You can visit a selected church, mosque, synagogue, temple, shrine, or other religious place.

How you organize your study and frame your questions are affected greatly by the religion and the region of your selected institution. If you select a Buddhist temple, for example, the Buddhist monuments in Sanchi in Madhya Pradesh state in India will offer a totally different opportunity for study from the Buddhist pagoda in Ueda, Japan. Buddhism is so complex that you may wish to focus your attention on one aspect, such as on Buddha himself who lived from around 563 to 483 B.C.; the beliefs such as dharma, karma, and pantheism; ethics and morality; rites and restrictions such as dietary laws, death rites, purification rites; or sacred orders of the priesthood or monasticism. In other words, you must tailor your study in a way that uses the resources of the institution well.

Some religious institutions are controlled from a central source (the Roman Catholic Church), while others are local and democratic. You will find synagogues to be of the latter kind. While synagogues typically serve three functions—a house of prayer, a house of assembly, and a house of study—they are essentially democratic institutions, established and maintained by the community of participating Jews. It might include extensive social, recreational, and philanthropic activities and reflect the desires of the local community. Your study of a synagogue, then, is a natural for discovering how a group of people attempt to make their institution culturally appropriate.

The buildings, that is, the structures, are a good place to begin. Be alert to the great contrasts among religions on what a building should look like. A Baha'i temple is constructed to reveal symbolically the spiritual unity of all people. A mosque emphasizes structurally the central place of prayer for the Moslem; its *mihrab* (decorated niche with pointed arch, a place of prayer) faces Mecca toward which prayer is directed. Much of its space, often courtyards, is designed for congregational prayers.

Regardless of what kind of religious institution, edifice, or holy place you select, keep in mind the following six categories of inquiry:

1. The location

2. The structure itself, inside and out

3. Ways that religious meanings are conveyed through architecture, symbols, holy people, art, and tradition

4. Uses to which the edifice or place is put

5. Its care and maintenance

6. The interface of the building or place with its surrounding community, including its religious ministry

We will now illustrate how you can use those six categories of inquiry. Our selected institution is a church of the Catholic faith. Again we remind you that many of these questions would not be appropriate in studying a Buddhist temple or, for that matter, the holy places of most other faiths. But you can see how the questions are framed and how they can be adapted to your study of a church from another Christian tradition, a Jewish synagogue, a Hindu shrine, a mosque, a holy river, cave, or mountain.

1. Examine its exterior. Can you locate works of religious art on the walls? What style of architecture is used for the building? If there are statues and gargoyles, can you identify what symbols are used? Does the church face the central square? If so, what other buildings face the square? Is there a public park in proximity to the square? Is it in use? Are beggars in sight? If so, how are they treated? Is a political manifestation in progress? If so, how is it carried out? How do observers respond? Are children free to play in or near the sanctuary? Do animals roam in or near the sanctuary? How do people respond to the animals? Do you think this is a wealthy or a poor church?

2. Enter the church. Quietly and respectfully examine the interior. Locate each of the alcoves from the main sanctuary. Attempt to determine the purpose(s) of each alcove. Which alcove is dedicated to the church's patron saint, the baptistry, the suffering Christ on the cross, the Mother Mary with the baby Jesus, the suffering Mary of the crucifixion, etc.? Think about the relative size of the various figures and their placement in the building. Which figures dominate? How is God represented? Jesus? The Holy Spirit? Mary? Apostles? Angels? Saints? Are all of the figures presented in white skin tones? Is the host culture's heritage reflected in any way? Do you see visible evidence of miracles attributed to this church?

3. How is the church being used by the people during the time you are present? (If mass is being said, it is quite acceptable for you to observe as a nonparticipant. When, during the mass, the peace of God is passed, you should greet your neighbor, shake hands, and pass the peace.) Do you notice more men or women in the sanctuary? Are they mostly old people, or young people too? Are priests or nuns in evidence? What specifically religious behaviors do you notice? Is there behavior which surprises you?

4. What type of religious art do you see? Is only one style in use, or is there a mixture of styles? Do any of these works create positive emotions in you? Negative ones? Are any sacred relics on display? To whom/what are they attributed?

5. Sit alone for five to ten minutes. Think about your own religious heritage. How is it similar to Catholicism? Different? How do you think your experience of this church building compares with that of the other persons in the sanctuary?

6. If workers are cleaning or repairing the sanctuary, how does this activity affect those who are worshipping?

7. Leave the church and look again at the exterior art work. How does it fit in with the paintings and sculptures of the interior?

8. Walk through the city blocks which surround the church. What types of homes and businesses are close to the church? Is this a poor town, a middle-class town, or a wealthy one? What criteria are you using to determine class level?

9. Observe public behavior in the vicinity of the church. Do you see any specifically religious behavior?

10. Talk with people in the city. Attempt to find out about the history, the patron saint, the celebrations, miracles, the priests or pastors, the mission, and so forth.

11. What is the relationship of the church to this community? For example, do all bus routes stop near the church? Does the church support hospitals, mission work, parochial schools, or other forms of public service?

12. Who are the priests and other religious workers who serve the needs of this congregation? Are they local people or foreign missionaries? How many priests are assigned to this parish? For how many persons are they responsible for pastoral care? Do you know how the staff of this church is paid?

13. Identify questions which this study has raised for you—about the church or community, about the role of religion in this community, about the relationship of religion to culture in general, or about your own religion.

Field Trips

Unless you have enclosed yourself in a room and capitulated to culture shock, you are inevitably going to get restless and want to explore this new land. In short, you want to see the country. Taking to the road is a natural part of international experience.

Whether field trips—visits to outlying places—are undertaken individually, in groups, or with your spouse and children, they have the potential to become rich educational experiences. But it is not automatic. Successful field trips require planning and a determination to learn from them. A quota of enthusiasm helps too.

Planning a field trip

Inventory the resources of the host country that you would enjoy seeing. Include natural resources, industry and agriculture, social institutions and their programs, festivals and special events, ethnic centers, etc.

Gather information about these resources from the tourist bureau, information centers, books about the host country, newspapers and magazines, cultural interpreters, and friends. Build a file of facts about the places to visit, the people whom you might contact when you arrive, and information about transportation, food, lodging, tickets, etc. Write out a list of questions you want to ask and information you wish to acquire, and be ready to add to it as the day unfolds.

Check the calendar. On what date does the festival fall? When is the game likely to be played? When are the national holidays? In what season do the turtles lay their eggs? Are the parks open then? What will the weather be like? Can you be assured of lodging during that time? When do the companies open their doors to visitors? Will the traffic be heavy?

Make necessary arrangements. Is a reservation required for the bus? The ferry? To hold a campsite? To get a room at the pension? Can you buy the ticket for the game now? Will a phone call facilitate your visit to the monastery?

What should you carry with you besides enough money? A special identification card or permit? Bottled water? A packed lunch? A bird guide? A second pair of walking shoes? Sunscreen?

On the way

1. Don't sit in a bus playing cards or look only for the next place you can buy souvenirs or take photos to show the folks back home. Observe the country you pass through for what it tells you about the people and the culture that constitute your host environment.

2. Notice road and communications systems. Are they efficient, effective, in good repair? How does your analysis reflect your American values? How do you think local people see these same systems?

3. Observe geographical changes and the concomitant changes in flora and fauna. Observe terrain, rock formations, evidences of erosion and deforestation, river routes, mountain passes. How does each of these natural phenomena affect personal life and national life, socially, psychologically, economically? How does temperature influence how people live?

4. Look for evidence of ecological awareness. How are local people acting as shepherds of the earth? How are they disregarding the earth's needs for renewal and survival? What relationships do you notice between humans, animals, and plant life?

5. Actively search for indices of the economic life of the communities you pass through: observe types of dwellings, presence or absence of communal buildings, density of housing, factories, clothing worn, tools in use, presence of banks or other types of financial centers.

When you stop

1. What appear to be the major resources of the towns and villages? What types of stores do you find and do they sell the goods you expect? Are there cultural centers, schools, theaters, galleries, libraries, recreational centers? Are there churches? Synagogues? Temples? What seems to be lacking in the area's resources by American standards? What cultural values are present in your observations?

2. Observe the presence or absence of people of different races. Do the people of different races mix with each other? Can you see any evidence of exclusion or discrimination?

3. If the trip involves tours, be ready to work at making the most of the guides, especially if they are informal or untrained. Language might be a barrier, but try hard to ask questions, even though it is a struggle.

4. When possible, talk with people in the towns and villages. What information do they give you about their hometowns, themselves, and their neighbors? Do they talk about national issues and problems, the country's strengths and beauties? Do they ask you about your country? They may take the lead by suggesting things to see and do. Respond positively; you may be rewarded with surprises.

5. Be ready to capture your personal reactions. Make sketches. Take (or buy) snapshots. Write poetry or prose commentary in your journal.

6. Relate what you are seeing and experiencing to what you have read or to prior experiences, to what you have learned in language classes or, if a student, in lectures. Do your senses teach you the same things you learned in other contexts?

After the trip, summarize your observations in your journal and analyze the experience in the context of the intercultural learning process in which you are engaged.

Note: it's a fair prediction that on any field trip, something, perhaps many things, will go wrong. A bus arrives late (or you can't find a gas station when you need one). The guide at the furniture factory doesn't show up. The heat in the sugar refinery is sweltering. There is too much noise in the power plant to hear the explanations. Someone needs a rest room. You are taken to see something you have absolutely no interest in.

The unpredictability of field trips makes them both a headache and an opportunity. The determined inquirer will find, even in a field trip's vagaries, a chance to learn something that might not have been available if everything had gone without a glitch.

Shopping

It is quite possible that gesturing and stuttering to a clerk about a loaf of bread will be your first independent attempt to communicate with someone in this foreign land. The need to purchase necessities is basic and should actually be fairly simple, even in a foreign country. In fact, it can be quite daunting, especially if you don't have a host family or experienced friend to help you through your initial attempts. Where should you shop? What do you call the thing you want to buy? How much should you expect to pay for it? Is it true you must deal with the salesclerk, the cashier, the packager, and the store guard all before you can leave with your purchase? Shops can be friendly little places or intimidating indeed.

But shopping is also a mode of entry into the culture. The way people shop, the goods available, the attitude toward customers and service are all indicators of the values of a society.

This exercise is designed to help orient you to shopping in your new culture both as a practical aid and a culture-learning resource.

Procedures for the project

During your first week or weeks in the host country, go shopping with your host family or a friend. Let them back you up while you make your purchases. As soon as you feel sufficiently confident, go out on your own, buying small, not very consequential items at first. Notice the kinds of stores. Do little general stores at street corners serve the neighborhoods? Are there food shops in narrow alleyways? Does your city or town feature a central market where vegetables, meat, and fish can be found packed on counters or hanging from beams like great sta-lactites? Do farmers have a weekly market in an open field or plaza? Can you find the supermarkets common to the American shopper? Talk with your host family or your friends about stores, shopping patterns, vocabulary, and etiquette.

Look up the words in the local language for the food and other items of interest to you. Write them down and then find out their prices. It is quite accept-able to ask prices without buying. When you have acquired the data, record your experience in your journal—what you learned about the different kinds of shops, about procedures in stores, about prices, about the people you dealt with, about language, and about your own performance. Some of these leading questions may help you as you reflect and write:

1. On which day of the week did you shop? Does the day make a difference in who is buying what? (In the U.S., which are the bigger grocery shopping days? Do you find that same pattern in the host country?)

2. Which shops are family-owned? Neighborly? Modern? Clean? To which shops does the family send a child to buy an item for immediate con-sumption, such as an egg, a stick of butter, or milk? Which shops special-ize in a few basic products? Which ones stock foreign products? Which ones have parking lots?

3. Do the shops accept checks? Give credit? Encourage bargaining?

4. Who supplies the shops? From where does the merchandise come? How is it delivered? Who puts it on the shelves? Can you see any evidence that producers compete for shelf space (as they do in American supermarkets)?

5. Who are the patrons? Do they interact with each other? Are they in a hurry, or do they make shopping a social occasion? Do they bargain? If so, is it a tense combat or a friendly game? Do you observe patterns in who buys what? How do the patrons directly or indirectly reveal their economic level? How do the shops cater to the needs and behavior of their clients' eco-nomic class?

6. As you study the goods that are available in the shops, what can you con-clude about your host country's agricultural production? Does it offer lots of prepared or processed foods? Does it depend on imports to stock gro-cery shelves?

7. Do you think that the shopkeepers and store owners observe the motto that "the customer is always right"? Do you sense in clerk and customer the informality of traditional culture? The respect and fear of authoritar-ian culture? The impersonality of technological culture?

8. Which shop do you like best? Least? Why?

Guide 42

The Uses of Photography

There are mixed feelings about the use of cameras and the taking of pictures by foreign tourists and travelers. Here are objections and cautions: (1) Cameras are the badges of tourists, who snap pictures and return home to show their albums without ever really seeing the places to which they travel. (2) Photography is, in many countries, a hobby of the rich, and distances the camera owner from those in the host culture who can't afford them. (3) Many people, irrespective of culture, resent being treated as a curiosity by tourists with cameras. It is important to ask permission before taking someone's picture and courteous to take the subject's name and address and to send him/her a copy of the photo (see comment re "faces" on p. 211). (4) In some cultures, especially Moslem, the making of images is forbidden or at least frowned upon. (5) It may be unwise to take photos around military installations, especially where there is some governmental antipathy toward the United States. (6) Preoccupation with getting the "great shot" can actually interfere with establishing good contacts with people and learning about the culture. "Better," says one program director, "to record an event in the mind than on film."

At first, when I was abroad, I didn't carry a camera. Later I started using it more. My conclusion: people should be given priority over cameras, but pictures can, in a special way, contribute to one's learning and to the quality of contact with people.

Using a camera for friendships

After you make friends with your hosts, most of them will enjoy having their pictures taken, especially if they know they are going to get a copy. Host families are quite happy to show off their photo albums.

Imaginative picture takers find interesting ways to move across cultures with their cameras. Volunteer workers at a refugee camp took pictures of families in the camps and gave them copies—which they, of course, treasured because the snapshots were the only ones they had. Another person in our program met a stain-covered banana plantation worker who was eating a packed lunch that his two children carried to him. After chatting awhile, the American visitor asked the worker if he could take a picture and later sent a copy back to him. I saw the picture; the banana worker must surely have been proud to receive it. Another American visitor was invited to a fiftieth wedding anniversary. She approached the family, offering to document the anniversary mass and reception with her camera. She later presented the couple with an album—her anniversary gift.

Using a camera for culture learning

It may be less obvious to you how one can use a camera for culture learning. Your doubts are understandable since American classrooms seldom use the camera for instructional purposes. In brief, you can use a camera to see, to document, and to express. All three uses are represented in the following examples of the kinds of things that can be done with a camera.

Collections. You might use a camera to help you see items of a kind. You might make a snapshot collection of architectural styles, trees, tools, markets, bridges, or leaded glass windows.

Incongruities. A friend of mine who has both a sense of irony and a keen eye looks with his camera for scenes and events that contain a strange juxtaposition: an aristocrat and a beggar woman, a jet plane and a yoke of oxen, a smile and a frown. His albums open the viewer's eyes to cultural complexities.

Faces. Faces reveal culture. (As do hands, feet, and posture.) If your camera is given the assignment to find faces, you will be looking at people far more carefully than the casual tourist. Taking pictures of faces presents a major problem: how can one get up close enough to record the subtle meanings in a face? When does a face shot invade privacy? A face shot is likely to be intrusive unless you have a friendly connection with the subject.

Textures. If you are an artist, you probably seek out interesting lines, colors, shadows, and light. And you know the artistic force of texture. So you use the camera to study where your host culture is smooth, gritty, jagged, undulating, curling, rippling, and the like. That study may direct you to a study of trees because of your attraction to the varied textures of bark.

People at work. I saw a series of black-and-white prints from a traveler who focused strictly on people in their regular line of work—the shoe repairman, the washerwoman, the diplomat, the vegetable huckster—always surrounded by the tools of their trades.

Activities documentation. You want to remember a special day, so your journal entry includes not only jottings and sketches but also snapshots. Use snapshots in the journal to illustrate a written text or to be the primary text itself.

Park project. Go to a national or regional park and roam the furthest reaches of the reserve, documenting the park's flora and fauna. Mount your photos, with captions, on wallboard and present them to the park director for display in the information office. (This will be appreciated especially in those parks that don't have sufficient funds for publicity of this kind.)

A procedures report. You wish to explain to an art class at home how your hosts made their clay pots. Your camera can serve well to show the breaking of the soil, the sifting, the mixing, the molding, drying, painting, and firing of the pots.

A natural wonder. You can't find words to describe the waterfalls, the jungle through which you rode on the elephants, the orchid show. Your camera helps you to express it.

A gift. A friend you have met in your host country is celebrating an anniversary. What might you give? How about a snapshot, enlarged and framed?

All of these ideas are intended for the amateur photographer. The professional or freelance photographer will have a far more complete strategy for getting inside culture. Study their works for windows into the nuances of culture. See, for example, the series of books by David Cohen and Rick Smolan, *A Day in the Life of....*

Some things to keep in mind:
1. Cameras get ripped off.
2. Cameras get wet; film wears out faster in hot, humid weather.
3. Film and developing are often more costly overseas than at home.
4. If you are going to send snapshots, you need addresses.
5. Make the five-year test. Which photos will retain their value in five years? The test may help you decide what and when to shoot.
6. Think about how you will present your snapshots. Slide presentations? Mounted on poster board? In an album? The form of presentation might guide your picture taking.

Guide 43

Generating Your Own Explorations

Some foreign sojourners, be they volunteers with nongovernmental organizations, business executives, tourists, or students, expect to buy a package deal in which the entirety of their time abroad is planned and programmed by someone else. Anyone reading this book is likely to be more independent and, probably, more adventuresome. You know there is much that you can do on your own, and, for many of you, there is no alternative. This guide is designed to help you plan your independent explorations to make them all the more valuable.

While the ideas here will be useful to anyone striking out on his or her own, my orientation is frankly toward students who are abroad as part of a group. It is they, especially, who are encouraged to pursue independent study projects in order to extend themselves beyond the inherent limitations of an organized program.

These too are the people I most enjoy working with. Here are just a few illustrations of the kinds of things these independent-minded people have dreamed up:

Doug Fike talked with radio station owners and managers in order to find who made the weekly listing of top pop music played on local FM radio stations.

Janet Kraybill and Korla Miller published a chapbook of journal entries from their term in China.

Lana Stoltzfus and Ingrid Hess volunteered to work with the "dying destitute" in a Calcutta clinic associated with Mother Theresa.

Tom Unzicker observed pottery making in rural Tanzania, then set up shop to use those methods and also to teach some methods he knew.

Dewey Mast rode to the end of a bus line, and from there walked to an isolated lowland village to see what life was like in such a remote spot.

Logistics

Your own project is likely to have three parts: (1) planning, which includes finding the time, getting permissions, obtaining finances, rounding up supplies, arranging travel, lining up interviews, etc.; (2) doing the project, which might require only an hour or might possibly occupy you for weeks, and (3) reporting the project.

These kinds of projects are valuable because they force you to hit the street, make your own arrangements, deal with red tape, confront the dead ends with your own ingenuity—the nitty-gritty everyday concerns that both test your maturity and foster personal growth as you go about solving the problems which arise. Even when projects don't work, they may provide valuable insights into the way things are (or aren't) done in the host culture and force you to deal in adult ways with your frustration.

Here are some possible projects

Attend:
- a baptism party, a funeral, a mass, an ashram ceremony
- a fifteenth birthday party, a fiftieth wedding anniversary, a name-day celebration
- a patron-saint festival, a Friday night community dance, a bone dance
- a bullfight, a soccer game, a surfing contest, a sumo match
- a political rally, a student demonstration, a labor protest, a meeting of the national assembly

Interview:
- the national symphony director or a renowned player of a unique local instrument, e.g., the sitar
- the former president of the country, a preeminent mullah
- the manager of the Toyota franchise, the IBM rep
- the nation's champion swimmer, a boxer
- the author of a recently released novel

Travel:
- walk the distance the rural baker walks to get his supplies
- cycle the route of a championship bike race
- go white-water rafting
- bounce your way on a round-trip by bus to a rural village or visit a bedouin settlement in the desert
- explore a jungle river

Make:
- a basketball backboard and hoop for local kids
- pizza for your host family or an artifact to celebrate *devali*
- posters to help your school announce its pageant
- a terrarium for the sick grandfather in your host home
- a scrapbook/photo album of your town

Analyze:
- the contents of the daily newspaper
- billboards within a kilometer of your house
- films made in your host country
- personal calling cards and company logos
- your family's favorite TV shows
- the design on a mosque or a Hindu temple

A final word of advice. If you are going to make the effort to do independent study, give attention to how you will report it. Discipline yourself to work carefully in order to give appropriate form to your experience: a speech, a video, an album, an essay, a set of slide transparencies, a series of letters, a collection of sketches. Reportage should not be an afterthought, but rather your considered best work.

III. Case Studies

Introduction

A case study has come to mean a close examination of some exemplary or provocative slice of life. It may be developed from an event, a set of facts, an individual's behavior, possibly a story you hear, a joke, words of counsel offered to you, or a question put to you in the field. In the case study, you are given the setting, the principal actors, the decisions made, the action or the words, and possibly some of the consequences. It's your task to review the evidence, make observations of the people and their behavior, assess the crucial factors related to causes and effects, and evaluate what happens. You may be asked to speculate on hypothetical outcomes if any of the variables have been different.

The rationale for case studies is as convincing as it is simple: you can learn from experience, particularly if you study experience a little at a time. The case study serves well to isolate a segment of experience and, like the televised replay, run it over again and from several different angles. You will miss the benefits of the case study if you merely get a whiff of its flavor. Case studies are bones to be gnawed on. You've got to identify, think, react, and evaluate.

The guides that follow are lifted from international travel, study, and service experiences. All of them are based on fact, although names and details are altered to protect the privacy of the people involved.

Questions and issues for discussion are provided. They lend themselves far better to discussion than merely to private reflection, so even if you are not part of a group, try to find someone to read and discuss them with you.

Connections

How does one communicate across cultures? If there were only an easy answer! Even after long and tedious efforts, you still stand at the edge of your culture and wish that by magic you could somehow understand and participate in theirs. Here's one student's account.

May 24

Today was the first day for me to go out and do something. In the morning I went out alone to hear the national symphony (yes, a Sunday morning concert). After I got home from the concert my host family took me along to my "sisters" in Heredia for dinner. The whole family was there because, as I found out when we walked through the door, it was my host mother's birthday. I felt rather bad because I hadn't acknowledged it, but no one had told me it was her birthday. That kind of thing happens to me a lot, not knowing what's going on. For instance, we often have people coming over and I think they're family, but I'm not sure because we've never been introduced and I feel stupid asking someone who they are and if they're part of the family. I feel like an outsider.

Although it was nice having a change of scenery for once, it was not my idea of fun. Most of the time I just sat and half-listened to what was going on; they talked so fast I didn't understand anything. No one talked to me either so I just sort of twiddled my thumbs. I decided to try and learn something from the experience (like a good student) and was aware that these are affectionate people, but that was the extent of that. I was definitely beginning to have my doubts when I heard strange "music" coming from part of the house. Since I love music and play the piano myself, I decided to go investigate. My host brother-in-law had bought an electronic keyboard/minisynthesizer a month ago and they were messing around with it. They let me join in and then left. I wished I had some of my music with me, but I still went on playing it for awhile anyway. It reminded me how much I missed my piano and music.

Then my brother-in-law came back in and we started to talk. He asked me questions about what I was studying and about the States. He told me that he was studying philosophy, social work, and theology, so we talked about that and I told him about religion classes I have had and other such stuff. It was good to have a person want to carry on a conversation. It was the first time anyone here had taken an interest in me.

(excerpted and adapted from journal of Zoann Haarer)

Questions for discussion

1. Think of Zoann's journal entry as a composition in three parts, a beginning, a middle, and an ending. Describe the events of each part. Describe the writer's cultural orientation in each part. Describe the writer's frame of mind in each part.

2. Have you ever been culturally displaced? To the best of your ability, describe how it feels.

3. In the middle of the journal entry, and perhaps in the middle of the afternoon, "doubts" creep in. What kind of doubts do you suppose they were? What is a first-aid suggestion for such occasions of doubt?

4. The cultural bridge that the student crosses over has to do with something quite familiar to her—music. (Notice she had attended a concert earlier in the day, and she has a piano and music at home.) What are your interests that could possibly serve as cultural bridges?

5. In this particular case, who had to make the first move? How might the day have ended if that initiative had not been taken? How might the day have ended if she had declined to play the instrument because, in not having music along, she might have made mistakes?

6. Who was rewarded in this meeting? What was the nature of the reward?

A Rock Concert

What is cultural sensitivity? How far should one be expected to go in accommodating other cultures? Case studies may help to define and even answer such questions. The event described in this case study was critical enough so that when I asked one of my students at the end of his three-month term whether there was any unfinished business between him and me, he said, "Yes, I am still angry about not going to that concert!" What was provocative for this student may be provocative for you.

An ethical dilemma

A big rock concert by Bruce Springsteen and the E Street Band, Peter Gabriel, Sting, Tracy Chapman, and Youssou N'Dour was to be held in the next town. I personally wanted to go, even though as the adult director of our college's study program I might be considered something of an old fogey. I had thought I might go with my American students as a group, even though the twenty students were to arrive just three days before the concert. But now I had to ask myself this question: Should I refrain from allowing or enabling my group of American students to attend the concert considering the following:

—The stated intent of the concert (to support human rights) is nearly lost to a spreading declamation here that such events encourage moral decadence, including drug consumption.

—An op-ed essay openly doubts that the concert will support true human rights—liberty, respect for life and the dignity of people, equal treatment, conscience in work, the common quest for the public welfare, a spirit of reconciliation, and openness to spiritual values.

—The simple, democratic, and rather religious populace is startled over recent revelations that its terrain is becoming a major transshipment station for cocaine and that apparently some well-placed officials are involved in the activity.

—A local TV sports commentator asks how it is that this country promotes a "Say No to Drugs Day" (September 5) and then follows it the very next week with an activity (the concert) which, in his opinion, says "Yes to Drugs."

—A priest, known for his openness and tolerance, pleads with his parishioners on Sunday to stay away from the stadium, and the archbishop opposes the concert.

—The price of a ticket—$15 (or one thousand colones)—is considered a terrible waste of money in a land where per capita income is considerably less than $2000 a year. (Within the sound of the concert will be people in shack towns, hurting from hunger.)

—The majority of our host families will not permit their own children to attend.

—The event occurs in the first week of the students' visit—the very time of their welding relationships with their families.

—The six-hour concert will end after the buses have stopped running and will greatly complicate the students' getting home.

   Should we go and enjoy our music or should we stay home in deference to public opinion and in respect for our hosts?

Questions for discussion

1. What is your opinion of musical performers of this sort? Of their music? Their lyrics? Their lifestyles?

2. What do you know of the human-rights concerts produced internationally by performers such as these in the late 1980s? What did they accomplish?

3. As you read the account above, what are the reasons (explicit or implied) that local people opposed the concert? What are some additional questions that troubled the supplier of this case study?

4. Which of these objections are unique to this one country? Have you heard any of the objections in other parts of the world? Have you heard any of them in your own home community?

5. Which of the objections (by the community or the writer) are, in your judgment, illogical? Based on inadequate information? Prejudiced? Expressions of an exaggerated sensitivity to others? Which objections are reasonable? Based on credible conviction? Derived from documented fact?

6. If you were a member of this student group, just arriving in this country when the concert was being produced, and you were asked to stay away for the reasons mentioned above, what would you do?

7. What principles will you use in resolving conflicts between your personal preferences and your host culture's preferences? Will it make any difference to you if your hosts' standards are more liberal than yours? More conservative than yours?

Shoes

The next case has to do with early glimpses of a culture different from yours, when you encounter strange incidents and begin to wonder what they mean. When the event happened, nobody suspected it would turn out to be material for a case study. It was a small occurrence that was over quickly. Only later did my traveling companions begin to talk about it.

The focus of attention

Our trip brought us down off the meseta and onto the hot Pacific coastal plain of rice, African palm and Brahman cattle. We felt the heat and saw the little cottages and wondered what was on people's minds, so soon after Hurricane Gilbert's heavy flooding of their area.

As we entered the village of Parrita, we noticed a cluster of several hundred people, many of them school children in uniform, out in the hot sun, gathered around a person giving a speech.

To our surprise, we discovered that it was the winner of the 1987 Nobel Peace Prize, the untiring worker for a new era in Central American cooperation, a persistent opponent of United States' foreign policies—President Oscar Arias.

We stopped the bus, of course, grabbed our cameras, jumped out into the tropical heat, heard the final paragraphs of the speech, and walked closer, hoping for a glimpse of *the man*.

And then, almost as though the honored guests had finally arrived, the Costa Ricans stepped aside and in seconds we were there—in his very presence. We gave to him the customary Costa Rican greeting. He talked to each of us and listened to our answers. When our Spanish faltered, he spoke English. Those with cameras snapped as fast as they could.

At that moment, a little girl tapped Valerie on the elbow. Valerie first thought it was the usual pushing and shoving of a throng, but the girl tapped again. Valerie looked at the girl and saw her finger, pointing to Valerie's feet.

"Reebok," the little girl said, in admiration.

Questions for discussion

1. Establish the physical setting in which this event occurs. What does the account tell you of the socioeconomic context of the local people? What can you infer about the foreign travelers' socioeconomic level?

2. The travelers are attracted by what? By whom? Why?

3. Take your time to think about the significance of U.S. citizens meeting Arias in this way. What can they do to make the most of this moment? How might they "use" the event when they return home?

4. The villagers seem not to care that the visitors go right up to their president. What might be some reasons for the villagers' attitude? Imagine that you were a local resident of Parrita. How would this event look to you? What would be your reaction to the visitors?

5. Describe the visitors' conduct. Describe the president's.

6. The little girl's attention, which is supposed to be focused on her president, is drawn away to the visitors. Contrast the visitors' object of attention and the little girl's object of attention. Why would she notice shoes? Why would she notice the label? What does this say about her? About her culture?

7. If the little girl is indicative of the populace, what are some big issues that the president and his country now face? More specifically, how does a whetted appetite for consumer goods affect a country's political and economic agenda?

8. What is the quality of communication in this cross-cultural event? Is it a meeting? Is it a meeting of equals? Is there communication? What messages are delivered? What messages are received?

9. Which of the following reactions from the travelers an hour later would be understandable and defensible: delight, pride, shame, confusion, regret, appreciation, guilt, accomplishment?

10. Take a quick inventory of the possessions you brought with you into your sojourn abroad. Try to define their significance from the point of view of the little girl.

11. Do the people of your host culture put a priority on acquiring consumer goods? Is theirs an exaggerated yearning for goods? Which items do they want? What keeps them from acquiring these items? How can you, a resident of a country where consumer goods are easy to come by, establish and maintain mutually satisfying relationships with local residents?

Eclipse

You aren't in a foreign land long before you want to make judgments about the culture. You smell odors that turn your stomach. You hear grating noises. You see unsavory sights. You flinch at strange behaviors. You encounter your cucarachas everywhere.

Is it fair to judge another culture? Are you qualified to make the judgment? How can you handle the evaluation process responsibly?

Try this case.

This superstitious culture

In the third week of my stay in Williamstown we had that total eclipse of the sun. Remember? Well, I heard about the coming eclipse from day one. People were scared. They were actually predicting the end of the earth. Radio announcers were saying what to do to protect yourself. Doctors—medical doctors—were giving all kinds of spooky advice. When the day finally arrived, people stayed in bed. Actually. Shops were closed. My sister didn't go to the bathroom, thinking that the urine would be black. Pregnant mothers hid to protect their fetuses. I went out, of course, but I was the only one in the street. Well, when my sis saw that it didn't kill me, she came out too. Just us two saw this marvelous 100 percent eclipse of the sun. Here, let me show you some pictures. Had you told me before I went that the culture was so superstitious, I wouldn't have believed it. Oh, incidentally, at the clinic for the next month, every ailment was linked in one way or another to the eclipse.

Questions for discussion

1. If you had been in this town, would you have gone outside to look at the eclipse?

2. Do you think that the visitor is justified in being critical of the town's attitudes and conduct regarding the eclipse?

3. Do you think that the local residents would have been justified in being critical of the visitor's attitudes and behavior?

4. By what criteria (or standards) might the town be judged? What is the source of those standards?

5. What historical and cultural factors have contributed to their current orientation? Does an understanding of such factors modify your own evaluation of them?

6. What are some of the obstacles in the way of their accepting a scientific viewpoint on such phenomena? Do those obstacles affect other aspects of their lives?

7. Can you find anything positive about their orientation to nature's mysteries? Explain.

8. Are any such attitudes and behaviors ever expressed within your own culture? In what kinds of situations?

9. Can you think of any limitations that a scientific worldview might impose upon people? Should the scientific worldview receive scrutiny?

10. In trying to make an appropriate response to one's host family and neighbors in such a situation, do you think it worthwhile to try talking about their orientation to eclipses and your own? Or should you just keep quiet and go your own way?

Money Manipulation

You've been concerned from the very first week that your behavior as an international guest be consistent with your own ethical standards and yet appropriate to your hosts' cultural ways. You've encountered some minor issues that puzzle you, but you get by. Now comes one for which you can find no ready answer.

Changing money

My host country has a serious financial problem related somehow to its unbalanced trading. Sorry, I can't explain it yet. But I do know that the government sets an official rate for exchanging my dollars for their money. It is illegal to change money on the streets at a different (more favorable) rate. People can be arrested, fined and imprisoned for this. Furthermore, the government says that a citizen may take only a set amount of money out of the country each year—a very small amount at that. Do you get the picture? So, here I am, a newcomer, not knowing what's going on, a tad anxious about money, and finding that even going to the bank to change money is nerve-wracking. Out of the blue, the brother of my host father stops by the house. He's a gentleman, educated, respected and respectful, a business executive, so on and so forth. His daughter—that would be my host cousin—will be studying in the States in two years. There's no way he can send out that amount of dollars to pay her tuition, so he's got a plan. Instead of my exchanging dollars at the bank, I should have my parents send that amount of dollars to his sister (a sister of my host father) who lives in Los Angeles. I am supposed to tell my host father's brother the amount sent, and he'll give me local currency at the official bank rate. Should I do it?

Questions for discussion

1. In your country would there be anything illegal in exchanging money in this way?

2. Do you think that this proposed arrangement for exchanging money violates the letter of your host country's laws? The spirit of the laws? Who might help you to answer those questions?

3. In your own habits, do you tend to follow the letter of the law? In what cases? On what occasions do you fudge a bit?

4. If you carry out the plan, who stands to gain from the deal? To lose? If a million residents of your host country did this kind of thing, who would be the losers?

5. What have you learned up to this point about the typical individual's orientation to law in your host country? Is law-keeping an ethical issue? Do people internalize laws? Is law-keeping or lawbreaking a private matter, or do people regulate each other's lives in regard to the law? Do people often try to get around laws? How?

6. Does your social and ethical obligation to your host family modify this situation? Do you owe it to them to negotiate with your host father's brother? What is the consequence to your family relationship if you say no?

7. Do the rules of the program of which you are a part give you any guidelines or restrictions in this regard?

8. What would be the consequences to you and your host family if due to some unexpected turn of events the arrangement were exposed?

9. If you agreed to do this, what would be your rationale? If you declined to do it, what would be your reasons? Which of these reasons would you state to them?

Language Idiot

In intercultural settings, a ready topic of conversation is language. No wonder: language affects survival, generates relationships, offers up opportunity, provides insight, and, not least, helps to define self-worth. What we think of ourselves and what others think of us is shaped by our ability to talk.

A case study may show the power of language to enhance and, conversely, to demean.

Rebecca, how I love/hate you

I could not have been more pleased when Bill informed me that I'd be living with a host family that is related to the host family Rebecca was assigned to. It meant I'd see Rebecca often and we might become friends. In any event, she'd be a companion during the time when we were adjusting to our families. I have always admired Rebecca from a distance. Although quiet, she had always impressed me, especially with her intelligence.

After six weeks, I can affirm Rebecca's intelligence and add that she is a whiz in learning German. Growl.

Here's my fate. Although I study diligently, listen to the tapes, and try to talk with my family, I'm not learning the language fast or well. Meanwhile Rebecca has been advanced to the first group. She hears it, she says it.

When our two host families get together, she has become the favored one. Questions are addressed to her. People actually turn their faces from me to her. They address me through her, as though I were deaf. And lately I have been able to see their nonverbal gestures having to do with my not knowing what's going on.

I'm a language idiot. I am terribly down on myself. It seems the harder I try, the worse I feel both about my inability to learn German and about my inferiority to Rebecca.

Questions for discussion

1. Through the evidence in the written account is it established that the storyteller is actually a slow language learner? What is the basis for her coming to that conclusion?

2. Is it likely that two people, any two people, would learn language at the same rate?

3. Do you think it unusual that the hosts would tend to give attention to the faster language learner? Name some other ways that people express preference when dealing with two rather similar individuals. What, for example, is the effect upon preference of a person's physical body, skills, educational level, sex, and race?

4. How might the storyteller reclaim her own sense of worth in areas of her life apart from learning language? Should she speak to her host family about her reactions to their preferential treatment of Rebecca?

5. Apart from her continued study and practice of the language, how might the storyteller handle her (temporary, we hope) discomfort?

6. Does this case study bring to your mind an instance in which you preferred one person over another? What effect do you, especially in retrospect, think it had?

7. What can the storyteller do to maintain a satisfactory pace of culture learning and cross-cultural adaptation despite her difficulties with language learning?

My Host Father

Here's a case study that gradually emerged in a journal. The writer valued his privacy and was guarded about discussing his personal affairs. He did not like to reveal his feelings to others. Instead, he wrote about his situation in his journal, returning to it many times. The case is presented as an unbroken whole with ellipses indicating the starting and stopping of entries in the journal.

Being male

     ...in contrast to my host mother's warm welcome, my father was distant tonight. He seemed to speak nothing but soldier-like commands. He told his children to carry my luggage to the room, told his wife to fix food. He even made his younger son get his pipe and tobacco for him.... He doesn't do a stitch in the house. She even puts his food on his plate.... Three out of four nights he's not around. Working, they say. He is apparently a rep for a company in office equipment and computers.... When he talks, I can't understand him, and although I ask him to slow down, he doesn't. He uses idioms and a way of talking quite different from my language teachers and even my host mother.... I'll not forget the day. He said he'd take me to a football (soccer) game. We began by bar hopping, where he was loud and obnoxious and I felt out of place. At bars we picked up his friends and eventually squeezed into the stadium

when the game was a quarter over and they were a quarter intoxi-
cated. In the stands, he and his friends became totally offensive.
Racial insults. Comments and whistles directed toward women. Most
of the stories these guys told were too fast for me to understand.
After the game we went somewhere and only after we were in the
house did I realize we were with prostitutes. He went into a room
with a woman and I remained in a sort of hallway. I didn't know
what to do. When he returned we drove home. He didn't say anything and neither did I. This morning at the house, he was again
the commander, but didn't seem to recognize me.... I have the impression that he thinks I am effeminate.... By this time I notice how
the atmosphere of the house changes when he is around. His children look up to him as a king. They obey him. But I would rather be
around my host mother and siblings than with him.... What kind of
male is he and what kind of male am I?

Questions for discussion

1. If the guest is accurate in his perceptions, what might be some of the
   cultural expectations placed upon the male? Which of the behaviors might
   be more idiosyncratic than cultural?

2. The account does not indicate that the guest noticed any evidence of the
   father physically abusing his family. Do you think that the family was
   psychologically hurt by him?

3. From the comments made by the guest, what do you suppose might be
   some of the cultural influences that color his own point of view? How
   might his own cultural makeup put him at a disadvantage in this new
   culture?

4. When looking across cultures, one's perceptions can be distorted. In what
   ways might the guest's perceptions be faulty, or at least incomplete?

5. Do you think that the guest should have confronted the host father about
   his outside-the-home conduct? Should the matter have been shared with
   anyone else?

6. There are cultural observers who'd claim that this picture of a man and his
   family is not atypical. What is your reaction?

7. Why do you suppose this material remained a private journal topic rather
   than a matter for group discussion? Do you think it wise to work through
   this kind of trauma privately? Would he have enhanced its value as a culture-learning experience by talking about it with others?

Dating and Sexual Relationships

What do you suppose are the recurring issues in counseling international students enrolled in colleges and universities in the United States? Thomas and Althen (1989) indicate that all of the following bring international students to the counselor's office:

- the initial adjustment to a new culture
- academic difficulties stemming from the novelty of the academic system
- the impact of developments back home, such as wars, radical changes in government, and economic difficulties
- social isolation, depression, paranoia
- financial difficulties
- anxiety brought on by fear of immigration authorities
- cross-cultural male-female relationships

The latter one was emphasized by a counselor who said recently that he had not yet found informational tools to help students in cross-cultural dating. "A person ends up in court accused of date rape," he said, "after a series of misread cultural cues."

The confusion about male-female relationships encountered by international students on American campuses has its counterpart when Americans travel abroad. Eager to make friends, Americans may discover they have given signals they never intended. And they learn, sometimes too late, that they have read signals incorrectly. Each culture has its own long-established (and very complex) ways of encouraging, facilitating, regulating, and punishing activities in dating and mating—ways often confounding to outsiders.

A program director, a male, offers the following step-by-step progression into a common male-female disaster experienced by an American female in a Mediterranean setting.

Twenty steps to disappointment

Step #1. By tradition, the Mediterranean female—not the male—rules a social relationship. She decides *whether*, *when*, and *where* to date, engage in sex, or get married. The man, by contrast, is a creature of the street, hunting, pursuing, and if allowed to do so, conquering. Despite the male's testimonials of victories, it is the female who rules through restraints and restrictions which reduce her vulnerability.

Step #2. The American woman doesn't understand this and has little motivation to want to comprehend it, especially in a day of liberation when she believes that she indeed is in control of herself and not in need of old-fashioned restraints. In the cross-cultural dating scene, this leaves her vulnerable but she doesn't know it.

Step #3. Thanks to films, TV, and magazines, the Mediterranean male thinks he knows all about the American female—that she is liberated from the traditions that limit Mediterranean females; that American females when they leave the house decide, without the permission of their elders, where they are going and how: by bus, taxi, or backpack; that they are expansive and impulsive, that they laugh freely, talk boldly, and choose what they want to drink. And, of course, he *knows* that they hop into bed without the moral hassles of the Mediterranean woman. (The American female, of course, would categorically reject the assertion that any Mediterranean male knows anything at all about her.)

Step #4. The American woman arrives in a Mediterranean country, perhaps leaving a boyfriend back home, perhaps never having dated, and not particularly anxious for a fling with a guitar-toting romantic crooner. She dislikes people trying to stereotype her or predict her social behavior.

Step #5. The Mediterranean male notes the arrival of a tall, light-haired, attractive American female.

Step #6. International living, to the American female's surprise, is more difficult than anyone had reported. How awkward to meet people, to talk across language barriers! And how disgustingly primitive, the actions of Mediterranean males on the street, who have no respect for women.

Step #7. Also to her surprise, the host family expects more of her than she had anticipated, including family rules about going out, rules about whom you go with, where you go, how you go, and when you get back. She hadn't expected to reenter childhood.

Step #8. But if the restrictions at first seem strange and not a little quaint, the American female remembers her resolve to fit into the cross-cultural setting. After all, the rules don't really affect her, so she doesn't resist.

Step #9. The Mediterranean male, finding the right time—on a bus maybe, or in a restaurant, at a dance, in the park, at the school—begins his move. Friendly. Modest. Genteel. The conversation moves quickly—his interest (like hers) in education; his struggle to surmount his past; his dreams; his ideals. And he tells her something she has perhaps not heard—that she is a beautiful woman.

Step #10. The American female is taken off guard by three things: (1) Here is a handsome, sensitive Mediterranean male who is different, not a macho; (2) he respects her; and (3) she had not been conscious of being "beautiful." American males had never told her that, at least as simply and romantically as this person had.

Step #11. The Mediterranean male invites further contact, asks when they can again meet.

Step #12. When her host family says they don't know this man whom she met on the street and don't approve of her seeing him again, the house rules metamorphose (in the female's opinion) from outdated idiosyncrasy to unjust restriction.

Step #13. The American female knows her own strengths, knows what she can and can't handle, and trusts her judgment. She secretly breaks the house rules and meets the male again.

Steps #14. The conversational and behavioral details of the subsequent meetings need not be specified here. However, some elements may be described: (1) the American female proceeds to play a role to which she is culturally accustomed, characterized by appreciation, trust, and candor and (2) to the Mediterranean male, her behavior has practically no convergence with that of the local women who know what his intentions are and how to parry them. Instead the American's behavior, from his culturally determined perspective, gives him the right to conquer.

Step #15. The relationship becomes intense quickly and then sexually intimate. Most of the American female's energies are now redirected toward this relationship, with the subsequent slacking off of attention to previous cross-cultural activities and commitments. Love is a many-splendored thing, even across cultures.

Step #16. At the moment when the American female chooses to say the word "no," that verbal declination is easily nullified in the mind of the Mediterranean male by the many times he saw a nonverbal "yes," so he continues his conquest. An emotionally entangling affair follows.

Step #17. The ecstasy of the cross-cultural affair is gradually or abruptly threatened. It may have to do with the female's disquiet that he is secretive about his family. She might be annoyed by his single-minded interest in sex. He may miss appointments or create one too many excuses. She might overhear gossip about him and learn that he is married or in some other way compromised.

Step #18. Anxious or horrified, she tries to talk things out with him, but her language is not as strong as his reassurances. Talking accomplishes nothing. People who might have been consultants to her at an earlier stage are now not available because they will have nothing to do with the affair. She struggles alone.

Step #19. Sooner or later the American female recognizes that the relationship cannot endure and that her deep emotional investment will be lost.

Step # 20. Back in her home community, the American female says to herself, "How could I have been so stupid...?"

(memo from a program director)

Questions for discussion

1. Do you think that the program director who supplied this case study knows what he is talking about? Does he understand cultures? Does he represent fairly the two cultures in the case study, especially the Mediterranean culture?

2. Does he fairly represent males and females? Do you think a female program director would say the same thing in the same way?

3. What is the nature of the social function performed by the host family in this case? What does their opinion imply about their culture's understanding of individual decision versus communal decision? What does their approach to dating imply about their culture's understanding of personal standards versus external guardianships?

4. What are some benefits to the student in first talking with her family before making a social appointment? What are some things the family might wish to tell her about the man, if she truly wants their counsel? What are some inconveniences to the guest in clearing her social agenda with her host family? In this cultural setting, if the international guest on her own makes arrangements to see the stranger, what might be some unintended messages communicated to the family?

5. Do American families fulfill that same social function? How does decision making in your hometown compare with that in this case study? If you were assigned to live in this town, how would you deal with this family-oriented procedure for making a social calendar?

6. Do you tend to criticize the male's role in this cross-cultural dating relationship?

7. Do you tend to criticize the female's role in this relationship?

8. Can the female be justified in expecting males in the country to take her verbal "no" to mean no? Is a male justified in "getting" what he can get?

9. Do you suppose that the "shipboard-romance syndrome" does in fact influence people during travel and study abroad? What makes a term abroad especially suitable or unsuitable for pursuing romantic relationships? For behaving in ways one did not at home?

10. What do you imagine to be factors not mentioned in this case that would complicate short-term cross-cultural sexual relationships?

11. A director once said that any cross-cultural dating by members of her program was an issue that justified her intrusive participation. What do you think of her opinion?

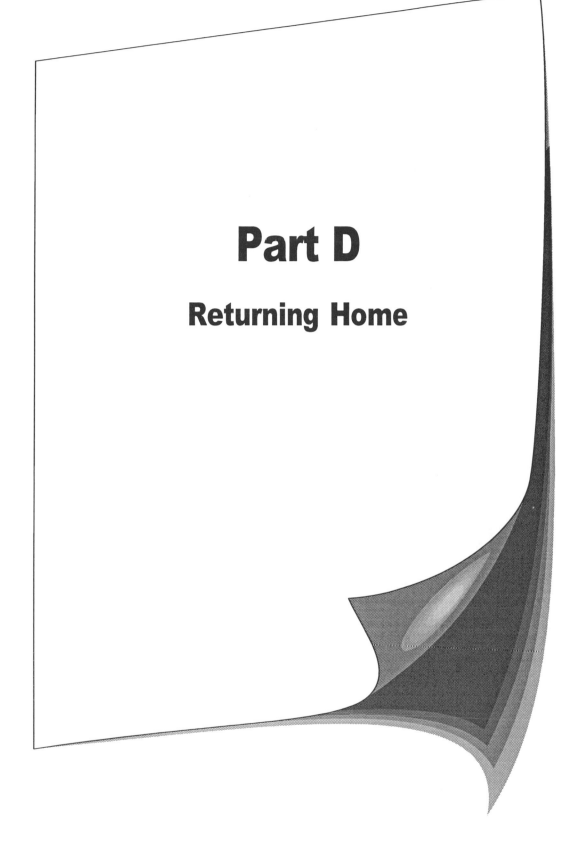

Part D

Returning Home

Introduction

An experienced traveler, actually an ethnomusicologist who has searched the nooks and crannies of the earth for indigenous music and musical instruments and who has made it her career to sojourn among strangers in order to learn their music in context, once admitted that the most difficult part of her travels was the first six months after each return home.

This admission is not new or unusual. The most famous traveler in the history of the Western world, Odysseus, is shown in Tennyson's "Ulysses" to be home at last on his island of Ithaca with his beloved wife and son. But instead of reigning happily ever after, he is restless, gazing across the waters and longing for new adventures.

Many homecomers—a month or two later—can identify with Odysseus and the ethnomusicologist. Ruth Gunden, an international program director, summarized the situation as follows:

> Although most of us expect some difficulty in adjusting to life in an unfamiliar culture overseas, few of us assume that we will encounter adjustment problems coming home. Consequently we are inadequately prepared when we come back to handle the effects of the many changes that have occurred within us and at home. (Hockman 1989, 5)

The trauma of returning home has become, for some countries, a political issue. Youth go abroad to study and then after four years in the foreign land, decide not to come back. The consequence for the original country is a loss of its future leaders—the so-called brain drain.

For most, however, the issue is reverse culture shock, a subject scholars and theorists have studied but about which the research is still skimpy. Recall in chapter 1 (see pp. 4-5) our noting that the U-curve theory of cross-cultural adaptation had evolved into the W-curve theory to describe the fact that the person returning home goes through an adaptation process or culture shock similar to that experienced by the person going abroad.

It is a pretty good strategy, then, for the returning traveler to review the sections of this book devoted to culture shock, particularly Guides 24 and 25. In fact, most of Part B, section V is appropriate for reentry. The returnee can find freedom from the frustrations of returning home by naming the cucarachas (Guide 20), identifying the things about one's own culture which are now bothersome. He or she can continue action-reflection-response learning by making instructive modules out of the critical events that occur after having set foot on native soil (Guide 21). In identifying the isms of one's own people that now seem to loom large, the returnee can look afresh at the cultural landscape and come to new recognition of the cultural bedrock (Guide 22). The homecomer, who is out of sync and out of place, may now benefit from thinking through the time and space issues that weren't a problem originally, but now, after having adjusted to a different pace and a different sense of space, take on new significance (Guide 23).

Here in Part D, we offer three guides having to do with reentry. The first one is a case study of a sojourner who has developed a new attitude toward his home. We include it in order to emphasize that sojourners seldom return home in a neutral or impartial frame of mind. Just as they carry cultural baggage with them when they leave, so they carry a different set of baggage when they return. Often they don't realize how consequential are the new perspectives, attitudes, opinions, and lifestyles that they have adopted during the sojourn. Guide 52 features one particular attitude. As you work through this case study you might begin to identify other attitudes that would affect a homecoming.

Guide 53 presents testimonials from returnees. You will sense immediately that the words come out of deeply felt emotion. Be aware of the issues that give rise to such feelings, the struggles that are being faced, and the ways of dealing with them that have been found.

In the final guide, you are invited to continue your culture learning, but the context is now different. The same attitudes and skills which help you to be a culture learner in a new culture can be applied at home. Will you be, can you be, as diligent a culture learner at home as you were abroad?

My Fellow Americans

It happens often. When a sojourner comes to know a culture quite well and has adapted to the point of identifying with its people and integrating into their ways of living, he or she may experience a new array of feelings about home and country. In culture-shock theory its extreme form is called "going native" and is manifest in as thorough an imitation and adoption of the host culture's behaviors and attitudes as possible, accompanied by a denigration of those of the home country, praise for everything about the host culture, and condemnation of everything about one's own culture. (The opposite is the "fight" syndrome in which the home culture is seen as ideal while everything about the host culture is seen as wrong.)

Here is a case of going native. It involves an American who turns negative about his homeland.

To be or not to be a (proud) American

Steven went to Southeast Asia with no specific goal in mind other than to take a break from college. At the time he considered himself rather typical of American youth, except that he was restless and wanted to see the world. He chose Jakarta because a family friend lived there and knew of a community center where Steven could possibly teach English.

Now, three years later, Steven lives in Bangkok, Thailand, having resided in two other countries (Indonesia and the Philippines), and has worked in a variety of enjoyable jobs (usually related to language study). Simply put, he loves Southeast Asia.

245

Steven is well-read, studies language diligently, and moves in a circle of internationals that he himself labels "the politically disenchanted." "A good time" for him means sitting with friends at a street bar and chatting the evening away.

But when you listen to Steven, you hear quite a lot of snarling about the United States. It's a general loss of affection, but expressed in specific grievances—the U.S. involvement in the Cambodian political realignments, Philip Morris marketing cigarettes overseas, the U.S. military presence, the foreign businessmen who patronize the infamous prostitution centers and the tourists who ride the elephants, the American researchers who come with their questionnaires, the American-made films that dominate the marquees, the bias of the American weekly news magazines, and on and on. He has on occasion said that when he sees Americans on the streets of Bangkok, he flees, not wanting to be associated with the United States.

Steven doesn't think of himself as being a negative or cynical person. Just the opposite. People like to be around him because he is good-natured and even funny. But thoughts of America depress him. When asked how he will readjust in the States, he says that he has no desire nor plans to return.

Questions for discussion

1. Can you identify with Steven or does his disaffection turn you off? Explain why you are distant from or close to his current state of mind. Do your own feelings tilt toward the negative or the positive when thinking about home? Is that tilt moderate or extreme?

2. Have you ever in your international sojourning had negative feelings toward the United States? About what? Be as specific as you can in naming them.

3. Although you may be unfamiliar with Southeast Asia, what do you suppose might be local situations or customs that are so attractive that they come to be a measure for judging one's own culture? Have you, in your sojourning, found cultural elements that show up the weaknesses of your own culture? What are those elements? Why do they attract you?

4. Do you think Steven is just in a stage of culture shock? If he remains at this point of acculturation, what will be the long-range consequences for him? If he changes, what do you think will be the next stage in his development?

5. For a moment, put yourself into the mindset of the natives of Bangkok. How do you suppose they see Steven? To what extent is Steven seen as an American? Does Steven's own distancing himself from fellow Americans make any difference in how they see him?

6. Let us suppose that you live near Steven and occasionally spend an evening chatting with him. How are you going to respond to his criticisms of the United States? To his general negative attitude about home? Do you want to give him any advice? Is there any culture learning that Steven has yet to address? If so, what kind?

7. Have you ever been in the presence of someone from another country who has turned negative about his or her home? Have you known international students, for example, who do everything they possibly can, legally or illegally, to avoid returning to their homeland? What is your reaction to these situations? What do you think is an ideal accommodation to both one's new and old cultures?

8. Respond—agree, disagree, elaborate, illustrate—this comment by Sondra Thiederman in a book written for managers in the multicultural workplace (1991):

   As important as it is to become conscious of your culture and aware of your own cultural point of view, this does not mean that you are expected to change that culture radically or discard it. It is all right to like and value your own ways, and, in fact, studies have shown that appreciating one's own values and way of life does not make a person any more likely to be critical of other cultures.

   Managers need to be reassured that although they are being called upon to make adjustments and compromises in their interactions with culturally different workers, they are not being asked to change their essential personalities and cultural perspectives." (1991, 32-33)

9. How might Steven's present state of mind affect his return home?

Reentry Experiences

Cynthia Hockman left her American college campus to spend time overseas study-ing and volunteering. Upon her return she went through reentry shock, an experi-ence that was, at first, somewhat private. But she got to thinking about it and decided to talk with other returnees. What she discovered was the material for a chapbook, later published by Pinchpenny Press, entitled *Returning Home* (1989). The book is a type of open-microphone in which students tell of their experiences and feelings upon reentry.

We have adapted several of the statements for this guide. Although the testi-monials might surprise and even astonish you (does a returnee *really* feel that way?), tuck them in a corner of your memory. Upon your own return you may wish to recall some of the statements that express your own feelings.

Returnees remember

Immediate and initial shock: I hated coming back. The first day—getting into Chicago—I didn't even want to be there. I got into the van and I was yelling at the driver to slow down because I thought he was driving too fast. Everything seemed to be flying by. The driver stopped at a Burger King or something and I didn't feel like going in at all.

Things have changed: I was struck by how many things had happened that I didn't know about. I was almost mad in a way—like, "Why didn't you guys tell me?"

Nobody understands: I was angry with my parents and with everybody for not understanding why I was depressed. I just cried at the drop of a hat, and they didn't understand, but I didn't know how to explain to them. They were tired of listening to all my stories. (And I could never make the stories sound the way they really were!) It was frustrating.

I'm homesick...but I'm home: I cried and cried on the plane and on the bus.... I didn't want to come back, and so when I saw my parents, it was nice meeting them, but my mind was still back in my host country.... After a certain point my parents and friends didn't want to hear about it anymore, and I had absolutely no one to talk to.

Some people are so naive: Many people view China as Red China, ideology China, but when I think of China, I think of my students. It makes me mad when people say stuff like, "You couldn't go many places, could you?" or "The KGB watched you, didn't they?" The KGB? This is China, not the Soviet Union.

Am I happy to be an American: Once I got to the U.S., I was repulsed. The grocery store scene was the worst. I walked in and counted over a hundred different kinds of pop and more than that many kinds of breakfast cereal. It made me sick because it just isn't necessary. I was amazed at how much excess we have and how I had never even thought of it as excess.

Life at home bores me: I was sitting around one day after I got home. It was a cold December day. I think it was drizzling. I was so tired of lying around. My overseas travels were such a big adventure and all of a sudden I had no stimulus whatsoever. I had nothing to look forward to except going back to school. I remember getting up, putting on some sweats, and just running. All of a sudden I realized that this was cathartic and I ran as fast as I could—ran and ran and ran.

Why do I feel like this: Part of reentry shock is feeling guilty about my overseas experience—feeling like mine wasn't as good as other people's—and maybe I didn't like it as much as I should have—and maybe I didn't have the best attitude all the time—and feeling like somehow I failed.

Dealing with culture shock, round two

Let's reintroduce Guides 24 and 25 as we think further about those testimonials. Review the *stages* of culture shock. At what likely stage were the students when they *reported* on their feelings? When they *experienced* their feelings?

On the basis of the accounts above, list some of the *symptoms* of reentry shock. How are they similar and different from culture shock?

What do you suppose are the *causes* of reentry shock? Name some situational factors (the home scene), niche factors (not being able to find where you fit in), activity factors (not being engaged yet in significant activities), and self-concept factors (not being able to figure out who you are).

Guide 24 claims that "culture shock is not all bad." Hockman echoes that sentiment: "Many of the uncomfortable feelings associated with return have helped me to expand my world, making me more keenly aware of other cultures. I have

249

learned to be more grateful. The shock I felt when I returned to the United States has helped teach me the value of living not only for myself but for others as well" (39).

Hockman closes her chapbook with specific suggestions for coping with reentry. They're yours for future use:

1. Expect things to be different.

2. Continue to write in your journal.

3. Talk with others who've been overseas and have gone through reentry shock.

4. Talk with a counselor to help you sort through your feelings.

5. Cook a typical meal of your host culture for family or friends.

6. Read the international press.

7. Recognize and get to know people in your home community who are newcomers from overseas. Help them in their adjustment to the United States.

8. Take a course at the local university in international literature, politics, development, art, or ecology.

9. Form or join a discussion group.

What suggestions do you wish to add to Hockman's list? For example, you may wish to include something about keeping in contact with friends in the host culture, preparing an informative photo or journalistic report of the experience to be shared at home, or addressing social and political issues that your international experience has highlighted for you. The next guide expands on yet another antidote for reentry shock—continuing your culture learning at home.

Culture Learning at Home

Having become an active culture learner abroad, you should have developed attitudes and skills which will enable you to be a better culture learner at home. Strangers are in your midst in the United States. Some have just arrived, others have been here for generations. You may take them for granted until circumstances, such as living abroad, turn you into a stranger too and increase your capacity to see them, to reach out to them, and to try to learn who they are.

In addition to being better equipped for culture learning at home, you also are more qualified to assess and react to the issues currently revolving around cultural pluralism in American society. From its beginning the United States has been perceived as an intersection of cultures. This idea, articulated early on by Alexis de Tocqueville in *Democracy in America*, evolved into the melting pot concept. In more recent decades, however, the focus has shifted from the image of a melting pot to that of a cultural "salad." A new emphasis is placed on "unmeltable ethnics" and on the United States as a society of diverse cultures joined together in a cultural mosaic. The issue has come to the fore in the controversy which has swirled around the concept of multiculturalism in the school curriculum. *Time* magazine devoted a cover story to this debate on July 8, 1991. We lift a variety of opinions from the story and invite you—and hopefully a discussion group that you may be a part of—to read and respond to them from the cross-cultural perspectives you have developed as a result of your experience. Who are we? What do you want us to be? Or to put it in *Time*'s words, "Do Americans still have faith in the vision of their country as a cradle of individual rights and liberties, or must

251

they relinquish the teaching of some of these freedoms to further the goals of the ethnic and social groups to which they belong? What kind of people do Americans now think they are, and what will they tell their children about that?"

The initial paragraphs come from *Time* staff writers. Later paragraphs are labeled by author.

From "Who Are We?" *Time* magazine, July 8, 1991

All 56 of the signatories [of the Declaration of Independence] were white males of European descent, most of them wealthy property holders. Like some of his co-revolutionaries, Thomas Jefferson... owned slaves.

It is now fairly commonplace to learn American history in the context of who has oppressed, excluded or otherwise mistreated whom.

Gone, or going fast, is the concept of the melting pot, of the U.S. as the paramount place in the world where people came to shed their past in order to forge their future. Instead there is a new paradigm that emphasizes the racial and ethnic diversity of American citizens, of the many cultures that have converged here, each valuable in its own right and deserving of study and respect.

Ultimately, multicultural thinking, for all its nods toward pluralism and diversity, can lead to several regressive orthodoxies. One is the notion that truth is forever encapsulated within collective identities, that what white males or females or blacks or Hispanics or Asians know about their experiences can be communicated only imperfectly to people beyond their pales.

There is no guarantee that the nation's long test of trying to live together will not end in fragmentation and collapse, with groups gathered around the firelight, waiting for the attack at dawn.

(*Time* staff writers)

Hey, hey, ho, ho, Western Culture's got to go!

(a student demonstration)

African-Americans, Asian-Americans, Puerto Rican/Latinos and Native Americans have all been the victims of an intellectual and educational oppression that has characterized the culture and institutions of the United States and the European American world for centuries.

(Task Force on Minorities, commissioned by New York State Education Commissioner Thomas Sobol)

It is politically and intellectually unwise for us to attack the traditions, customs and values which attracted immigrants to these shores in the first place.

(Kenneth T. Jackson, Columbia University)

The primary reason youngsters need to study multiple cultures is to learn how to develop multiple perspectives.

(Edmund Gordon, Yale University)

In a complex society, there are many different elements, and we should view this as a unique opportunity to build the strength of the whole.

(Chang-Lin Tien, UC-Berkeley)

Unity is the completed puzzle, diversity the pieces of the puzzle. And until we recognize every piece, we cannot have true unity.

(Antonia Hernandez, Mexican-American Legal Defense Fund)

The top priority should be to equip children for life in the modern world, to preserve and expand the unity America needs to function better, for the sake of all, and to avoid the destructive effects of intellectual tribalism.

(Henry Grunwald, Time, Inc.)

History should not teach a kind of uniform identity or a communality of American culture. So much of American history really does involve struggle and conflict and different groups trying to come to terms with one another.

(Clara Sue Kidwell, UC-Berkeley)

What we have in common...is a splendid continent...a history of a network of relations...unpleasant as well as pleasant memories...the Constitution and Bill of Rights...a future.... And we have denim jeans. That's a shared loyalty, from the Indians to the yuppies.

(Patricia Limerick, U of Colorado at Boulder)

One of the proudest things we have in our tradition is pluralism.

(Garry Wills, historian and author)

To break it down into what the Hungarians contributed, what the Russians contributed, the English, Irish and Germans contributed, I'm not sure that's a good idea. Are you willing to dilute the pure stream of history in order to investigate all the creeks that run into it?

(Shelby Foote, Civil War historian)

My impression is that the historic forces driving toward one people have not lost their power. The eruption of ethnicity is, I believe, a rather superficial enthusiasm stirred by romantic ideologues on the one hand and by unscrupulous con men on the other: self-appointed spokesmen whose claim to represent their minority groups is carelessly accepted by the media.

(Arthur Schlesinger Jr., author)

Your culture-learning agenda

In your journal draw up your cultural self-portrait. Describe your filiation—your cultural identity by birth, your family's cultural origins. List your affiliations—your cultural identity by choice, your group associations. Describe the cultural scene you grew up in. Describe those cultural identifications. Indicate by name and description some of the groups that you knew about during your teenage years, but separated yourself from at the time. What were some of the stereotypes you held of these groups? What were the origins of the stereotypes? At what moments of your life have you been most ethnocentric?

Now that you have been away from home and immersed in another culture and have moved on the culture-learning continuum from ethnocentrism toward ethnorelativism, what do you think of the melting pot concept ("The point of America was not to preserve old cultures but to forge a new, American culture" *Time*, 12) and the contrasting theory of multiculturalism in which diverse identities, languages, and customs are accommodated, accepted, valued, and, indeed, desired within a larger cultural mosaic?

Do you think that the people of the United States really do have "values, characteristics, and traditions which we share in common" (*Time*, 14)? Do you think that a Eurocentric bias discriminates against those from other traditions (*Time*, 16)? What is your opinion about history textbooks that no longer honor "the American gallery of national icons" but rather describe an "American history in the context of who has oppressed, excluded or otherwise mistreated whom" (*Time*, 13) or, conversely, enable students to value more consciously the contribution to the American tradition of people who have come from cultural backgrounds different from those of Western Europe?

As you think of returning home and of again becoming a part of the larger American cultural milieu and a participant in specific cultural groupings, what is your agenda for culture learning? What is your agenda for the group with which you identify most strongly? What new groups would you like to join? Which ethnic communities would you like to learn more about? Do you have any stereotypes that need revision? What are some prejudices you wish to eliminate? What are some cultural commonalities you want to advocate and strengthen?

Bibliography

Bibliography

Achebe, Chinua. *Things Fall Apart.* London: Heinemann, 1958; New York: Fawcett, 1969.

————. Adler, Peter. "Beyond Cultural Identity: Reflections upon Cultural and Multicultural Man." In R. Brislin, (Ed.). *Culture Learning: Concepts, Applications, and Research,* Honolulu: University of Hawaii Press, 1977.

————. "The Transnational Experience: An Alternative View of Culture Shock." *Journal of Humanistic Psychology,* 15, no. 4 (1975): 13-23.

————. "The Boundary Experience—Studies in Human Transformation." Ph.D. diss., Union for Experimenting Colleges and Universities, 1974.

Althen, Gary. *American Ways: A Guide for Foreigners in the United States.* Yarmouth, ME: Intercultural Press, 1988.

Andersen, Peter. "Explaining Intercultural Differences in Nonverbal Communication." In Samovar and Porter, (Eds.). *Intercultural Communication: A Reader,* (6th ed.), Belmont, CA: Wadsworth, 1991.

Argyle, Michael. "Intercultural Communication." In Stephen Bochner, (Ed.). *Cultures in Contact: Studies in Cross-Cultural Interaction,* New York: Pergamon Press, 1982.

Asante, Molefi Kete, William B. Gudykunst, with Eileen Newmark, (Eds.). *Handbook of International and Intercultural Communication.* Newbury Park, CA: Sage, 1989.

Bagdikian, Ben H. *The Media Monopoly,* (3d ed.). Boston: Beacon Press, 1990.

Barnlund, Dean C. "Communication in a Global Village." In Samovar and Porter, (Eds.). *Intercultural Communication: A Reader,* (6th ed.), Belmont, CA: Wadsworth, 1991.

———. *Communicative Styles of Japanese and Americans.* Belmont, CA: Wadsworth, 1989.

———. "The Cross-Cultural Arena: An Ethical Void." In N. Asuncion-Lande, (Ed.). *Ethical Perspectives and Critical Issues in Intercultural Communication,* Annandale, VA: Speech Communication Association, 1980.

———. *Public and Private Self in Japan and the United States.* Yarmouth, ME: Intercultural Press, 1989.

Barnsley, John H. *The Social Reality of Ethics: The Comparative Analysis of Moral Codes.* Boston: Routledge and Kegan Paul, 1972.

Basics and Tools: A Collection of Popular Education Resources and Activities. Ottawa: CUSO Education Department, 1988.

Bellah, Robert N., et al. *Habits of the Heart: Individualism and Commitment in American Life.* New York: Harper & Row, 1985.

Bender, David. *American Values, Opposing Viewpoints.* San Diego, CA: Greenhaven Press, 1989.

Bennett, Milton J. "A Developmental Approach to Training for Intercultural Sensitivity." *International Journal of Intercultural Relations,* 10, no. 2 (1986): 179-96.

———. "Overcoming the Golden Rule: Sympathy and Empathy." In D. Nimmo, (Ed.). *Communication Yearbook 3,* Philadelphia: International Communication Association, 1979.

———. "Towards Ethnorelativism: A Developmental Model of Intercultural Sensitivity." In R. M. Paige, (Ed.). *Education for the Intercultural Experience,* Yarmouth, ME: Intercultural Press, 1993.

Berger, Arthur Asa. *Signs in Contemporary Culture: An Introduction to Semiotics.* New York: Longman, 1989.

Bhawuk, D. P. S. "Cross-Cultural Orientation Programs." In R. Brislin, (Ed.). *Applied Cross-Cultural Psychology,* Newbury Park, CA: Sage, 1990.

Bochner, Stephen, (Ed.). *Cultures in Contact: Studies in Cross-Cultural Interaction.* New York: Pergamon Press, 1982.

———. *The Mediating Person: Bridges between Cultures.* Cambridge, MA: Schenkman Publishing, 1981.

Boucher, Jerry, Dan Landis, and Karen Arnold Clark. *Ethnic Conflict: International Perspectives.* Newbury Park, CA: Sage, 1987.

Boulding, Elise. *Building a Global Civic Culture: Education for an Interdependent World.* New York: Teachers College Press, 1988.

Brislin, Richard W. *Cross-Cultural Encounters: Face-to-Face Interaction.* New York: Pergamon Press, 1981.

————. *Culture Learning: Concepts, Applications, and Research.* Honolulu: East-West Center, East-West Culture Learning Institute, 1977.

Brislin, Richard W., et al. *Intercultural Interactions: A Practical Guide.* Beverly Hills, CA: Sage, 1986.

Brislin, Richard W., (Ed.). *Applied Cross-Cultural Psychology.* Newbury Park, CA: Sage, 1990.

Broome, Benjamin J. "Building Shared Meaning: Implications of a Relational Approach to Empathy for Teaching Intercultural Communications." *Communication Education,* 40 (July 1991): 235-49.

Campbell, Joseph. Phil Cousineau, (Ed.). *The Hero's Journey: Joseph Campbell on His Life and Work.* San Francisco: Harper & Row, 1990.

————. *In All Her Names: Four Explorations of the Feminine Divinity.* San Francisco: Harper, 1991.

Campbell, Joseph, with Bill Moyers. Betty Sue Flowers, (Ed.). *The Power of Myth.* New York: Doubleday, 1988.

Carroll, Raymonde. *Cultural Misunderstandings: The French/American Experience.* Chicago: University of Chicago Press, 1988.

Casse, Pierre. *Training for the Cross-Cultural Mind: A Handbook for Cross-Cultural Trainers and Consultants,* (2d ed.). Washington: Society for Intercultural Education, Training, and Research, 1981. (Out of print. Revised edition forthcoming from Intercultural Press.)

Chomsky, Noam. *Language and Mind.* New York: Harcourt Brace Jovanovich, 1972.

Cohen, David. *A Day in the Life of China.* San Francisco: Collins, 1989. (Part of a series with additional titles on Ireland, Italy, Japan, Spain, and Soviet Union with Rick Smolan as co-editor.)

Condon, John C. *Good Neighbors: Communicating with the Mexicans.* Yarmouth, ME: Intercultural Press, 1985.

————. *With Respect to the Japanese: A Guide for Americans.* Yarmouth, ME: Intercultural Press, 1984.

Condon, John C., and Fathi S. Yousef. *An Introduction to Intercultural Communication.* Indianapolis: Bobbs-Merrill, 1983.

Crossing Borders, Challenging Boundaries. Minneapolis: Augsburg College, 1988.

Cruz, Nadine. "A Challenge to the Notion of Service." *Experiential Education,* 14, no.5 (November-December 1989): 23.

Dodd, Carley H. *Dynamics of Intercultural Communication,* (2nd ed.). Dubuque, IA: W. C. Brown, 1987.

Eby, Kermit. "Let Your Yea Be Yea." *The Christian Century,* 72 (Sept. 14, 1955): 1055-57.

Ericson, Edward L. *The American Dream Renewed: The Making of a World People.* New York: Continuum, 1991.

Faulkner, William. "The Bear." In *Three Famous Short Novels,* New York: Vintage, 1961.

Fieg, John Paul, revised by Elizabeth Mortlock. *A Common Core: Thais and Americans.* Yarmouth ME: Intercultural Press, 1989.

Fike, Doug. *The Rising Tide: Essays for the Traveler.* Goshen, IN: Pinchpenny Press, 1981.

Forster, E. M. *A Passage to India.* New York: Grosset and Dunlap, 1924.

Frideres, James S., (Ed.). *Multiculturalism and Intergroup Relations.* New York: Greenwood Press, 1989.

Frost, Robert. "Education by Poetry: A Meditative Monologue." An address given at Amherst College, 1930. In *The Norton Reader: An Anthology of Expository Prose,* New York: Norton, 1973.

Furnham, Adrian, and Stephen Bochner. *Culture Shock: Psychological Reactions to Unfamiliar Environments.* London: Routledge, 1989.

Furtaw, Julia C., (Ed.). *The Video Source Book,* (15th ed.). Detroit: Gale, 1994.

Gelernter, Carey Quan. "Observations about people like you." *The News and Observer,* Raleigh, NC (August 4, 1991): 4E.

Gochenour, Theodore. *Considering Filipinos.* Yarmouth, ME: Intercultural Press, 1990.

Greene, Theodore Meyer, (Ed.). *Kant Selections.* New York: Charles Scribner, 1929.

Grove, Cornelius L. *Orientation Handbook for Youth Exchange Programs.* Yarmouth, ME: Intercultural Press, 1989.

Grove, Cornelius L., and Ingemar Torbiörn. "A New Conceptualization of Intercultural Adjustment and the Goals of Training." In R. M. Paige (Ed.). *Education for the Intercultural Experience,* Yarmouth ME: Intercultural Press, 1993.

Gudykunst, William B., and Young Yun Kim. *Communicating with Strangers: An Approach to Intercultural Communication.* Reading, MA: Addison-Wesley, 1984a.

———. *Methods for Intercultural Communication Research.* Beverly Hills, CA: Sage, 1984b.

Gudykunst, William B., and Stella Ting-Toomey, with Elizabeth Chua. *Culture and Interpersonal Communication.* Newbury Park, CA: Sage, 1988.

Gudykunst, William B., Lea P. Stewart, and Stella Ting-Toomey, (Eds.). *Communication, Culture, and Organizational Processes.* Newbury Park, CA: Sage, 1985.

Gullahorn, John Taylor, and Jeanne E. Gullahorn. "Extension of the U-Curve Hypothesis." *Journal of Social Issues,* 19 (July 1963): 33-47.

Haglund, Elaine. "Japan: Cultural Considerations." *International Journal of Intercultural Relations,* 8 (1984): 61-76.

Hall, Edward T. *Beyond Culture.* Garden City, NY: Doubleday, 1976.

———. *The Dance of Life: The Other Dimension of Time.* Garden City, NY: Doubleday, 1983.

———. *The Hidden Dimension.* Garden City, NY: Doubleday, 1966.

———. *The Silent Language.* Garden City, NY: Doubleday, 1981.

Hall, Edward T., and Mildred Reed Hall. *Hidden Differences: Doing Business with the Japanese.* Garden City, NY: Doubleday, 1987.

———. *Understanding Cultural Differences: Germans, French and Americans.* Yarmouth, ME: Intercultural Press, 1990.

Hamilton, Edith. *The Greek Way.* New York: W. W. Norton, 1971.

Hardin, Garrett J. "The Tragedy of the Commons." *Science,* 162 (1968): 1243-48.

Harrison, Lawrence E. *Underdevelopment Is a State of Mind: The Latin American Case.* Cambridge: Harvard University and Lanham, MD: University Press of America, 1985.

Hatch, Elvin. *Culture and Morality: The Relativity of Values in Anthropology.* New York: Columbia University Press, 1983.

Hecht, Michael L., Peter A. Andersen, and Sidney A. Ribeau. "The Cultural Dimensions of Nonverbal Communication." In Asante and Gudykunst, with Newmark, (Eds.). *Handbook of International and Intercultural Communication,* Newbury Park, CA: Sage, 1989.

Herskovits, Melville J. *Cultural Relativism: Perspectives in Cultural Pluralism.* New York: Vintage Books, 1972.

Hess, J. Daniel. *From the Other's Point of View: Perspectives from North and South of the Rio Grande.* Scottdale, PA: Herald Press, 1980.

———. *Vignettes of Spain.* Goshen, IN: Pinchpenny Press, 1975.

Hiebert, Paul G. *Anthropological Insights for Missionaries.* Grand Rapids, MI: Baker Books, 1985.

Hockman, Cynthia. *Returning Home.* Goshen, IN: Pinchpenny Press, 1989.

Hofstede, Geert H. *Culture's Consequences: International Differences in Work-Related Values.* Beverly Hills, CA: Sage, 1984.

Hoopes, David S. "Intercultural Communication Concepts and the Psychology of Intercultural Experiences." In M. Pusch, (Ed.). *Multicultural Education: A Cross-Cultural Training Approach,* La Grange Park, IL: Intercultural Press, 1979.

Hoopes, David S., and Kathleen R. Hoopes. *Guide to International Education in the United States,* (2d ed.). Detroit: Gale Research, 1984.

Hope, Anne, and Sally Timmel. *Training for Transformation: A Handbook for Community Workers.* Gweru, Zimbabwe: Mambo Press, 1984.

Hostetler, Julie. Unpublished study journal, 1989.

Hu, Wenzhong, and Cornelius L. Grove. *Encountering the Chinese: A Guide for Americans.* Yarmouth, ME: Intercultural Press, 1991.

Jain, Nemi C. "World View and Cultural Patterns of India." In Samovar and Porter, (Eds.). *Intercultural Communication: A Reader,* (6th ed.), Belmont, CA: Wadsworth, 1991.

Josephson, Harold, (Ed.). *Biographical Dictionary of Modern Peace Leaders.* Westport, CT: Greenwood Press, 1985.

Kauffman, Norman L., Judith N. Martin, and Henry D. Weaver. *Students Abroad: Strangers at Home: Education for a Global Society.* Yarmouth, ME: Intercultural Press, 1992.

Kennedy, Gavin. *Doing Business Abroad.* New York: Simon and Schuster, 1985.

Kim, Young Yun. *Communication and Cross-Cultural Adaptation: An Integrative Theory.* Clevedon, England and Philadelphia: Multilingual Matters Ltd., 1988.

———. *Interethnic Communication: Current Research.* Newbury Park, CA: Sage, 1986.

———. "Intercultural Personhood: An Integration of Eastern and Western Perspectives." In Samovar and Porter, (Eds.). *Intercultural Communication: A Reader,* (6th ed.), Belmont, CA: Wadsworth, 1991.

Kim, Young Yun, and William B. Gudykunst, (Eds.). *Theories in Intercultural Communication.* Newbury Park, CA: Sage, 1988.

Kluckhohn, Florence R., and Fred L. Strodtbeck. *Variations in Value Orientations.* Evanston, IL: Row, Peterson and Company, 1961.

Kochman, Thomas. *Black and White Styles in Conflict.* Chicago: University of Chicago Press, 1981.

Kohls, L. Robert. *Survival Kit for Overseas Living: For Americans Planning to Live and Work Abroad,* (2d ed.). Yarmouth ME: Intercultural Press, 1984.

Kolakowski, Leszek. *The Presence of Myth.* Adam Czerniawski, tr. Chicago: University of Chicago Press, 1989.

Koller, John M. *The Indian Way.* New York: Macmillan, 1982.

Korzenny, Felipe, Stella Ting-Toomey, with Susan Douglas Ryan, (Eds.). *Communicating for Peace: Diplomacy and Negotiation.* Newbury Park, CA: Sage, 1990.

Kraybill, Janet, and Korla Miller. *Two Voices: A China Journal.* Goshen, IN: Pinchpenny Press, 1981.

Landis, Dan. *Ethnic Conflict: International Perspectives.* Newbury Park, CA: Sage, 1987.

Landis, Dan, and Judith N. Martin, (Eds.). Theories and Methods in Cross-Cultural Orientation (Special Issue). *International Journal of Intercultural Relations,* 10, no. 2, 1986.

Lanier, A. R. *Living in the U.S.A.,* (4th ed.). Yarmouth, ME: Intercultural Press, 1988.

Leed, Eric J. *The Mind of the Traveler: From Gilgamesh to Global Tourism.* New York: Basic Books, 1991.

Leininger, Bruce. Unpublished study journal, 1990.

Lewis, Tom J., and Robert E. Jungman. *On Being Foreign: Culture Shock in Short Fiction, An International Anthology.* Yarmouth, ME: Intercultural Press, 1986.

Loewen, Jacob A. *Culture and Human Values.* South Pasadena, CA: William Carey Library, 1975.

Luce, Louise Fiber, and Elise C. Smith, (Eds.). *Toward Internationalism: Readings in Cross-Cultural Communication.* Rowley, MA: Newbury House, 1987.

Lustig, Myron W. "Value Differences in Intercultural Communication." In Samovar and Porter, (Eds.). *Intercultural Communication: A Reader,* (5th ed.), Belmont, CA: Wadsworth, 1988.

Lynch, James. *Multicultural Education in a Global Society.* New York: Falmer Press, 1989.

Lysgaard, Sverre. "Adjustment in a Foreign Society: Norwegian Fulbright Grantees Visiting the United States." *International Social Science Bulletin,* 7 (1955): 45-51.

Marshall, Terry. *The Whole World Guide to Language Learning.* Yarmouth, ME: Intercultural Press, 1989.

Martin, L. John. "The Contradiction of Cross-Cultural Communication." In Fisher and Merrill, (Eds.). *International and Intercultural Communication,* New York: Hastings, 1976.

Martin, L. John, and Ray Eldon Hiebert, (Eds.). *Current Issues in International Communication.* New York: Longman, 1990.

McKay, Virginia. *Moving Abroad: A Guide to International Living.* Wilmington, DE: VLM Enterprises, 1990.

McLean, George F., and Olinto Pegoraro. *The Social Context and Values: Perspectives of the Americas.* Lanham, MD: University Press of America, 1989.

Mead, Margaret. *Coming of Age in Samoa.* New York: Morrow, 1971.

———. *Sex and Temperament in Three Primitive Societies.* New York: Morrow, 1963.

———. "Some Cultural Approaches to Communication Problems." In L. Bryson, (Ed.). *The Communication of Ideas,* New York: Institute for Religious and Social Studies, 1948.

Merrill, John C. *Global Journalism.* New York: Longman, 1991.

Moore, David. "Power and Experience: Critical Perspectives on Field-Based Learning" (a review of *Power and Criticism: Poststructural Investigations in Education* by Cleo Cherryholmes, New York: Teachers College Press, 1988). *Experiential Education* (May-June 1989): 11-12.

Morse, Richard M. *New World Soundings: Culture and Ideology in the Americas.* Baltimore: Johns Hopkins University Press, 1989.

Murdock, George P. "The Common Denominator of Cultures." In R. Linton, (Ed.). *The Science of Man in the World Crisis,* New York: Columbia University Press, 1945.

Nida, Eugene. *Understanding Latin Americans: With Special Reference to Religious Values and Movements.* South Pasadena, CA: William Carey Library, 1974.

Nydell, Margaret K. *Understanding Arabs: A Guide for Westerners.* Yarmouth ME: Intercultural Press, 1987.

Oberg, Kalvero. "Culture Shock." Originally presented to the Women's Club of Rio de Janeiro, Brazil, August 3, 1954. Later published as "Culture Shock: The Problem of Adjustment to New Cultural Environments." *Practical Anthropology,* 7 (1960): 177-82.

Paglia, Camille. *Sexual Personae: Art and Decadence from Nefertiti to Emily Dickinson.* New York: Vintage Books, 1990.

Paige, R. Michael, (Ed.). *Education for the Intercultural Experience.* Yarmouth, ME: Intercultural Press, 1993.

Paige, R. Michael. "International Students: Cross-Cultural Psychological Perspectives." In R. Brislin, (Ed.). *Applied Cross-Cultural Psychology,* Newbury Park, CA: Sage, 1990.

Pandey, Janak. "The Environment, Culture, and Behavior." In R. Brislin, (Ed.). *Applied Cross-Cultural Psychology,* Newbury Park, CA: Sage, 1990.

The Partnership for Service-Learning. *Sixth Annual International Conference Proceedings.* Phoenix, Arizona, February 24-26, 1989.

Ramsay, William R. "Service-Learning as a Life-Style." *Experiential Education* (January-February, 1992): 23-24.

Reddi, Usha. "Media and Culture in Indian Society: Conflict or Cooperation?" *Media, Culture and Society,* 11 (1989): 395-413.

Renwick, George W., revised by Reginald Smart and Don L. Henderson. *A Fair Go for All: Australian/American Interactions.* Yarmouth, ME: Intercultural Press, 1991.

Richardson, E. Allen. *Strangers in This Land: Pluralism and the Response to Diversity in the United States.* New York: Pilgrim Press, 1988.

Richmond, Virginia P., et al. *Nonverbal Behavior in Interpersonal Relations.* Englewood Cliffs, NJ: Prentice-Hall, 1987.

Rohrer, Felicia. Unpublished study journal, 1990.

Rokeach, Milton. *Beliefs, Attitudes and Values: A Theory of Organization and Change.* San Francisco: Jossey-Bass, 1968.

———. *The Great American Values Test: Influencing Behavior and Belief through Television.* London: Collier Macmillan, 1984.

———. *The Nature of Human Values.* New York: Free Press, 1973.

———. *The Open and Closed Mind: Investigations into the Nature of Belief Systems and Personality Systems.* New York: Basic Books, 1960.

Rolbein, Seth. *Nobel Costa Rica.* New York: St. Martin's Press, 1989.

Ruben, Brent D. "Human Communication and Cross-Cultural Effectiveness." *International and Intercultural Communication Annual,* 4 (December 1977): 98-105. Reprinted in Samovar and Porter, (Eds.). *Intercultural Communication: A Reader,* (5th ed.). Belmont, CA: Wadsworth, 1988.

Samovar, Larry A., and Richard E. Porter, (Eds.). *Intercultural Communication: A Reader,* (5th ed.). Belmont, CA: Wadsworth, 1988.

———. *Intercultural Communication: A Reader,* (6th ed.). Belmont, CA: Wadsworth, 1991. (Now 7th edition, published in 1993.)

Sarbaugh, Larry E. *Intercultural Communication.* New Brunswick, NJ: Transaction Books, 1988.

Sauder, Chris. Unpublished study journal, 1991.

Savage, Peter. *The Safe Travel Book: A Guide for the International Traveler.* Lexington, MA: Lexington Books, 1988.

Schiller, Herbert I. *Communication and Cultural Domination.* White Plains, NY: International Arts and Sciences Press, 1976.

Schlabach, Gerald. *And Who Is My Neighbor?* Scottdale, PA: Herald Press, 1990.

Schlabach, Joetta Handrich. *Extending the Table: A World Community Cookbook.* Scottdale, PA: Herald Press, 1991.

Schrag, Myles J. Unpublished study journal, 1991.

Schultz, Steven. "The Shadow Side of Service." *Experiential Education* (January-February, 1992): 19-20.

Showalter, Stuart W., (Ed.). *The Role of Service-Learning in International Education: Proceedings of a Wingspread Conference.* Goshen College, Goshen IN, 1989.

Shweder, Richard A. *Thinking through Cultures: Expeditions in Cultural Psychology.* Cambridge: Harvard University Press, 1991.

Sikkema, Mildred, and Agnes Niyekawa. *Design for Cross-Cultural Learning.* Yarmouth, ME: Intercultural Press, 1987.

Singer, Marshall R. *Intercultural Communication: A Perceptual Approach.* Englewood Cliffs, NJ: Prentice-Hall, 1987.

Smart, Reginald. "Religion-Caused Complications in Intercultural Communication." In Samovar and Porter, (Eds.). *Intercultural Communication: A Reader,* (5th ed.), Belmont, CA: Wadsworth, 1988.

Spitzberg, Brian H. "Intercultural Communication Competence." In Samovar and Porter, (Eds.). *Intercultural Communication: A Reader,* (6th ed.), Belmont, CA: Wadsworth, 1991.

Spradley, James P., and David W. McCurdy. *The Cultural Experience: Ethnography in Complex Society.* Chicago: Science Research Associates, 1972.

Stevenson, Robert L. *Communication, Development, and the Third World: The Global Politics of Information.* White Plains, NY: Longman, 1988.

Stewart, Edward C., and Milton J. Bennett. *American Cultural Patterns: A Cross-Cultural Perspective.* Yarmouth, ME: Intercultural Press, 1991.

Storti, Craig. *The Art of Crossing Cultures.* Yarmouth, ME: Intercultural Press, 1989.

Summerfield, Ellen. *Crossing Cultures through Film.* Yarmouth, ME: Intercultural Press, 1993.

Thiederman, Sondra. *Bridging Cultural Barriers for Corporate Success: How to Manage the Multicultural Work Force.* Lexington, MA: Lexington Books, D. C. Heath, 1991.

Thomas, Kay, and Gary Althen. "Counseling Foreign Students." In Paul Pedersen, et al., (Eds.). *Counseling across Cultures,* Honolulu: University of Hawaii Press, 1989.

Tocqueville, Alexis de. *Democracy in America.* New York: Schocken Books, 1961.

Triandis, Harry C. "Theoretical Concepts that Are Applicable to the Analysis of Ethnocentrism." In R. Brislin, (Ed.). *Applied Cross-Cultural Psychology,* Newbury Park, CA: Sage, 1990.

Ulin, Robert C. *Understanding Cultures: Perspectives in Anthropology and Social Theory.* Austin: University of Texas Press, 1984.

Uniting Service and Learning. Sixth Annual International Conference Proceedings. New York: The Partnership for Service-Learning, 1989.

"Whose America?" *Time,* 138 (July 8, 1991): 12-17.

Wurzel, Jaime. *Toward Multiculturalism: Readings in Multicultural Education.* Yarmouth, ME: Intercultural Press, 1988.

Yum, June Ock. "The Impact of Confucianism on Interpersonal Relationships and Communication Patterns in East Asia." In Samovar and Porter, (Eds.). *Intercultural Communication: A Reader,* (6th ed.), Belmont, CA: Wadsworth, 1991.

Zuercher, Melanie. *Piti Piti Zouazo Fe Nich: Essays on Haiti.* Goshen, IN: Pinchpenny Press, 1981.